Landmark Visitors

Vendée
& Charente-Maritime

Judy Smith

For our granddaughter Acacia. We hope that you, too, will enjoy the sunny skies of Vendée and Charente-Maritime one day.

Thanks are due to

Eric – 'sherpa, chauffeur and chef' – your multiple talents were very much appreciated in the making of this book!

The very helpful staff of Offices de Tourisme throughout both *départements*

Published by
Landmark Publishing
The Oaks, Moor Farm Road West, Ashbourne, DE6 1HD

Abbaye aux Dames, Saintes

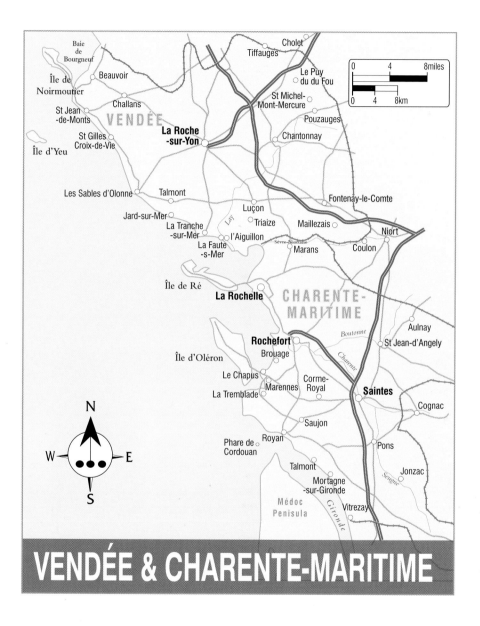

VENDÉE & CHARENTE-MARITIME

Contents

Welcome to
Vendée, Charente-Maritime

France is divided into exactly 100 *départements,* somewhat akin to the counties of Britain, each of them stamped with its own individual character. Standing side by side on the Atlantic coast, Vendée and Charente-Maritime may have something in common, but there is one very big difference.

The Vendée is well known, almost a household word, and conjures up images of sunshine, wide sandy beaches, rolling ocean and modern resorts – the stuff family holidays are made of. But mention Charente-Maritime and you have blank looks. It is only when you talk of its constituent parts – the ancient port of La Rochelle, the Roman town of Saintes, the islands of Ré and Oléron, the resort of Royan – that the faces light up again. Yes, yes, Charente-Maritime has plenty of interest! Together these two *départements* form the territory to which this book is devoted – but there has been just a little manipulation of the borders, because no one who has passed through the Cognac vineyards would not want to go on to Cognac itself, and an exploration of the Poitou marshes would be incomplete without its 'capital' Coulon, which is in Deux-Sèvres.

Top Tips

Cycling

This whole area is a cyclist's paradise - bring bikes or hire them when you arrive. The cycleway running the length of the Vendée coast and the network of tracks on Ré and Oléron are highlights.

The Marais Poitevin

The best way to get a feel for this green watery labyrinth is to hire your own boat for a couple of hours

Puy du Fou

The Puy du Fou

A whole day (and maybe evening) should be reserved for this most exciting and very different theme park.

Île d'Yeu

Take a day trip to this idyllic island and explore by bike or on foot

La Rochelle

This is surely the most fascinating city on the French Atlantic coast. Have lunch on the quayside, climb the harbour towers, wander through the arcaded streets and maybe visit the vast Aquarium or the ships of the maritime Museum.

Romanesque Art in the Saintonge

The hugely ornate stone carving on many of the churches in the vicinity of Saintes is something quite unique and well worthy of investigation.

Regional Produce

You simply cannot come to this area without sampling the oysters, and particularly the renowned 'green oysters' of the Marennes-Oléron basin. Add to that mussels, cognac, local wines and perhaps even eel from the Marais Poitevin

Oyster platter

France receives more visitors each year than any other country in Europe, and this coast has long been a favourite holiday destination for British families. The reasons are obvious. Sunshine hours here are almost on a par with the Mediterranean, although temperatures are less extreme. The sea, warmed by the passing Gulf Stream, offers comfortable bathing until late in the year. And travelling distances are not too great – La Rochelle, for example, can be reached by mid-afternoon if you take the overnight ferry to St Malo. Add to that the sandy beaches backed by pine forest, the assortment of islands with their subtropical vegetation, and the abundance of oysters on every menu and you are talking about an accessible paradise!

This book will take you to all the holiday destinations, to cities, towns and villages offering all manner of facilities, each of which is detailed. It will also take you on drives through the surrounding countryside – around the islands, along the ridge of the Vendéan Hills, beside the banks of the Gironde, along the valley of the Charente, down the long sunny Côte de Lumière and more. And if you would like to dig just a little deeper into the area, maybe to appreciate something of the past from which it has grown, or the present economy on which it thrives, it can fill in some of the gaps there too, and point you to some of the fascinating places that reveal the more workaday character of Vendée and Charente-Maritime.

Going back into the past, it is surprising to realise that for the better part of three hundred years, this territory was under British rule. In 1152, Eleanor of Aquitaine, who owned the south-west corner of France, married Henry of Anjou who owned the north-west. Henry had a good claim to the English throne, and when his mother's cousin Stephen died two years later, he suddenly found himself Henry II of England. To the dismay of the French court, England ruled half of France! Eleanor and Henry's oldest surviving son was Richard I (the Lionheart), and you will find references to all three of them throughout the area - but important though their story is, it is by no means the only one here. History-lovers will have a field day in La Rochelle, where the multiple towers guarding the harbour tell of the city's more-than-turbulent past, and you can still see the dyke with which Richelieu once tried to keep out the English, and the streets paved with ballast brought back by ships trading with the New World. The English are in the frame again at nearby Rochefort, where Louis XIV kept his arsenal and built his warships to do battle with them on the high seas. Then there is the Vendée, once the scene of a civil war, the uprising of the local people against the evils of the post-Revolutionary government. This saga of bravery and bloodshed is possibly one you have never heard before. A more peaceful slice of history belongs to the south, where in the Middle Ages, pilgrims passed through in their thousands along one of the major routes to Santiago de Compostela. Monasteries, churches and even a hospital survive from that time. It seemed best to include these stories in the place where they naturally occur (so that you are not always turning the pages), but you can find a very brief resumé of French history to set it all in context at the back of the book.

Vendée and Charente-Maritime may well be full of historical interest, but just as compelling are the traditional industries that still flourish on this west coast. Half of France's oysters come from here, and the 'green oysters' from the Marennes-Oléron area are said to have a particularly subtle flavour. Those you must certainly taste – and get a glimpse of how they are cultured – but there are also the mussels from around the Bay of Aiguillon. *Moules-frites* on the terrace of a restaurant with a view of the sea is obligatory! Then there is salt production on the marshes – the way in which the water is evaporated is intriguing, and the rectangular ponds with their glistening piles of salt provide plenty of ammunition for the camera. More picturesque scenes are to be found in connection with the fishing industry. Coastal harbours are alive with brightly coloured boats, many bearing a forest of cheerful marking pennants from the lobster pots. In particular, do not miss la Cotinière on the Ile d'Oléron, where you can not only see the catch landed but also watch the subsequent auction carried out at break-neck electronic speed from a special public gallery.

Those time-honoured enterprises contribute hugely to the fascination of this region – but you could add to them the vineyards of Vendée, Oléron and Ré producing their light quaffable wines, and in the south of the region, the great cognac houses where liberal measures of time and skill go into the creation of what is truly the aristocrat of spirits. Again you will find in these pages information on all these industries, and details of many, many museums and private establishments where you can get first-hand experience.

On a practical note, each of the six chapters in this book ends with detailed information about the places you might like to visit and the Tourist Offices that could be contacted before you go. The latter will be able to give you help with accommodation and will happily send you a screed of detail about the attractions of their area. Also to be found at the end of the chapters are particular suggestions for family outings. So much of this area is devoted to children that you will be spoiled for choice, but I have tried to recommend 'free' outings as well as those that involve digging in the pocket. At the same time, some ideas for rainy days have been included here – although hopefully you will not have too many of those. And since no self-respecting Frenchman would consider his investigation of a region complete without a dip into its gastronomic possibilities, a few specialities not to be missed have been offered in each area.

Finally I must say what great pleasure working on this book has been, and what an enormous amount my husband and I have learned about an area that we really thought we knew well. Many years ago, the owner of a gîte in which we were staying told us that his lifetime ambition was to take a holiday in each of France's *départements* (he had managed all 95 on the mainland and was on to *outre-mer* at the time). This set us thinking – we could never rival his achievement, but what about a short-list of the most interesting? Which *départements* would be on it? After many, many years of exploring in France, we conclude that both Vendée and Charente-Maritime would find a slot in our top 10, but which one would be where – well, what do you think?

I wish you many happy holidays in this absolutely delightful corner of France.

1. The Vendée Coast

The Vendée coast boasts an abundance of the traditional family holiday ingredients – sun, sand and sea.

The sun shines here for around 2,500 hours a year, which in practical terms means that you can expect an average 8 hours a day in July or August. The golden sands stretch in an almost un-broken line from Noirmoutier in the north to la Faute in the south, a distance of some 70 miles. And the sea is warm, tempered by the Gulf Stream, making bathing a possibility until late in the year. Admittedly, wide beaches facing the open ocean are sometimes more suited to surfing than swimming, but there is a more than adequate endow-ment of sheltered spots, often backed by pinewoods offering welcome shade. And the sea provides a wealth of other entertainment, sailing, kayaking, and fishing.

Along this coast the well-known resorts succeed each other as you travel south – St Jean de Monts, St Gilles-Croix-de-Vie, Les Sables d'Olonne, la Tranche-sur-Mer, each of them well-geared to the needs of a family holiday, and buzzing with activity throughout

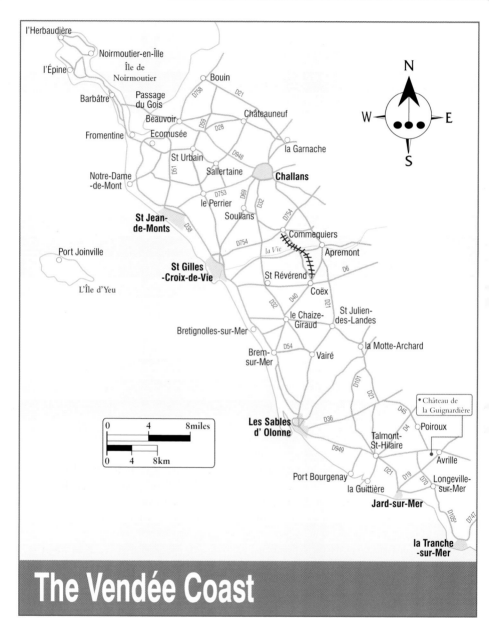

The Vendée Coast

the summer months. Only the very north of the *département* is set apart from this hurly-burly, a peaceful corner that is not much penetrated by the holiday throng, and yet it is well worthy of your attention.

The Marais Breton

The Vendée meets its northern neighbour Loire-Atlantique in an area of low-lying marshland known as the Marais Breton. In a landscape of flat fields criss-crossed by drainage channels and dotted with reed beds, the few towns and villages stand prominently on low hills that were once islands in the sea. The sea itself has receded to the mud-flats of the Bay of Bourgneuf, which is now the domain of the oyster farmers rather than the sunbathers of the south. A short drive will give you a feel for this very different area, but before setting off, it is worth devoting a few minutes to the town of Challans at the eastern edge of the marsh.

With a population around 19,000, **Challans** is the second largest town in the *département* of Vendée. Even so, there is little remarkable about it – that is, unless you come on a Tuesday. On Tuesdays, sleepy Challans wakes up and parties, with a vast and colourful market that extends its tentacles into every nook and cranny of the town. Among the more usual stalls you may well find vans selling guinea fowl or black chickens, as well as the large marsh-bred ducks for which Challans has long been renowned. And when you have taken your fill of it all, like the stall-holders you can retire to the Les Routiers restaurant (*La Noue*) in the nearby Place Victor Charbonnel where an excellent 3-course lunch with wine is served at more-than-modest cost.

Challans offers one more diversion before you leave – this is the place to make your acquaintance with the work of the Martel brothers whose sculptures you will then recognise throughout the length and breadth of the Vendée (see box P13). Behind the church a long frieze (a memorial to the artist Charles Milcendeau) depicts marshland life, in the school grounds opposite the Maison des Arts a Vendéan woman carries a pitcher of milk on her head and above the cinema on the Rue Carnot (the road to Beauvoir and Noirmoutier) another frieze incorporates scenes of traditional dancing.

Autrefois Challans

Not content with its exciting weekly market, Challans surpasses itself in staging four market extravaganzas every year. On two Thursdays in July and two more in August, more stalls than ever are set out and the whole population dresses up in the clothes of a hundred years ago. Children play hoop and stick in the streets, horse-drawn carriages bounce along the roads, musicians tune ancient instruments and folk dancers twirl and sway on the sidelines. The day ends with an evening of feasting and dancing for all. To see *Autrefois Challans* or to avoid it, get the dates from the website www.autrefoischallans.com.

The Martel Brothers

Twins Joel and Jan Martel were born in Nantes in 1896. They spent their whole lives together, sharing a studio and producing works of a cubist nature which were much in demand in their time. Their large sculptures were commissioned for war memorials and personal memorials (including that to the composer Debussy) and their reliefs, which often depicted peasant life, grace many town centres and important buildings in this western part of France. They were also well-known in Paris where they exhibited their characteristically co-signed works on many occasions. The twins died within 6 months of each other in 1966.

A tour of the marsh

Total distance 66km (40 miles)

This may be only a short drive, but allow a whole day, because there is more than enough to stop and linger over. Leaving Challans, first turn northeast on the minor road to the village of **la Garnache**. Beside the crossroads on its outskirts, the medieval château behind the wall on the right was partially destroyed on the orders of Louis XIII during his pursuit of the Protestants. With ramparts, keep and sections of round towers, enough remains for it to host guided tours during the summer months. A museum of local history (costumes, furniture, tools and utensils) has been created in one of the rooms and fine English and French gardens are laid out.

From la Garnache, the D71 leads west across the marsh, and in 5km or so you reach a T-junction near the village of Châteauneuf. To the right here (follow the signs), the grey ruins of the twelfcentury **Abbey of Île Chauvet** lie beyond a very well preserved latter-day mansion, both of them concealed in woodland. The abbey's finest feature is its Romanesque doorway, but you may also visit the monks' dormitory, the kitchen and the cellars.

Returning from the abbey to the village, the wooden observatory on the right offers a good view of the most conspicuous wildlife of these flat lands, the storks. Posts with platforms have been erected in the surrounding fields and several pairs have obligingly moved in and built their nests. If you want to see more of the storks, a well-marked 21km (13 mile) 'stork trail' (*Sentier des Cigognes*) starts from the observatory.

The main attraction of **Châteauneuf** itself is Le Petit Moulin, a picturesque windmill built some 300 years ago and still grinding corn. For most of its life the mill has been in the hands of the Vrignaud family and today it is M Vrignaud who introduces you to the creaking, clanking machinery and temperamental sails while Mme Vrignaud turns out the delectable pancakes that complement the visit.

From Châteauneuf you could head north-west into a part of the marsh that has been fully reclaimed only in the last hundred or so years (bear right at a cross at the end of Châteauneuf, then at a T-junction in 4 km (2.5 miles), turn right). On a slight rise above the

Martel Sculpture - Perrette et le pot au Lait

flat, cattle-grazed terrain, the village of **Bouin** was once the haunt of smugglers, although its more legitimate prosperity came from extensive salt workings. The current industry of the village is oyster-farming and at any of Bouin's three local ports (Port du Bec, Port des Champs, Port des Brochets) you can get an idea of what goes on here. Essentially the baby oysters are allowed up to four years to mature and to fatten on the particularly rich mud of this bay (see P169 for more details of oyster farming). Each of the ports is no more than a jumble of unassuming huts and rickety jetties lining a tidal inlet, but these are the places to buy your fresh oysters – and if you don't fancy doing it yourself, you can bowl along to the very popular Mord'eau restaurant beside the lock at Port du Bec, where half a dozen with a glass of chilled Muscadet will slip down very

nicely. The most interesting way to reach this restaurant is via the coast road from Port des Champs, which passes the wind farm (Parc Éolien). If you can bear to stand under the huge blades, you can find an information board on one of the turbines.

South of Bouin the D758 leads to the larger village of **Beauvoir-sur-Mer** – despite retaining its title, it is now 4 or 5 km (3 miles) from the sea. The Office de Tourisme in its main street offers lots of information on the marshland, including a first-class map of circular walks entitled *Sentiers Pédestres et Équestres* for those who would like to experience the marsh on foot (the routes shown are also waymarked on the ground, so they are easy to follow).

From Beauvoir a causeway known as the Passage du Gois leads out to the island of Noirmoutier, but you can return to that another day. For the moment, this is an exploration of the marsh and the very best place to find out about life in former times here is the **Ecomusée du Marais Breton Vendéene** (also known as the Ecomusée du Daviaud), south of Beauvoir at **la Barre-de-Monts**. This superb ecomuseum comprises a collection of widely scattered and well-preserved farm buildings – the low single-roomed farmhouse backed by the animals' quarters, the grain store, the dairy, the machinery shed. Challans ducks and chickens roam free, and there are also local breeds of sheep, cows and donkeys to charm the children. In summertime you can observe the working of the saltpans, and there may well be demonstrations of country crafts, *yole* punting or folk dancing. An observa-

Life on the marsh

The *bourrine* and the *yole* were essential elements of one-time life on the *marais*. The *bourrine* was a long, low cottage, made of clay and thatched with reeds. In its single room with a fire at one end the whole family (often three generations) would sit, eat and sleep. If you visit the *Bourrine à Rosalie*, you can see the beds that were often raised on high legs because of the ever-present risk of flooding.

Bourrine at Ferme de Daviaud

The *yole* was a flat-bottomed boat, the equivalent of today's family car, and the only means of getting to church, to school or to market. It was propelled along the channels by means of a long pole, known as a *ningle*. The *ningle* was also used for vaulting the ditches by farmers and others who wanted to cross the watery terrain. At Le Daviaud you may well see displays of ditch-vaulting, but do not be encouraged to try it yourself!

tory overlooking the flat fields affords distant views of avocets and egrets among others – if this appeals to you, take binoculars.

South of the ecomuseum (keep ahead on the same minor road and then turn right at the junction), a 70m (230ft) high water tower with a *Salle Panoramique* offers its visitors the best possible view of all the marsh – and out to sea, the islands of Yeu and Noirmoutier. Headsets with English commentary are available to help you distinguish the features.

Back on terra firma again, the D82 east followed by the D119 north (from le Plaud) will bring you to the **Bourrine à Rosalie**, a very well-preserved example of a traditional marsh dwelling that was lived in until as recently as 1971. Now you can wander through its two rooms of memorabilia and make the acquaintance of the donkey in the garden.

The road from the Bourrine à

Le maraîchinage

In the empty landscapes of the marsh there could be little privacy. Fine Sunday afternoons would see a procession of eligible young ladies strolling along the dykes, each of them carrying a very large umbrella. This naturally brought out the young men, and if any of them was offered an umbrella – well, naturally enough they could put it up and who knows what went on behind it. This *maraîchinage* was accepted practice, and everyone determinedly turned a blind eye!

Rosalie back to Challans first passes the **Rairé Windmill**, a very old mill said to have been continuously in use since the sixteenth-century. Again you can be taken on tour, and end the visit with a purchase of newly-ground flour. Beyond the mill lies the village of **Sallertaine**, and this must be your final port of call. From July to September, Sallertaine is taken over by artisans of all kinds. The village achieved fame when the author René Bazin described it in his book *La Terre qui Meurt* (The Dying Land–1899), and instigated the restoration of its church that now houses changing exhibitions. In addition to the many artisans' premises, the village boasts a state-of-the-art bread making museum (English headsets – and taste the bread at the end) and offers guided canoe trips around its 'island'.

Noirmoutier

The long thin island of Noirmoutier separates the shallow oyster-filled Bay of Bourgneuf from the more holiday-orientated sandy beaches of the south. Islands have a certain intrinsic appeal and this one seems to attract everyone holidaying in these parts. Visit it at your peril in the height of summer! Traffic jams aside, Noirmoutier is a fascinating place with villages of low, whitewashed houses, an interesting main town, some attractive coastline and an obvious display of its past and present economic ventures in the form of salt production, market gardening, oyster farming and fishing.

The island has a curious shape, a long slender stalk of land swelling to a bud at its tip. The stalk is connected to the mainland by a bridge of some 700m (2,300ft) built in 1971, and more excitingly by the Passage du Gois, a causeway across the seabed passable only at low tide. Whichever route you come by, you will arrive at the main road through the centre of the island, the scene where the summertime congestion starts. If it is simply a beach you are looking for, you could avoid this by turning left off the main road as soon as you have crossed the bridge. This lesser road now parallels the coast and there are many signed access points. These west-facing beaches are wide, sandy and backed by rather bare dunes, but there are views across to the Île d'Yeu and plenty of space for everyone. **Barbâtre**, the little town on this road, is a blend of traditional cottages and shops meeting the needs of the holidaymakers.

At the top of the stalk, where the 'bud' begins, the road divides at the little town of **la Guerinière**. It has its own distractions in the form of a rather quaint museum of rural life (Musée des Traditions de l'Île) and a butterfly farm tucked away behind the local supermarket. To the left of la Guerinière are the salt marshes, while ahead the road leads to the island's main town, **Noirmoutier-en-l'Île**, where there is a lot to see and do. Most popular with families is the huge *Océanile* waterpark on the outskirts of the town. Further on, at the heart of Noirmoutier-en-l'Île, it is the solid fifteenth-century château flanked by pepperpot towers that dominates the scene. Across a grassy courtyard you can gain entry to its keep, where the three floors display a rather bewildering miscellany of model boats, Jersey pottery and modern art. The most publicised exhibit is an upholstered chair riddled with bullet holes – the chair in which the unfortunate Vendéan Général d'Elbée, already injured and unable to stand, was obliged to sit to face his Republican firing squad in 1794. Far more impressive than all these exhibits is the summit watchpath. From here you can look out over the town and over all the low-lying island and even pick out the far distant bridge to the mainland.

Beside the château rises the spire of St Philbert's church, built on the spot where the saint himself founded an abbey in 674. In the ninth-century crypt below the altar the tomb is empty – although a couple of relics remain in a casket, St Philbert himself was long ago taken elsewhere to escape marauding Vikings. Below both ancient buildings a long quay-lined channel cuts into the heart of the town. There is a buzz here – restaurants and cafés with outside tables overlook the line of moored boats and a cheerful tourist train tootles off on its journey around town. On the far side, the Sealand aquarium housing local and exotic species draws the families, and not far away the boat-building museum (Musée de la Construction Navale) extols the craftsmanship of yesteryear's marine carpenters. A walk further along this quay, past all the working boatyards, will bring you to what amounts to a ships' cemetery, a collection of broken ribs and holed hulls emerging more picturesquely than you might expect from the tidal mud. Across the channel behind you have one of the best views of the town, with château and church standing side by side.

The prettiest part of the island is just north of Noirmoutier-en-l'Île. The **Bois de la Chaise** is a forest of holm

---

Take a walk

Escape the crowds at Noirmoutier-en-l'Île by taking a walk up the Jacobsen Jetty (on the château side of the channel), heading between mudflats on the sea side and the Marais de Müllembourg salt pans on the other. The latter area is a bird reserve, so take your binoculars! This path is part of a 7km (4 miles) circular route marked with yellow flashes (it continues along the coast to the Plage des Dames before returning through the town) and the whole is described on an information board on the quayside and on a leaflet to be found in the Office de Tourisme.

---

oaks and umbrella pines that in February and March is brightened by the golden yellow pom-poms of mimosa, another of the island's exports. Backed by these woods, the **Plage des Dames** is the most beautiful spot on the island – and everyone knows it. Parking space here is at a premium (consider walking – see the box!). The beach is a lovely horseshoe of golden sand, with the woodland spilling down the only bit of rocky coastline on the island. The long arc of white bathing huts is a relic of the early days of this beach's popularity, and somehow it adds to rather than detracts from the scenic appeal. Following a path through the woods you first pass a long jetty reaching into the sea (you can walk out) and then a lighthouse, the Phare des Dames. Further round the path reaches the next cove, the Anse Rouge with its Tour Plantier before descending to Souseaux beach.

If you decide to continue the journey

by road, the next place north along the coast is **Le Grand Vieil**. Here the sparkling white houses with blue shutters, red roofs and hollyhocks at the door are shown off to their best advantage. Cur-

Opposite page: Moulin de Chateauneuf;

Below: Market hall at Challans

rently rather a fashionable place, it was once a fishing village, and those doors and shutters that are now decorously painted in matching blue were decked out in the same medley of vivid colours as the boat hulls at sea.

Beyond le Grand Vieil the road bends and twists its narrow way along the north coast to the port of **l'Herbaudière**. Here the brightly

Port des Champs

Régates du Bois de la Chaise

In early August every year a surprising variety of tall ships and other historic sailing craft meet here to take part in three days of competitions, held off the Plage des Dames. Naturally not all is serious, and the races are interspersed with fireworks and feasting, and conclude with a festive 'parade' into the harbour at Noirmoutier-en-l'Île.

coloured working boats come and go as they have for centuries, although today the catch is more commonly the noble fish caught with a line (sole, sea bass, sea bream, etc.) than the formerly popular sardines. Shellfish are also caught, and many boats carry the colourful pennants that are used to mark the position of lobster pots in the water.

Noirmoutier potatoes

In this north-western tip of the island, you will already have noticed the flat potato fields, perhaps earthed up into ridges. Early Bonnotte potatoes from Noirmoutier grace the tables of some of the best Parisian restaurants, and although this is not a vast enterprise, the quality ensures that it is a lucrative one. Grown in a soil naturally rich in seaweed fertiliser, these are arguably the world's finest of their kind. Prices vary of course, but you can expect to pay several times that of Jersey Royals at home.

South of the potato fields lies another area of economic importance to Noirmoutier. This low-lying land is divided neatly into rectangular saltpans. Narrow roads and tracks pass between them and several enterprises offer guided visits and sales for the holidaymaker. The salt industry has seen a revival – having reached an all-time low of around 30 *sauniers* working the pans in the 60s, there are now three times that number as Noirmoutier salt has acquired gastronomic importance. On the coast, the attractive almost tropical little town of **l'Épine** is the capital of this salt producing area and is worth a visit in its own right.

From l'Épine the road leads back to la Guerinière, where it passes the four windmills that have perched on these dunes for nearly 200 years. Beyond is the island's main road, the D38. If you want a glimpse of Noirmoutier's other industry, oyster culture, you could cross that road and continue between the oyster *claires* to the port of **Bonhomme** on the opposite shore.

Soon though it will be time to return to the mainland—for an alternative route, it may just be possible to take the causeway known as the **Passage du Gois**. Following the D38 down the 'stalk' of the island, Le Gois is signposted at a roundabout about 7 km (4 miles) from la Guerinière. But before you turn off, make sure you have consulted the tide tables (you can get them at any tourist office, and there is one by this roundabout). Depending on the tidal coefficient, you can expect to cross the Gois only for about an hour on either side of low water.

The Gois and its Foulées

The name Gois comes from *goiser*, a verb in local patois meaning to paddle or to flounder. The Passage du Gois is a natural phenomenon, a 4.5km (3 miles) long sandbank created where currents from the Bay of Bourgneuf in the north meet currents from the south. Known from antiquity, it was paved only in 1924, when platforms on stilts were added as refuges for those caught by the tide. At its greatest height, around 4m of water covers the causeway! Today no one should need to take advantage of those refuges (although several do every year) because tide tables are posted at both ends of the crossing and warning lights flash when the tide starts to rise. Locals who come here at low tide to collect clams and other shellfish seem remarkably confident of their ability to escape in the nick of time!

The Foulées du Gois is an event held on a Saturday in either May or June, the actual date depending on the tides. After local runners have raced across the causeway at low water, thirty or so elite runners set out just as the sea begins to cover it. By the time they are in the middle they are already at the mercy of the conflicting currents and reaching the far shore is no easy matter. The slowest may have to swim! If you would like to watch this spectacle, check out the details on www.fouleesdugois.com.

Île d'Yeu

Noirmoutier is not the only island off the Vendée coast. 20km (12 miles) out to sea sits the Elysian Île d'Yeu, and every day throughout the summer months boatloads of enthusiastic visitors make the crossing from either Fromentine in the north or from St Gilles Croix-de-Vie. Yeu (originally known as *Oya*) is a fascinating island. A mere 10x4 km (4 x 2.5 miles) in size, it has a healthy economy based on its fishing industry, and a population of 5,000 biased in favour of youth (25% are under 25). Despite its distance from the coast, it has only been an island for the past 5000 years or so, before which, of course, it was a peninsula. Prehistoric man must have reached it on foot, and it seems that for him this far-flung spot was a sacred site. Today you can still find many menhirs and dolmens on Yeu. The first inhabitants of the island as such are thought to have been monks in the sixth-century and although Viking invaders destroyed the original monastery, by the tenth-century monks of a different order had returned. Since then Yeu has had some military importance, as witnessed by the fourteenth-century Vieux Château on its southern shore and by the nineteenth-century Fort de la Pierre-Levée above Port Joinville, large enough for a garrison of 400 men, and subsequently used as a prison.

Forgetting the more sombre side of Yeu, it is its wonderful coastline that draws the visitors. They arrive at its main town, **Port Joinville**, on the north coast – and most seem to make their way directly to the cycle-hire bases on the quayside. Yeu is perfect for cycling, just the right size to explore in a day, and criss-crossed with designated cycle tracks – although a couple of taxis and a tourist train will offer to take the strain out of things for those who prefer,

Passage du Gois

and it is also possible to opt for one of the five waymarked walking routes and just take in a part of the island. But it is the cyclists that have the best of it on Yeu, easily coasting around the whole island and reaching the places that cars never can.

Leaving Port Joinville, the cycle trail takes you first past the little bays of the north coast to the Dolmen de la Planche à Puare, a curious 'cross-shaped' dolmen with lateral chambers. From there on, the coastline becomes wilder and more rocky. The much-photographed Vieux Château on its craggy perch is reached by a path through thickets of blackthorn – remote as it is, it is a spot not to be missed, and the château offers regular guided tours. Beyond the château are cliffs with caves (le Gouffre d'Enfer),

Plage des Dames

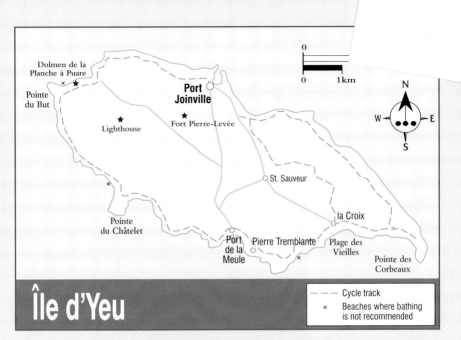

Dolmen de la
Planche à Puare

Pointe
du But

**Port
Joinville**

Lighthouse

Fort Pierre-Levée

St. Sauveur

Pointe
du Châtelet

la Croix

Port
de la
Meule

Pierre Tremblante

Plage des
Vieilles

Pointe des
Corbeaux

0   1 km

N
W   E
S

Île d'Yeu

- - - - Cycle track
×   Beaches where bathing
       is not recommended

and then a welcome arrival at possibly the prettiest spot on the island, Port de la Meule. Beside its well-cradled harbour, overlooked by a tiny white chapel, an informal restaurant provides the necessities for restoring the energy. A *crêperie* a few paces up the road shares the role. On the trail again, most people

Tourist train at Noirmoutier-en-l'Île

23

pause to test the *Pierre Tremblante*, a huge, finely poised logan stone that is supposed to rock when touched – if you can find the right spot. And on a hot day, everybody stops at the most beautiful beach on the island, the Plage des Vieilles. A dip in the sea here is wonderful after an energetic cycle ride – although almost any beach you pass on Yeu is safe for bathing (see the map).

From the Plage des Vieilles it is possible to return directly to Port Joinville on the *piste cyclable*, or to continue through the pine-woods along a coast that faces north-east, and is reminiscent of the Vendée again. For those who care to continue, there is still the lighthouse in the centre of the island and the Fort of Pierre-Levée above Port Joinville to explore. But eventually most day visitors make their way to the bars on the harbour side at Port Joinville where they can overlook the colourful fishing fleet and enjoy a drink while waiting for the boat to go home.

Noirmoutier salt

Of course it is not essential to confine your visit to Yeu to a day trip – there is plenty of holiday accommodation on the island. But you need to be a bit careful. Potential visitors should bear in mind that the island is addic-

Philippe Pétain (1856–1951)

The final role of the Citadel at Port Joinville was as a prison for Maréchal Pétain in the years following the Second World War. Pétain first distinguished himself in World War I with his defence of Verdun, and in consequence became something of a national hero. In World War II he became prime minister in June 1940, following the fall of France, and led the repressive Vichy government in collaboration with the Nazis. At the end of hostilities he was convicted of treason, but in view of his age (then 90), his sentence of death was commuted to life imprisonment. Pétain was taken to Pierre-Levée on the Île d'Yeu where he remained for almost six years.

On falling ill, the Maréchal was taken to a house on the Rue Guist'Hau, where he subsequently died. The house now bears a commemorative plaque, and Pétain lies buried in the cemetery on the outskirts of town–his grave facing in the opposite direction from all the others.

A memorial

The granite Statue de la Norvège beside the harbour tells a sad tale. By a Scandinavian sculptor, it commemorates the day in January 1917 when the local lifeboat went out to help the crew of a Norwegian cargo boat that had been holed by a torpedo. The men were rescued – but in terrible weather conditions, the lifeboat was blown to the coast of Brittany, by which time six islanders and five Norwegians had lost their lives.

tive, and an old saying goes *Oya deux jours, Oya toujours* – loosely translated as 'come here for a couple of days and you're here for life!'

The Pays de Monts

Lending their name to the resorts (Notre-Dame-de-Monts, St Jean-de-Monts), the *Monts* are not exactly mountains but rather the high dunes that flank the most northerly coast of the Vendée. Until the seventeenth-century this 'dune country' was an island, cut off from the mainland by the flooded marsh behind. Now it marks the start of the long line of holiday beaches for which the Vendée is re-nowned. Golden sands stretch for 25km (15 miles) from Fromentine to the rocky headland at Sion-sur-l'Ocean. Behind the sands, the dunes are covered in marram and couch grass, and further back still, the forest of maritime pines dates back to the nineteenth-century when it was planted here in an attempt to stabilise the ever-shifting sand. Today that forest offers sweet-smell-ing shade, and in its depths are several

waymarked walks and a fine cycle track that skirts its inland edge.

Just outside the forest, the road that parallels the cycle track makes a much pleasanter way of heading south than the campsite fringed D38. About a kilometre along this winding road (from its junction with the bridge road to Noirmoutier) you could halt in the little car park on the right and climb the long series of steps to the top of the dunes. Here a raised wooden viewing platform, the **Pey de la Blet**, just pokes its head above the trees and allows you views of the nearby bridge and out to sea, a shadowy prospect of the Île d'Yeu.

Further on, where both road and cycle track reach the edge of **Notre-Dame-de-Monts**, stands the Maison de la Dune et de la Forêt. Packed with information about the local environ-ment, it serves as a learning resource for schools, but also welcomes holidaymak-ers with its annual exhibitions. From here a road leads inland to a roundabout

On your bike

The Vendée claims to have a more extensive network of cycle routes than any other *département* of France. This coastal trail is the best of all. Stretching from Noirmoutier to Bourgenay, south of les Sables d'Olonne, it only very rarely takes you onto the most minor of roads and even gets you through the big resorts without tangling with anything motorised. With cycle hire readily available in every town (just ask at any Office de Tourisme), this is something that everyone can enjoy.

Monument de la Norvège

Les Sables d'Olonne - Vendee Globe

on the main D38. The little tourist office nearby is one of the best stocked on this coast.

Notre-Dame-de Monts welcomes its visitors with an exuberance of bright blue paint and a roundabout sprouting three colourful sails, telling you immediately what the town is about. Notre-Dame-de-Monts is a windy place! Sailing, windsurfing, sand-yachting and kite-flying are the facilities on offer here, and not far from those three sails is a splendid diversion known as the Jardin du Vent. In a small enclosure topped by the sails of a mill you can play games with the wind and sound, catch the tinkles of distant chimes in a concave mirror, whisper down underground tubes and propel yourself on a wind-powered roundabout (anyone with experience of sailing will have this whipping round).

Despite its allegiance to the wind, Notre-Dame-de-Monts has a very pleasant seafront, well-adorned with palm trees and other semi-tropical vegetation in which generous car parking spaces are discreetly concealed. The beach here is as fine as any on the coast, yet Notre-Dame-de-Monts is far less commercialised than the resorts to the

The work of the devil

Naturally a phenomenon like the Pont d'Yeu has a story attached! It is said than when St Martin wanted to visit Yeu to convert its inhabitants, he could find no-one to take him across by boat, whereupon the devil offered to build a bridge for him in one night. The price for this would be the soul of the first person to cross. The deal was agreed – provided only that the bridge was completed before the cock crowed at dawn. Thinking to buy time and make the bird more sleepy than usual, the devil then gave it some local wine. Unfortunately this made the excited bird crow straight away – and so the bridge got no further than you see today.

Vieux Chateau

south. For even more seclusion, there is car parking behind the dunes at the south end of the town, with further beach access.

Just south of Notre-Dame-de-Monts (walk down the beach or turn where signed off the A38), the fine sand is broken briefly by a natural phenomenon known as the **Pont d'Yeu.** The Pont is actually a rocky promontory some 3km (2 miles)long yet only 50m (165 ft) or so wide, pointing directly to the Île d'Yeu out to sea. Completely covered at high tide, at low tide it attracts shell-fishers who need to know when to take their leave. For those who get it wrong, poles on the shore show the line in which to walk!

South of the Pont d'Yeu, the beach, dunes and forest continue to **St Jean-**

Port de la Meule

de-Monts. For over ten years the coastal resort of St Jean has put children centre-stage, and now claims itself the 'main town in the Vendée for children and families'. In media-speak, St Jean is 'Station Kid'! Certainly there is plenty for children to do here, from games and swings on the famed 8km (5 miles). Plage des Demoiselles to cycling or roller-blading along the designated track on the promenade or swinging through the trees at the arboreal adventure park. Roads leading from the seafront are lined with restaurants and cafés, and with shops offering nets, buckets, inflatables and all the paraphernalia of the beach. Adults are not entirely forgotten, and can pamper themselves at the thalassotherapy (seawater therapy) centre by day and go on to party all night at the multitude of bars and the seafront casino. Behind all this razzmatazz the old town still exists, gathered around its church, and all members of the family can enjoy the colourful market stalls that are set out here every day of the week in summertime (otherwise Wednesday and Saturday only).

Outside St Jean more family-orientated excursions include the Ferme des Pommettes (at le Vieux-Cerne, 4km/2.5 miles north) where the little ones can feed the animals, and **le Perrier** (5km/3 miles east) where all the family can take a trip on the marsh in a flat-bottomed *yole*. Most popular of all is the Atlantic Toboggan water park south of the town at les Becs, a miscellany of pools and water-slides with shady corners perfect for a hot day.

St Gilles-Croix-de-Vie and around

South of les Becs, the D123 continues through the forest to St Hilaire-de-Riez, at which town you could turn right to Sion-sur-l'Ocean and the **Corniche Vendéenne**, with the first cliffs on this journey south. Between outcrops of rock, the coves here are very popular, and there is even a little 'swimming pool' that refills at each high tide. Constant erosion by the crashing waves has left a line of five rock stacks, known as **les Cinq Pineaux**, separated from the cliff. Further on a sign points you to the **Trou du Diable**, a huge hole in the rock. All is best seen from the footpath that skirts these cliffs (there are places marked out for parking on the opposite side of the road) and if you continue on this past the lighthouse at Grosse Terre point you can descend to a shore of rockpools.

By car the road leads on along the Corniche de Boisvinet, lined with fine *Belle Époque* villas, and then down into the town and along the harbour-side. Technically you are in the fishing port of **Croix-de-Vie** here – the more holiday orientated **St Gilles-sur-Vie** lies across the estuary of the river. The towns were officially united in 1967, but each retains its own character. Croix-de-Vie still brings in its catch, which nowadays is mostly sardines and other 'blue fish' such as anchovies.

Other boats, too, leave from this quayside – in summertime a small ferry makes the quick hop across the river to St Gilles, a sailing ship takes visitors out on fishing trips (half or whole day) and much larger craft take passengers out to the Île d'Yeu. Upstream of all this, a lively marina accommodates something like a thousand pleasure boats. If you have just a few minutes to spare on this quayside you could call in to the **Maison du Pêcheur**, a tiny whitewashed fisherman's cottage carefully preserved from the 1920s. It is tucked away in a narrow street of similar buildings, opposite the tourist office.

Across the river in St Gilles the scene is very different. Although St Gilles is much older than its partner (there was a settlement here before Roman times) it is now firmly the domain of the holidaymaker. Just across the twisted mouth of the river lies the very popular Grande Plage, backed by the Dune de Garenne. Parking is plentiful along the roadsides behind the beach, but if all else fails, you could think of coming on the ferry from less congested Croix-de-Vie, or maybe going to the far south end of the beach where in the Dune de Jaunay there is more space.

Sardines

The taste of sardines is all in the preparation and canning, and the local firm of Gendreau has raised this to an art form using traditional methods. Finest of them all, the 'vintage' sardines known as *Millésimées* actually improve with keeping, and should be turned every 6 months. Each tin is marked with its year and given a serial number, making you feel you have one of a limited edition! Gendreau has a small sales outlet shop on the quayside, where you can purchase various preparations of sardines along with other local produce from the sea.

Finally, St Gilles is a great place for those who love markets–there are five a week all year round and even an extravaganza held on the quayside every evening in July and August. Local produce is there in plenty, but it seems that every craftsman for miles around descends on St Gilles at some time. With demonstrations of horse-shoeing, bread-baking, sardine-canning and the rest these markets are guaranteed entertainment for the whole family.

An inland tour from St Gilles

This short inland drive takes you as far as Apremont, an ancient village with an old grey-stone château overlooking a leafy lake shore – a far cry from the busy resorts and populated beaches of the coast. But this tour is not just about scenery. In fact there are so many places to stop and visit on the way out – and on the way back – that you will probably decide to come back again another day.

Leaving St Gilles heading north, pass through St Hilaire and then turn right on the D69 in the direction of Soullans. Almost immediately you will see signs to the **Bourrine du Bois Juquaud** on the left. This chocolate-box-pretty ensemble of traditional nineteenth-century thatched farm buildings increases its appeal in summertime with the addition of donkey cart rides, displays of country dancing and the like. Set in woods, its adjacent parking area offers glimpses of the *bourrine*, and is a pleasant spot to stop for a picnic.

Pause at the Bourrine du Bois Juquaud if you will, but just up the road is another museum housed in a

Vélo-rail

This ingenious adaptation of disused railway lines seems slow to catch on in Britain, but an afternoon on the vélo-rail can be great fun. Two people are needed to pedal the heavy metal platforms whose flanged wheels fit the tracks. Two more passengers can sit between them. The vélo-rail here runs from Commequiers to the village of Coëx, some 10km (6 miles) distant. The hard work comes when trolleys travelling in different directions meet – both crews are needed to lift one of them off the line!

Sand artist at St Jean

bourrine – or actually two in this case. The **Musée Milcendeau-Jean Yole** celebrates the lives of two talented local men who lived at the turn of the twentieth-century. The more flamboyant of the two by far was Charles Milcendeau, whose home this was. An artist who painted chiefly local scenes and rural inhabitants, his real love nevertheless was Spain – and in one of the *bourrines* he has covered the walls in brightly coloured creatures and added Moorish shapes to the windows to remind him of that country. In the other building Milcendeau's paintings of local life are displayed and you are offered English handsets to explain them. Huge windows look out over the marsh and complement the artist's portrayals of its wildness.

Jean Yole (a pseudonym), the second Vendéan commemorated in this

Summer on the beach at St Jean

museum, was a physician, a writer and a politician. His achievements will probably make far less impression on the English visitor, but for French-speakers some of his texts relating to the Vendée are displayed at designated points in the garden.

On now through Soullans and south-east to **Commequiers**, a village that is far from short of diversions. Its medieval château complete with moat and eight round towers stands quietly crumbling at one end of town, while the other end attracts most of the visitors with its (almost) juxtaposition of vélo-rail terminus and working tannery. The one needs strong muscles, the other a strong stomach, but both are neverthe-less well-subscribed.

From Commequiers it is only a few minutes drive to your goal at **Apre-mont,** where a two-towered château perches picturesquely on a rocky outcrop overlooking the River Vie. The château was built in 1534 by one Philippe Chabot de Brion, Admiral of France and a friend of François I. Medi-eval visitors here arrived mostly by river, and access was via the *voûte cavalière*, a steep tunnel hewn through the rock. It can still be explored today—and you can also climb through the empty rooms of the tall east tower with a view of the river and town below.

Views from the château are interest-ing but are not in the same league as those from the *salle panoramique* in the nearby water tower, whose entrance fee is curiously combined with that of the château. From this lofty room you can see the distant sea—and appreciate how flat is this landscape, where water towers like so many mushrooms are the only features to raise their heads above the horizon.

Back on the ground again, and Apremont's riverside offers two distinct diversions on account of the dam that divides it. Upstream of the dam, the lake with its sandy shore is a good place

On the jetty at St Jean-de-Monts

for a swim and can make a welcome change from the busy beaches of the coast. Downstream, canoes and pedalos are for hire at a base by the name of *Venise d'Apremont*. Even so, the shady leafy banks of the River Vie below Apremont are happily a far cry from sun-baked Venice.

Returning from Apremont to St Gilles, the horticulturally-inclined have two potential treats. The first of these is 7km (4 miles) to the south at **Coëx**, where beside the church, a rather garish notice that hardly does it justice announces the **Jardin des Olfacties**. This colourful garden is nurtured particularly for its scents – there are delicate roses, highly-fragrant herbs, overpowering sweet woodbine. To the delight of children there are also chocolate-smelling pelargoniums, a caramel tree and a game to test your nose (although English translations are provided elsewhere, this particular exercise is French only). Other attractions include a Japanese garden, a rainforest and a 'Hell's Path' of toxic plants. And while in Coëx, it is well worth calling in to the church to enjoy the intense and symbolic colours of the modern stained-glass windows by Vendéan Louis Mazetier.

Further along the D6, near the roundabout known as 'Quatre Chemins', there are more scents at the Roseraie de Vendée. Almost a thousand varieties of roses are carefully labelled and categorised here and various rose-based products such as jams and syrops are offered for sale.

The Roseraie is actually 2km (1.5 miles) west of the village of **St Révérend** and in getting to it you could possibly have spotted the other attraction of the village, the handsome Moulin des Gourmands. This is yet another of the Vendée's windmills inviting in the visitors, and in this case the tour includes the whole process from the corn growing in the field to the bread on the table, with a boulangerie and a rather up-market crêperie to do the honours at the end of the day.

Bretignolles, Brem, and beyond

South of St Gilles, the road soon crosses the River Jaunay – if you could be tempted to follow the river inland, you would reach a dammed section, the Lac de Jaunay, with several boat hire locations and a 13km (8 miles) walking and biking trail around its perimeter. But here we are heading south, and the D38 neatly skips past the next place, **Bretignolles-sur-Mer** although from the road signs it appears to pass through it twice over! But do not miss out on Bretignolles–ignore its first appearance, and at the second, turn right off the D38. Bretignolles is home to **Vendée Miniature**, an unassuming name for what is the most detailed and fascinating model village you are ever likely to see. A video over the entrance door explains that this was the work of one couple, Marie-Françoise and Yves Aubron, over 10 years. Beyond, as night changes to day and back again, the cock crows, the church bells ring, a train puffs by and tiny moving models of village folk pursue their daily tasks amid working machinery. Everything here is a precise and perfect re-creation of its original, from the carts in the farmyards to the slates on the church roof.

Reaching the end of Vendée Miniature, you may well feel you want to go back to the beginning and start all over again (this is possible!), but at last it will be time to move on. The road continues to the seafront, which to the north is rocky. To the south is La Parée beach, wide and sandy, revealing some interesting rockpools at low tide. South of Bretignolles, the next sandy beach is that of la Normandelière, and beside the road that returns from here to the D38 stands the **Dolmen of Pierre-Levée**. The story goes that the devil, surprised at meeting the Virgin Mary in this place, let go of the rocks he happened to be carrying. Be that as it may, this was clearly a burial chamber – excavations at the beginning of the twentieth-century revealed a skeleton, shards of pottery and other artefacts.

Back on the D38 again, you are in wine-growing country. It is surprising that there are vineyards so close to the sea, but these vineyards have been here a long time. The Romans were the first to plant their vines in this area, local monks continued the venture, and very much later Richelieu himself declared a particular liking for this wine, since when the best wines of this region became known as *'vins des Fiefs du Cardinal'*. VDQS status was achieved in 1984. The vineyard here is that of Brem, one of four producing Fief-Vendéen wine (the others are Mareuil-sur-Lay, Vix and Pissotte), which may be white, rosé or red. To sample it here, you could call at Cave Michon, signed beside the road. There is also a small wine museum with *dégustation* and sales at **Brem-sur-Mer**, the next village south.

There is not a lot of distance between Bretignolles and Brem on the D38, but here you will find first the **Parc des Dunes** (a children's adventure park with water slide, bouncy castles, ballpool, trampolines and lots more) and then a particularly good maize labyrinth (**Labyrinthe**), incorporating a treasure hunt (fortunately with clues in English). If these are not for you, you might like instead to turn left at the entrance to Brem and follow signs to the **Église St Nicholas**. Built in 1020 the old grey building looks its age – St Nicholas above the west door is only just discernable and the carvings around the door are weathered beyond recognition. In the whitewashed interior, paintwork removed in the 80s disclosed traces of medieval frescoes.

Leaving Brem for the south, the more peaceful road is the D80 running along the edge of the lovely Forêt d'Olonne.

On the other side of the D80 the **Olonne salt marshes** stretch to the

---

Take a walk

Maritime pines, holm oaks, false acacias and others clothe the high dunes of the Forêt d'Olonne. From a roadside car park on the D80 (Parking de la Grande Pointe, the third of the pull-ins on the right), a track winds beneath the canopy of green to the wide sandy shore, a distance of about a mile. The same site boasts a 1.8km (1 mile) *Sentier Botanique* in which trees have been given name plaques for identification (French and Latin only).

Quayside at St Gilles

horizon. Turning to the left on the D87 you will reach the village of **Île d'Olonne**, which, although flanked by the marsh, is far from being an island. Here the little Musée de la Petite Gare, housed in a one-time station, tells the story of the local industries of wine-growing and salt production. A turn right on to the D38 will bring you to an ornithological reserve (on the right), with its well-equipped observatory manned by volunteers (some speaking

English) and welcoming visitors. Ducks, geese, swans and a variety of waders rest here on their migrations. Further along, more of the local story is told in the **Musée des Traditions Populaires** in **Olonne-sur-Mer** (which is definitely not on the sea!). Furniture, costumes and a schoolroom form the main displays, but you will need a fair knowledge of French to get the best from it.

Les Sables d'Olonne

Les Sables d'Olonne is the best known and most fashionable of the Vendée resorts. Its most enduring image is that of a long golden beach backed by the raised wide promenade known as the Remblai, overlooked by white rectangular blocks of expensive apartments and luxury hotels. Fashionable restaurants abound, and at one end of the beach a glass-enclosed swimming pool and smart casino look out to the ocean. This is the Les Sables of the holiday brochures, but the town has another life. Around the corner from the casino is a harbour filled with trawlers and other vessels that bear witness to this being one of France's chief ports. The most important catch in les Sables is cod. The town also has a long tradition of seafaring and exploration. The port owes its existence to Louis XI who in the fifteenth-century had the estuary dredged and installed shipbuilding yards here. Many great navigators left from Les Sables d'Olonne, but, as often happens, the most notorious seems the best remembered (see box).

The old town of Les Sables lies between the port and the seafront, and is worth taking time to explore. Amid its lattice of narrow streets is one named the Rue de l'Enfer (Street from Hell), which appears in the Guinness Book of Records as the narrowest in France – some 40cm wide at its minimum point, it presumably qualifies as a 'street' because house doors open on to it.

The Rue de l'Enfer actually leads off the Rue des Halles, a road lined with interesting shops, where you will also find the handsome covered market with its mosaic façade. In full swing every morning except Monday, the juxtaposition of slabs of fresh fish and mounds of local fruit and vegetables should bring out the chef in everyone. Opposite the market, the church of Notre-Dame-de-Bon-Port is a Gothic edifice built by Richelieu in 1646, and in the streets and squares around are elegant buildings dating from the same period.

One corner of Les Sables not to be missed is the Île Pénotte, where walls and doorways are adorned with the imaginative shell mosaics of a local artist. Some, like Neptune or the kite-flying scene, are obvious large-scale murals; others are cameos tucked away in hidden corners, equally delightful. The Île Pénotte is most easily found from the clock tower on the seafront – almost opposite this is the Rue Travot,

Nau the Olonnais

Any town could be forgiven for disowning a son like Nau the Olonnais, but Les Sables simply dons its rose-coloured spectacles and accords him a slot in one of its museums. Born in Les Sables in the seventeenth century, François Nau went out in a local ship to Martinique, where he joined a gang of buccaneers. A bloodthirsty career of unbelievable ferocity followed and Nau the Olonnais became the all-time terror of the Caribbean. Eventually his exploits became too much even for his crew, and they deserted him, leaving him to be found by local Indians. Sadly they ate him!

and from this road the first alleyway on the right leads to the shell-adorned quarter.

More shells – about 45,000 of them – are to be found in the **Museum du Coquillage** near the fish market at the top end of the port. This is one diver's private collection, shells from all over the world arranged scientifically but also artistically, and the colours alone will make you gasp. Other exhibits include crabs, sharks, turtles and alligators. And if you fancy attempting a shell collage yourself, or maybe want to take home a big conch in which you can hear the sea, all are on sale at the end.

The Museum du Coquillage is at the top end of the fishing port, and from here you can take a pleasant stroll along the quays, enjoying the comings and goings of the trawlers on one side and the medley of interesting shops and cafés on the other. Reaching the entrance to the fishing port you can look across the water to the small commercial port and maybe spot the odd cargo boat beyond. From this end of the quay a little ferry boat plies backwards and forwards across le Chenal (the entrance channel) to the other very different district of les Sables known as **la Chaume**.

On a long spit of land guarding the entrance to the harbour, la Chaume was once the fishermen's village and even now it seems to have escaped the incursions of tourism. Its most conspicuous feature is the square crenellated **Arundel Tower**, built in the twelfth-century by one Duke of Arundel who invaded this coast, and then stayed for 60 years. Alongside the tower, the Château St-Clair houses a small museum of all things nautical (Musée de la Mer et de la Pêche), including the story of Nau the Olonnais. And down at the tip of la Chaume, pleasant gardens surround a one-time fort, which was itself built on the site of an eleventh-century religious establishment (Prieuré St Nicholas). An

The Vendée-Globe Challenge

The Vendée-Globe round-the-world race was devised in 1989 by French skipper Philippe Jeantot, and is now held every four years. Not without reason is it dubbed the 'Everest of yacht racing'! Yachtsmen applying to take part must first prove themselves with a solo crossing of the Atlantic. The conditions of the race are then simple – they must sail single-handed, not anchor at any time, and receive assistance from no one. Certain waypoints define with reasonable breadth the course to be taken, and in this way approximately 24,000 miles are covered in around 100 days. Britain, of course, had her finest hour when Ellen MacArthur came a more-than-honourable second in 2000/2001.

The race departs from Les Sables some time in November (next in November 2012) and for maybe a month beforehand the yachtsmen and their highly specialised and hugely expensive craft can be seen in and around Port Olona. It is definitely worth a visit at this time – but you will not be the only one to think so!

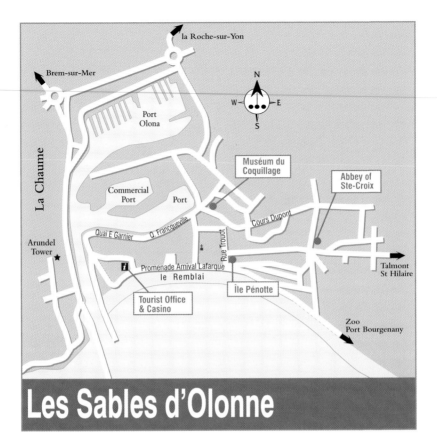

la Roche-sur-Yon

Brem-sur-Mer

Port
Olona

N
W — E
S

La Chaume

Muséum du
Coquillage

Abbey of
Ste-Croix

Commercial
Port

Port

Quai E Garnier   Q. Francqueville

Cours Dupont

Rue Troutt

Arundel
Tower
★

Talmont
St Hilaire

Promenade Amival Lafarque
le Remblai

Île Pénotte

Tourist Office
& Casino

Zoo
Port Bourgenany

Les Sables d'Olonne

impressive mosaic backs a monument to sailors lost at sea.

At the other end of la Chaume, the first bridge across le Chenal leads to **Port Olona**, a pleasure boat marina that since 1989 has gained fame as the starting point of the Vendée-Globe Challenge Race. There are more than a thousand craft of all kinds moored here, many of them truly 'floating palaces' that are well worth a few minutes' marvelling time.

Still in la Chaume but on the opposite side of the road bridge from Port Olona, very much humbler boats leave to take summer visitors upstream to the ancient saltmarshes known as **Les Salines**. The trip includes demonstrations of how the basins are flooded with water, and of how the crystals of salt

produced by evaporation are skimmed from its surface (see P114 for details). The same site can also be explored at lesser cost on foot, following a trail that leads between the saltpans. It starts at the canoe hire base about 3km (2 miles)north of Les Sables at L'Aubraie.

Before leaving Les Sables, it is worth calling in at the **Abbey of Ste-Croix**, at the eastern end of the town away from all the holiday scenes. No longer a haunt of the Benedictines, the smart seventh-century edifice has now been given over to a museum of modern art. The ground floor is devoted to the strange shapes and sometimes erotic images of Romanian artist Victor Brauner, while above are the curious brightly-coloured characters painted on wood and other bizarre materials by Vendéan Gaston Chaissac. Model ships and paintings by local fishermen are tucked away in the roof for a final browse – and somewhere or other there will almost certainly be a temporary exhibition.

The fashionable suburbs of Les Sables extend along the coast to the south, and that of **la Rudelière** is home to a lake, another casino, a *thalassothérapie* (seawater cure) centre and a small zoo. Like other establishments of its kind, the **Zoo des Sables d'Olonne** now declares its aims to be education and breeding of endangered species. With that in mind, families can spend an enjoyable afternoon in the shade of its abundant vegetation, watching everything from flamingos to big cats, including the graceful watery antics of otters and penguins.

Beyond la Rudelière the sandy beaches give way to rocky reefs and the seascape takes on a wilder look. At a pull-in on the right-hand side of the road you can walk down to le **Puits d'Enfer,** a huge cleft in the rock most spectacular at high tide, when the water crashes in its depths. A coastal path skirts the cliffs affording views of other lesser crevices and eroded stacks in the foaming water.

Shell murals in the Île Pénotte

Talmont, Jard and the south

Travelling south again, the road swings inland behind a forest, leaving the wild cliffs that were once the haunt of smugglers to those who venture forth on foot. Eventually both footpath and road arrive at **Port Bourgenay**, a new development created around a large harbour built in 1985.

From Port Bourgenay the road continues through woods, past a children's amusement park (Belière Loisirs), and on to the remote **Plage du Veillon**, effectively a long spit of sand at the mouth of the River Payré. As the naming of a campsite and a bar on the way have reminded you, dinosaur footprints have been identified on the rocks of this beach. A couple of restaurants tucked in the dunes now offer their seafood platters in the most appropriate of settings.

Plage du Veillon is the end of the line. From there you must retrace your steps to Port Bourgenay and then take a right

Musée des Traditions Populaires, Olonne-sur-Mer

turn into the oddly-named village of **Querry-Pigeon**. There skilled glass-blower Jean-Michel Gautier will divert you with a demonstration of his skills – and a signed left turn through the pastel-coloured 'toytown' hinterland and past a golf course will bring you to the most recent addition to this holiday scene, a huge aquarium complex unlike any other. The 7th Continent, opened in 2006, comprises three rooms each surrounded on all four sides by gigantic glass tanks, thus making you feel you are in the depths of the sea.

Back on the road north again and you soon reach a much longer-established museum, the Musée Automobile de Vendée. A family passion since 1950, the 160 or so vintage cars of this collection now stand in a huge hangar beside the D949 (just west of its junction with the D4). Most impressive are the vehicles from the earliest days of motoring, and a rare and capacious Léon-Bollé touring saloon from 1904. Cycles, motorcycles and wall-posters from the same period are also on display.

7km east of the museum on the D949 lies **Talmont-St-Hilaire**, with immediate glimpses of flag-topped ruins rising above the town as you arrive. Talmont's eleventh-century castle formed part of the dowry of Eleanor of Aquitaine, and so came into the possession of her son, Richard the Lionheart. He liked the area for its hunting and its wine, and so had the castle restored – its present state of destruction was largely achieved by Cardinal Richelieu's persecutions in 1628. But Talmont shows you what a bit of imagination can do with a ruin. With little more than the keep standing, there are nevertheless enough secret pas-sageways, narrow staircases and added 'bridges' to be a delight for inquisitive children. And in the grassy courtyards beneath, they can get a taste of medieval skills in jousting from a rotund Shetland pony, or firing a reduced-size crossbow. Other animations appeal to adults – and everyone can enjoy a summertime *visite nocturne*, when sound, lighting and even olfactory effects work their magic in bringing the castle's history to life as you walk around.

Leaving Talmont, a drive down the west side of the Payré estuary brings you to **la Guittière**, a village par-ticularly famous for its oysters, but also offering demonstrations of the work of the local salt-farmers, and guided bird-watching expeditions on the same terrain. Across the marshes from here lies **Jard-sur-Mer**, an attractive sandy-beached resort with many of its houses and even campsites tucked deeply into the encroaching pine forest.

Just east of Jard, and still bordered by

Take a walk

The road west from Jard along the edge of the pine forest passes the now abandoned seventeeth century Abbey of Lieu-Dieu, strangely surrounded by farm buildings. Further on the road ends at a parking area where a broad track leads over wooded dunes to the attractive Plage des Mines. From this track a signed path takes you through a protected site of holm oaks and pines to the wild Point du Payré at the tip of the estuary, with views of the Veillon cliffs opposite. It is possible to return on a path skirting the shore.

the pinewoods, sits the little village of **St Vincent-sur-Jard**. Its beach, flanked by the long sweep of the Longeville Forest and with views out to the Île de Ré, is one of the most attractive spots on the Vendée coast. Here it was that Georges Clemenceau, great French politician of a century ago, chose to spend the last ten years of his life, and from a local fisherman, rented an unpretentious low tiled cottage, right on the shore. It has been preserved exactly as it was at the time of his death.

To the north of St Vincent, the countryside is particularly rich in menhirs and dolmens dating from some 3000 years BC. The area has been much studied – particularly by an institution known as **CAIRN** (Centre Archéologique d'Initiation et de Récherche sur le Néolithique) in the village of **St Hilaire-la-Forêt**. This establishment can be visited, and in addition to its more serious side that details all the important prehistoric megaliths of western France, you can see a Neolithic house, take in a range of videos relating to Neolithic life and marvel at the skilled demonstrators who chip axe-heads, hurl spears using a *baton-propulseur*, and start fires by rubbing flints, all for your entertainment.

Having visited CAIRN, you will be keen to get out there and find some megaliths. Just up the road is **Avrillé** where the **Menhir du Camp de César**, 7m (23 ft) high and the largest in the Vendée, looks somewhat out of context in the gardens behind the *mairie*. Apparently this 'king of menhirs' was not always alone–there were three menhirs on this site until 1825 when the *mairie* was built. The Office de Tourisme at Avrillé (on the road to Luçon) has maps showing the positions of other megaliths in its domain. Just outside the area of the map is the one that really should not be missed, the **Dolmen de Frébouchère**. A dolmen of the large Angevin type, it can be found by following the signs off the road to Longeville (and dodging a couple of odd dolmens jutting into the minor road on the way). And while in the area, you might pay passing respects to the **Fontaine St Gré** (also signed off the Longeville road), a spring that has some remarkable magic powers.

Still in Avrillé, 14 other menhirs are to be found together in the grounds of the **Château de la Guignardière** that stands beside the road to Les Sables d'Olonne. Presenting a most attractive façade overlooking a 'swan lake', the château itself is worth a look around (its rooms are furnished in styles from different periods) but it is the grounds that attract the visitors. Menhirs and deer park are certainly there, but an inventive mind has added a diversion by the name of *L'Adventure Historique*. Following clues relating to lost civilisations you will find yourself fishing in a pond, measuring an obelisk, hunting a rain-god in the undergrowth, decoding messages and more – cleverly, it is suitable not only for families but for everyone, and elderly ladies, young couples and other unlikely groups are all there enjoying the game!

If after la Guignardière you are still looking for family distractions, 6km (4 miles) to the north at **Poiroux** is La Folie de Fanfarine, a lakeside woodland centre with bee-keeping exhibition, and a few games of its own (including a maze).

But back to the coast again now, and

Jardin des Olfacties, Coëx

through the white houses of Longeville the road leads on to **La Tranche-sur-Mer** (you could take time out to cast your eyes on the curious lichen-covered gritstone Menhir qui Vire, just out of Longeville – it apparently turns around at midnight). La Tranche, with its 13km (8 miles) of beaches is one of the most popular resorts on the coast, but has nevertheless retained the narrow streets

Georges Clemenceau (1841–1929)

Born into a farming family in Mouilleron-en-Pareds (see P68), Clemenceau was a radical in politics. His early career was stormy to say the least, even resulting in a short spell in prison at one point, although he held a seat in government for 17 years. Defeated in 1893, he went into journalism – and as editor of the newspaper *L'Aurore*, famously published Émile Zola's open letter 'J'accuse!' in response to the Dreyfus affair. Later he returned to government and

Bust of Georges Clemenceau

became Prime Minister for three years between 1906 and 1909 and for a further three years from 1917 to 1920. In power at the end of World War I, he was instrumental in putting together the post-war Treaty of Versailles. Clemenceau's ferocious political fighting earned him the epithet *le Tigre* (the Tiger). He was also a superb orator, with many notable quotes to his name (he declared the office of President to be 'as superfluous as a prostate gland' – but only after he had failed in his attempt to secure it!). On the British scene, he was a contemporary and good friend of Lloyd George, with whom he had much in common. His friendship with Claude Monet inspired him to create an 'impressionist-style garden' at his house on the beach.

Château de la Guignardière

of white-washed houses that give it its charm. At the highest point of the town a lighthouse emerges above holiday villas tucked in the pines. It perches on no more than a high dune, and from nearby you can gain access to the Pointe du Grouin du Cou, where the huge waves rolling in from the Atlantic are popular with surfers. West from here stretches the Forêt de Longeville, with many good walks and cycle paths in its depths. More woodland to the north (on the road to Moutiers-les-Mauxfaits) harbours *Indian Forest*, an ambitious arboreal adventure park where a day on the high-level circuits and death-slides could be rounded off with an overnight sojourn in a tree house.

In driving to la Tranche you will have noticed that on the inland side the land-scape has become a perfectly flat tree-less cattle-grazed plain. This is the start of the Marais Poitevin, a land reclaimed from the sea, and although there is yet another resort to the south (la Faute), it truly belongs to that marshland scene and has been included in Chapter 3.

Château de Talmont

Places to Visit

Offices de Tourisme

Challans
Place de l'Europe BP 245
85302 CHALLANS Cedex
☎ 02 51 93 19 75

St Jean de Monts
Palais des Congrès
67, Esplanade de la Mer BP 207
85160 ST JEAN DE MONTS
☎ 02 51 59 87 87

St Gilles Croix-de-Vie
Boulevard de l'Égalité BP 457
85804 ST GILLES CROIX-DE-VIE
Cedex
☎ 02 51 55 03 66

Les Sables d'Olonne
Centre de Congrès les Atlantes
1, Promenade Joffre BP 146
85104 LES SABLES d'OLONNE Cedex
☎ 02 51 96 85 85

Talmont-Saint-Hilaire
Place du Château BP 18
85440 TALMONT-SAINT-HILAIRE
☎ 02 51 90 65 10

Places of Interest

La Garnache

Château de la Garnache
☎ 02 51 35 03 05
Open Jul and Aug, daily 2–7pm (Sun from 2.30pm) and Wed evenings from 9pm; mid to end-Jun and first half of Sept, Mon to Fri 2–6pm.

Châteauneuf

Abbaye de l'Île Chauvet
☎ 02 51 68 13 19
Open Jul to Sept, daily except Sat 2–6pm.

Le Petit Moulin
☎ 02 51 49 31 07
Open Jul and Aug, daily 11am–7pm; Feb to Jun, Sept and Oct, daily 2–7pm.

La Barre-de-Monts

Ecomusée du Marais Breton (le Daviaud)
☎ 02 51 93 84 84
Open May to mid-Sept, 10am–7pm (7.30pm in high season) daily except Sun, Sundays and public holidays 2–7pm; Feb to Apr and mid-Sept to mid-Nov 2–6pm daily (Sun 3–6pm). Closed Mon and public holidays.

Salle Panoramique
☎ 02 51 58 86 09
Open Jul and Aug, 10am–7pm (Sun and public holidays 3–7pm); May, Jun and Sept 10am–12noon, 2–6pm (closed Mon); Feb, Mar, Apr and Oct 2–6pm (again closed Mon).

Sallertaine

La Bourrine à Rosalie
☎ 02 51 49 43 60
Open Jul and Aug daily 10.30am–12.30pm, 3–7pm; Jun and Sept 2.30–6.30pm daily; May to mid-Jun 2.30–6.30pm weekend and public holidays only.

Moulin de Rairé
☎ 02 51 35 51 82
Open daily, Jul and Aug 10am–12noon, 2–6.30pm; Jun, Sept, and school holidays between Feb and May 2–6pm.

Musée de la Mie Câline (bread-making museum)
☎ 02 51 35 40 58
Open Jul and Aug daily 10am–7pm.

La Route du Sel (Canoe trips)

☎ 02 51 93 03 40.
Guided visits to the marsh, including dawn and evening forays, available daily in Jul and Aug. Book at the office in Sallertaine (or any Office de Tourisme). Independent canoe hire is also possible at the base between 10am and 1pm and 2pm and 5.30pm daily.

Noirmoutier

Musée des Traditions de l'Île (la Guérinière)

☎ 02 51 39 41 39
Open Jul and Aug 10am–7pm, Apr to Jun and Sept to mid-Oct 2.30–5.30pm.

L'Île aux Papillons (Butterfly Farm) (la Guérinière)

☎ 02 51 35 77 88
Open Jun, Jul and Aug daily 10am–7.30pm; Apr, May and Sept weekdays 2–7pm, weekends and public holidays 10.30am–7pm.

Océanile (Noirmoutier en l'Île)

☎ 02 51 35 91 35
Open end of Jun to early Sept daily, 10am–7pm.

Le Château (Noirmoutier en l'Île)

☎ 02 51 39 10 42
Open late Jun, Jul and Aug daily 10am–7pm; mid-May to early Jun, Sept and Oct (and first few days of Nov.) daily except Tues 10am–12.30pm, 2.30–6pm.

Sealand aquarium (Noirmoutier en l'Île)

☎ 02 51 39 08 11
Open Jul and Aug 10am–7pm daily; Feb to Jun and Sept to mid-Nov 10am–12.30pm, 2–7pm daily.

Musée de la Construction Navale (Noirmoutier en l'Île)

☎ 02 51 39 24 00
Open mid-Jun to early Sept daily 10.30am–12.30pm, 2.30–7pm; Apr to mid-Jun and rest of Sept daily except Mon 10am–12.30pm, 2.30–6pm.

Île d'Yeu

Two companies operate crossings to the Île d'Yeu.

Compagnie Yeu Continent

☎ 0 825 85 3000
Makes at least two crossings in each direction daily throughout the year (more in Jul and Aug), starting from Fromentine, with times varying each day.

Compagnie Vendéenne

☎ 0 825 139 085
Operates from mid-April to the end of September from Fromentine, La Fosse (Barbâtre) on Noirmoutier and St Gilles Croix-de-Vie, offering high-speed crossings in each direction at suitable times for a day trip.
The company also provides a daily service from Les Sables d'Olonne to Yeu between mid-July to late August, and on certain other dates in the summer months. Some crossings in the winter season from Fromentine.

Le Vieux Château

☎ 02 51 58 32 58 (OT Île d'Yeu)
Open Jul and Aug daily 11am–6pm. OT has details of certain other opening dates outside those times.

(cont'd overleaf)

(cont'd from previous page)

Places to Visit

Notre-Dame-de-Monts

Maison de la Dune et de la Forêt
☎ 02 28 11 26 37
Open Jul and Aug, Mon to Fri 10am–12.30pm, 3–6.30pm. Also Wed in Apr, May, Jun and Sept 2.30–5pm.

Jardin du Vent
☎ 02 28 11 26 43
Open Jun to Aug daily 10am–7pm; Apr, May, Sept and autumn half-term 2–6pm daily except Mon.

St Jean-de-Monts

Arbre et Adventure
☎ 06 22 61 45 98
Open Jul and Aug daily 9am–11pm; Apr, May, Jun, Sept and Oct, 10am–7pm almost daily. Telephone to confirm openings outside high season.

Thalassotherapy Centre
☎ 02 51 59 18 18
Open Mon to Fri all year round (except latter half of Nov and Dec), 9am–12.30pm, 2–5.30pm.

Ferme des Pommettes
☎ 02 51 59 02 26
Open Jul and Aug daily 10am–7pm; latter half of Jun and beginning of Sept, daily 2–7pm; Apr to mid-Jun, weekends and school holidays 2–7pm.

Le Perrier

Promenade en Yole
☎ 02 51 55 58 03
Open daily except Sat, Jul and Aug 2–6pm; latter half of Jun and early Sept 3–6pm.

Les Becs

Atlantic Toboggan
☎ 02 51 58 05 37
Open from mid-Jun to early Sept daily, 10.30am–7.30pm.

St. Gilles Croix-de-Vie

La Bourrine du Bois Juquaud
☎ 02 51 49 27 37
Open Jul and Aug 10am–12.30pm, 2–7pm (Sundays and public holidays 3–7pm only); May, Jun and Sept 10am–12noon, 2–6pm (Sundays and public holidays 3–7pm only), Apr daily except Mon 2–6pm; Feb and Mar weekdays 2–6pm; rest of year school holidays (except Mondays) 2–6pm.

Maison du Pêcheur
☎ 02 51 54 08 09
Open Apr to Sept daily except Tues and Sun 2.30–6.30pm.

Soullans

Musée Milcendeau – Jean Yole
☎ 02 51 35 03 84
Open Jul and Aug daily 11am–7.30pm (Sun 3–7.30pm); May, Jun and Sept daily except Mon 10am–12noon, 2–6pm (Sun 3–7pm); Feb, Mar, Apr and Oct daily except Mon 2–6pm (Sun 3–6pm).

Commequiers

Le Vélo-Rail
☎ 02 51 54 79 99.
Jun, Jul and Aug several departures daily 10am–4.30pm; Apr, early Sept and autumn half-term, daily except Tue, 2 and 4.30pm; May, Wed, weekends and public holidays 2 and 4.30pm. Reservation strongly advised.

Tannerie

☎ 02 51 55 93 42

Open to the public daily except Sun throughout the year 8am–12noon, 2–7pm. Also closed Thursdays out of season.

Apremont

Le Château

☎ 02 51 55 73 66

Open daily; Jun, Jul and Aug 10.30am–7pm (6.30pm Jun); Apr and May 2–6pm; first half of Sept 2–6.30pm.

Coëx

Le Jardin des Olfacties

☎ 02 51 55 53 41

Open daily mid-Apr to mid-Jun and Sept 2–7pm; mid-Jun to end August daily 10.30am–7pm.

St Révérend

La Roseraie de la Vendée

☎ 02 51 55 24 03

Open mid-May to mid-Oct daily 2–7pm.

Le Moulin des Gourmands

☎ 02 51 60 16 72

Open Jul and Aug 10am–7pm daily; Apr, Jun and early Sept, 2–6pm daily except Sat; May 2–6pm Sundays and bank holidays only.

Bretignolles/Brem-sur-Mer

Vendée Miniature

☎ 02 51 22 47 50

Open Jun, Jul and Aug 10am–7pm daily; Apr, May and Sept 10am–12noon, 2–6.30pm daily, but closed Sun mornings.

Parc d'Attractions des Dunes

☎ 02 51 90 54 29

Open early Apr to early Sept daily 10.30–7.30pm.

Le Labyrinthe

☎ 06 65 32 27 95

Open Jul and Aug daily 1–7pm (last entry 6pm).

Île d'Olonne

Observatory

☎ 02 51 33 12 97

Open Jul and Aug daily 9.30am–6pm; late Jun and early Sept 10am–5pm; certain dates in Apr (Wed) for spring migrations.

Olonne-sur-Mer

Musée des Traditions Populaires

☎ 02 51 96 95 53

Open Jul and Aug, Mon to Fri only 3–6.30pm (also Tue and Thur 10am–12noon)); Apr, Jun and Sept weekdays 2.30–5.30pm; rest of year Tue only 2.30–5.30pm.

Les Sables d'Olonne

Muséum du Coquillage

☎ 02 51 23 50 00

Open Jul and Aug daily 9am–8pm; Jun 9.30am–7pm; May 9.30am–12.30pm, 2–7pm; rest of year daily except Sun morning, 9.30am–12.30pm, 2–6.30pm.

Musée de l'Abbaye Ste Croix

☎ 02 51 32 01 16

Open mid-Jun to Sept 10am–12noon, 2.30–6.30pm; Oct to mid-Jun 2.30–5.30pm.

(cont'd overleaf)

(cont'd from previous page)

Places to Visit

Musée de la Mer et de la Pêche

☎ 02 51 95 53 11

Open mid-Apr to Sept daily 3–6pm. Also 10.30am–12.30pm Jun to Sept.

Les Salines

☎ 02 51 21 01 19

Boat trips, visits on foot and canoe hire daily from Apr through to end Sept. Call for reservations.

Zoo des Sables d'Olonne

☎ 02 51 95 14 10

Open Apr to Sept 9.30am–7pm (7.30pm Jul and Aug); Feb (from half-term), Mar and Oct 1.30-6.30pm.

Talmont-Saint-Hilaire

La Belière Loisirs

Open Jul and Aug daily 10.30am–9pm; Jun and early Sept 10.30am–7.30pm (but closed Mon in Jun); late May and late Sept weekends and Wed only 2–7.30pm; Apr and early May daily 2–7.30pm

Le 7eme Continent (aquarium)

☎ 02 51 32 30 00

Open Jul and Aug daily 10am–7pm; Apr to Jun, daily 10am–6pm; rest of year, daily except Mon 2–6pm (but open Mon also in school holidays).

Musée Automobile de Vendée

☎ 02 51 22 05 81

Open daily Jun to Aug 9.30am–7pm; Apr, May and Sept 9.30am–12noon, 2–6.30pm.

Château de Talmont

☎ 02 51 90 27 43

Open daily Jul and Aug 10.30am–7pm (medieval events on weekdays, château visits at weekends); Apr to Jun 10.30am–12.30pm, 2-6pm; Sept to early Nov 2–6pm. Night visits (Nuits de Richard) are possible on weekdays in Jul and Aug and certain nights in Jun and Sept.

St Vincent-sur-Jard

Maison de Clemenceau

☎ 02 51 33 40 32

Open mid-May to mid-Sept daily 10am–12.30pm,2–6.30pm; rest of year daily except Mon 10am–12.30pm, 2–5.30pm.

St Hilaire-la-Forêt

Cairn

☎ 02 51 33 38 38

Open Jul and Aug daily 11am–7pm; Apr to Jun, Sept and Oct daily except Sat 2–6pm.

Avrillé

Château de la Guignardière (with l'Aventure Historique)

☎ 02 51 22 33 06

Open daily, mid Jun to end Aug 10am–9pm; mid-Apr to mid-Jun and Sept 11am–8pm.

Poiroux

La Folie de Fanfarine

☎ 02 51 96 22 50

Open Jul and Aug daily 10.30–7pm; Apr to Jun and Sept, daily except Sat, 2–6pm; Oct and early Nov Sundays and holidays only 2–6pm.

La Tranche-sur-Mer

Indian Forest

☎ 02 51 48 12 12

Open daily from Easter to early Nov, but note that times are different for different activities (these include paint ball, bungy jumping, bouncy castles, etc., as well as the tree-top trails). Reservations advisable.

For the family

Beaches

Younger children might be happier on the quiet beaches of Notre-Dame-de-Monts, while older ones will love St Jean, where coloured symbols (fish, house, engine, etc.) on tall posts help children find their parents–and vice versa–when the sands are crowded. St Gilles has the best of both worlds with beach clubs at one end, peace at the other. But there are marvellous beaches all along this coast – nowhere could be better!

Cycling

The coastal cycle track is superb for families who have never known such freedom in the UK. Cycle hire is available in every resort, and in many campsites too, but you save expense if you bring your own.

The markets

St Gilles (including the evening markets) are a treat for the whole family.

A rainy day?

Head for somewhere that has a variety of museums – in this area, possibly les Sables d'Olonne (Muséum du Coquillage, Musée de la Mer et de la Pêche, Abbaye de Ste Croix). But there are plenty of options – see the preceding list.

Larger 'museums' will occupy more time. Try the 7th Continent Aquarium at Port Bourgenay, and the not-too-far-away Automobile Museum

If it is stormy as well, go to the Corniche Vendéenne north of St Gilles and watch the waves crashing against the rocks. Another good spot for dramatic effects is the rocky coast south of les Sables d'Olonne where, in a westerly gale, spray shoots up from the thundering depths of the Puits d'Enfer.

A taste of the region

Shellfish

In the north of the region, oysters from the Bay of Bourgneuf. In the south, it has to be mussels.

Other food from the sea

At St Gilles, look especially for the Sardines Millésimées; at Les Sables d'Olonne, for fresh cod.

Patisserie

Forget about the sea and look in the patisserie (or on the market) for le Tourteau Fromagé, usually seen as a pile of pie-shaped cakes that look distinctly burnt on top. They aren't – this is simply a very light, not-too-sweet cake made with goats' cheese, and quite delicious.

2. Inland Vendée

The landscape of Inland Vendée is for the most part *bocage*. This commonly used French word can be translated simply as countryside, but it implies countryside of a particular sort – a farming territory of hedged fields, narrow lanes and scattered woodland. In the Vendée, the *bocage* extends from its northern border as far south as Fontenay-le-Comte, where vast cereal plains take over briefly, before the watery landscapes of the Marais Poitevin. The gently rolling terrain of central Vendée is known as the *bas bocage*, while the hilly country of the north-east goes under the title of *haut bocage*.

It goes without saying that leafy green inland Vendée is much quieter and less visited than the coast. Nevertheless, with an eye to all those holidaymakers who might be looking for an escape from the beach for the day, a few attractions have been established. In addition to these, the capital of the department, la Roche-sur-Yon, has a tale to tell and well merits a visit, while to the north and east of the town, the manor houses, forests and even windmills bear witness to the events of the post-Revolutionary Vendéan War. In the south, the Mervent-Vouvant forest is back on the tourist trail again, but

outdoor enthusiasts will enjoy its facilities for walking, mountain-biking and lake swimming. On the edge of this forest, Vouvant's charms have secured it a place among the élite *plus beaux villages* of France – and the nearby time-warped town of Fontenay-le-Comte is one that should not be missed.

La Roche-sur-Yon

Built on high ground above the River Yon, La Roche was a small town decimated by the Revolution when Napoleon's eye fell upon it in 1804. He was seeking a new regional capital for the Vendée, somewhere central from which he could quickly deploy troops should there be any recurrence of insurrection. With a population of merely 400 souls, la Roche usurped the position of regional capital from the more sophisticated Fontenay-le-Comte to the south (which was actually named Fontenay-le-Peuple at the time, as was more in keeping with a town of the Republic). The name of la Roche-sur-Yon itself was formally changed to 'Napoléon' – but that was only the first of many identity changes the town was destined to experience. The emperor promptly did away with most of the old town, set about rebuilding, and ordered his new capital to be fortified. He was not amused on returning a few years later to find its defensive walls had been built from 'wattle and daub', since the unfortunate military engineer could find no stone in the region. La Roche had to wait some 20 years before its new structure was finally completed – a large central square and a grid of streets in the shape of a pentagon, from which the main roads radiated like the spokes of a wheel. It does not make for the most attractive of towns in twenty-first-century eyes, but it does

An identity crisis

In the nineteeth-century La Roche seemed obliged to take its name from whoever was in power at the time – and in such a volatile political climate, it changed its name no fewer than eight times! After being re-baptised *Napoléon* in 1804, ten years later it briefly reverted to *la Roche-sur-Yon* when he fell from power, before becoming *Bourbon-Vendée* under the restored monarchy. In Napoleon's 'Hundred Days' return, it was *Napoléon,* in the second restoration it was *Bourbon-Vendée* again, and when the monarchy was finally abolished in 1848 it was back to *Napoléon* once more. With Napoleon III declaring himself emperor, it became *Napoléon-Vendée* (the name you can still see on the railway station), but when defeat in the Prussian War brought in the third Republic, the political football was allowed to rest, and la Roche-sur-Yon retrieved once and for all its original identity.

have a story to tell.

Paying homage to the great man, the Place Napoléon is the very heart of La Roche – a rectangle rather than a square, it was once the parade ground of 20,000 men. On one side a huge statue of Napoleon on horseback surveys the scene, while the encircling road is flanked by a fine array of neoclassical buildings, among them the Hôtel de Ville and the Église St Louis, said to be the largest church in the Vendée. Outside the Place Napoléon it is more difficult to find features of interest, although a walk into the Rue Clemenceau (from the Hôtel de Ville end of the Place) reveals the bizarrely art deco post office building and venturing in the opposite direction there are some buildings surviving from the original town around the Place de la Vieille-Horloge. Devotees of the work of the Martel brothers (see P13) might like

---

On your bike

On the bed of an old railway line, a 28km (17½ mile) long tarmacked cycle track links La Roche with Coëx in the west. On the way, cyclists pass through the attractive Forest of Aizenay (walks and VTT trails) and could stop off to visit the ruined twelfth-century Abbey of Lieu-Dieu at la Génétouze.

Another treat for the inhabitants of la Roche is the lake of Moulin Papon, created by a barrage on the Yon immediately to the north of the town (take the road to Dompierre-sur-Yon). A 9km (5.5 miles) footpath encircles the lake, and cyclists can take advantage of this along with some minor roads to complete their own circuit.

---

to take in their sculpture of a Vendéan couple in front of the station – and while there, a walk to the more distant platform gives a view of the distinct words *Napoléon-Vendée* crafted in stone above the entrance across the track.

One other feature of la Roche-sur-Yon to remain from its Napoleonic past is the National Stud (left at end of Rue Clemenceau). Originally rearing horses for military purposes, it is now home to 45 stallions of varying breeds, who are housed in the most elegant of quarters. Breeds represented range from draught horses to thoroughbreds, and all are proudly shown off in the hour-long summertime tours.

The Vendée at War

In the years following the Revolution, the green valleys of northern Vendée were the scene of some of the most poignant events of the Vendéan uprising and its sad conclusion. Here you can visit the manor house where brave Vendéan General Charette was captured, witness the recreated scenes in the Forest of Grasla where a hunted community made its retreat, and be moved by the modern memorial and list of victims in the martyr village of Les Lucs-sur-Boulogne. All these incidents took place little over 200 years ago, and are much alive in the Vendéan memory.

Driving on the relatively empty minor roads of France is always a pleasure, and heading north from la Roche-sur-Yon towards les Lucs-sur-Boulogne, you could not do better than take the D2 to **le Poiré-sur-Vie**. This is lovely undulating green countryside, and le Poiré itself sits on the flank of a valley with a lake at its feet. In this attractive spot the watermill (Moulin à Elise) has been restored and now gives noisy, splashy demonstrations of its important former role. There are picnic tables nearby, but if you don't fancy doing it yourself, the mill also houses an inviting crêperie.

North from le Poiré, the D4 rolls on to **Les-Lucs-sur-Boulogne**, on the way passing manor houses that are cited in the *Charette* trail. That can be embarked upon another day (see P58) – the village of Les Lucs, with its Mémorial, Historial, church windows and commemorative roundabout, deserves a day to itself.

It was late February 1794 when a column of Republican soldiers walked into les Lucs and massacred 564 of its inhabitants who had taken refuge in the church. The church itself was burned to the ground. Two hundred years later, Alexander Solzhenitsyn was invited to open a 'Memorial' to those victims – deep in riverside greenery below les Lucs, it is a building of severe grey slabs, intentionally sombre. Inside there is little light to pick out the steles on the floor of the 'crypt' or the curious river that runs through. Agricultural implements fashioned as weapons are hauntingly illuminated, and in the background water drips quietly, adding to the atmosphere. This is not really a place to take young children. Outside in the light again, a footbridge crosses the river and a path winds uphill to the Chapelle du Petit-Luc, rebuilt on the original site from the stones of the one that was destroyed. On the marble slabs of the chapel walls are engraved the names of all those who lost their lives. It is their accompanying ages that makes most impact.

Back in the valley again, the 2006 addition to this scene (a respectful distance away) is the **Historial de la Vendée,** a state-of-the-art museum that in its vast halls sets all the history of the *département* in context. You could be forgiven for not noticing the Historial as you arrived – set just below a rise of ground, its undulating roof is covered in turves of grass, making it almost invisible, and leaving the verdure of the valley undisturbed. The enormous space in this museum is divided on one side into seven separate areas – Prehistory, Antiquity, The Medieval Millennium, The Modern Epoque, The War of the Vendée, The 19th and 20th Centuries, The Third Millennium–while on the other side is a section devoted entirely to children with child-sized exhibits. Each of the seven historical areas is colourfully crammed with tableaux, video screens, talking figures, paintings, artefacts and lots of buttons to press for interaction. Each also has its own *spectacle*, a video show put on at regular intervals in its mini-theatre area. Happily, there is a generous provision of headphones to translate the whole thing into excellent clear English. Only the children's side is 'French only' but there is still plenty English children can do, such as 'cooking' in the kitchen area or illuminating the countries where foods are produced on the big world map. Interestingly, this very French children's section seems almost entirely devoted to food – the child is father of the man!

The Historial sensibly allows you to come and go all day for your entrance

Moulin de Rambourg

fee – such a miscellany of information clearly requires a break from time to time to do it justice. Outside there are picnic tables along the river and the Mémorial site to be visited.

But do not leave without finding the very-real helicopter, which for some reason is in a room of its own in the Antiquity section. Seats inside the helicopter are at a premium, but even those who don't manage to secure one can sit on the side and still experience a rush of blood as it dips and hovers over all the most important sites of the Vendée.

Maison de la Rivière, St Georges-de-Montaigu

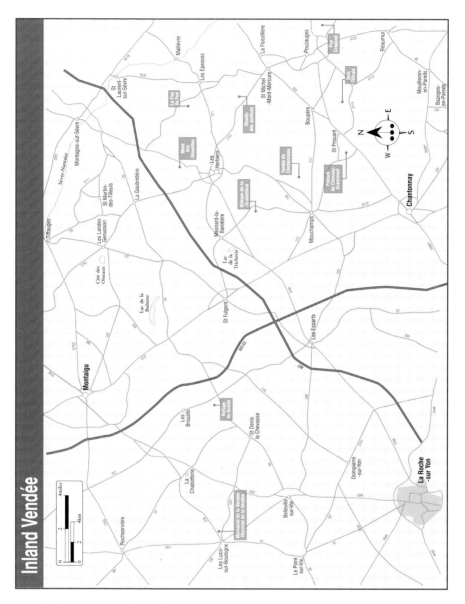

Back up in the village of les Lucs, it is worth going into the church of St Pierre to take a look at its 20th century stained glass windows, with their shocking scenes of the massacre and of the martyrdom of the priest (for a French commentary of this, try the buttons behind the organ). And finally, if you had come to les Lucs on the fast road from la Roche rather than the country route, you would have arrived in the village at a roundabout of memorial pillars, with a carillon of bells alongside. You might like to head out that way to

The Vendéan War

The Revolution of 1789 was born of a long period of dissatisfaction and political unrest in France. In its aftermath, the people of the Vendée (then known as Bas-Poitou) began to take stock of the new situation – and found all to be far from well. For a start, the taxes they were now required to pay exceeded those they had once rendered to the monarchy. And the new regime had taken away the power of the church and persecuted its priests, who were much revered in devoutly Catholic Bas-Poitou. The final straw came when conscription was demanded at a time when they felt little allegiance to their country.

Peasant leaders emerged at this point, and were joined by some of the local aristocracy. Mustering at St Florent-le-Vieil on the Loire, the 'whites', as they were known, soundly defeated and drove out the Republican 'blues' in March 1793. Over the long summer most of the Vendée as far as Angers and Saumur changed hands. In October the Vendéans were defeated at Cholet. Retreating to St Florent again, one of their leaders, Bonchamps, memorably refused to execute 5,000 Republican prisoners. At this time, almost 100,000 Vendéans crossed the Loire and headed north in an attempt to take a port on the Cotentin, through which they hoped to obtain help from the English. They did not succeed, and in their dispirited attempt to return to their homeland, were easy prey for the Republican armies, who were far less chivalrous than their adversaries had been. Finally Republican General Turreau sent in his 'infernal columns' (colonnes infernales) to lay waste to every potential pocket of resistance remaining in the area. The capture and subsequent

take a look.

From Les Lucs you could continue north to **Rocheservière**, where the church at the top of the hill has likewise been invested with a series of stained glass windows recalling another terrible massacre in February 1794. Whether you go that way or not, the next port of call on this circuit of the Vendéan Wars must be the Logis de la Chabotterie, near the village of St Sulpice-le-Verdon, with its tale of charismatic General Charette. Only about 10km (6 miles) from les Lucs, the two sites have been connected by a signed cycle route, for those preferring a more tranquil mode of travel.

La Chabotterie is a typical Vendéan *logis* of the sixteenth-century, with manor house, outbuildings and gardens all enclosed in a defensive wall. It would make an interesting visit in its own right, but the events of March 1796 have given it an added dimension. The ten rooms with their eighteenth-century furnishings look genuinely inhabited, and background sounds and voices add to the effect. The kitchen has the prize exhibit, the actual table on which Charette was laid to have his wounds dressed after his capture. The tour includes a French video of Charette's life and a *parcours spectacle*, a rather claustrophobic series of caves where waxwork-like talking figures tell some of the tale. English translation sheets are offered for all this, but in looking down to read them you execution of General Charette in 1796 effectively brought an end to what became known as the Vendéan War.

In subsequent years, and particularly in the last century, many memorials to the innocent victims of this war have been created. Most poignant is the one at Les-Lucs-sur-Boulogne, but there are also many church windows throughout the area that bear their own witness to the terrible events.

The Vendéans' battle-cry of Dieu et mon Roi (God and my King) is no longer relevant, but the two red hearts surmounted by a cross and a crown that

Mass in the Woods (Rochservière)

every Vendéan stitched to his breast has found an echo in the insignia of today's département of Vendée (although the crown is now often barely discernable).

would lose some of the effect. Outside there are lovely French formal gardens and a very high-class restaurant. A path across fields and through the woods (10 minutes each way) takes you to the spot where the capture was effected, now marked by a granite cross.

One more site in connection with the Vendéan War remains to be visited. Following the D18 south-east you reach the edge of the Forest of Grasla. A turn left on the D6 and then left on the D7 will bring you to the entrance to the **Refuge de Grasla**, a forest site where at the height of Republican repression, many threatened families went into hiding. The site has been evocatively restored, with clusters of primitive thatched huts scattered in the woodland. Some are furnished and inhabited as they might have been – the priest sits writing at his desk, his rough straw bed in the corner; the table is set for a not-too-sumptuous meal; the wounded soldier lies dying on his bed. Outside washing dries on the lines, a pot hangs from wooden beams above the fire and the wood is tidily stacked in piles. But there is no one in sight. The inhabitants have obviously heard you coming and made a quick exit – which is exactly what they did when General Terrand's troops found their way here while looking for Charette in 1795. This story has a happy ending. No one was captured at Grasla. Around two thousand people spent six months living here over the terrible winter of 1794/5

General Charette

François-Athanase Charette de la Contrie was born in a manor house near Ancenis on the Loire in 1763 and followed his father into a career at sea. After ten years roaming the world he returned home and was at the manor of Fonteclose, near Challans, in March 1793 when a peasant mob came to beg him to be their leader. They were excited by their recent victory at Machecoul, but Charette himself was initially unmoved. Eventually he conceded to their demands, and by December 1793 he had extended his command to become General-in-chief of the Catholic Army of Bas-Poitou. In this role he defeated Turreau, and in February 1795, negotiated peace with concessions for the rebel Vendéans. By the summer he had renewed hostilities and was conspiring to restore Louis XVIII to the throne. His plot was foiled, but Charette was clearly still a threat to the Republicans, and he was finally captured at la Chabotterie on 23 March 1796 and executed at Nantes six days later. For those interested, a leaflet available at la Chabotterie details other places associated with the life of Charette.

and then went back to their homes in peace. The Refuge de Grasla is open throughout the summer months, but if you come here on a Sunday afternoon (and certain Thursday evenings), you will find the forest taken over by a group of actors in period costume, who bring the whole scene to life with their production 'Sur les pas d'Amandine'.

The Refuge de Grasla is the last of the important Vendéan War sites, although some 25km (15 miles) to the east is the village of **la Gaubretière**, in whose cemetery (known as the Panthéon) several Vendéan generals lie buried, along with many local victims of an assault by the *colonnes infernales*. A few kilometres north of la Gaubretière, the Martyr Chapel at **St Martin-des-Tilleuls** records more names and ages, and carries two memorial stained glass windows.

Whether or not you go on to those sites, you have travelled well north in the Vendée at this point, and while here there are other places worth a visit. To the north at St Georges de Montaigu, the 18th century water mill has become the **Maison de la Rivière**, with various interactive exhibits on river life, and pleasant walks in the green depths of its valley. Not far way is the **Lac du Bultière**, a paradise for fishermen that also has a 9km signed footpath around its perimeter. North again, near Les Landes-Genusson, another lake serves as an ornithological reserve.

La Cité des Oiseaux is hardly a city but rather a remote reed-fringed stretch of water that is home to a variety of waterfowl and waders. Seasonal migrations provide added interest and are eagerly awaited by those who frequent the two-level observatory and nearby shaded dyke, which are open to all. At one corner of the lake, a stone cottage houses a museum that, with the aid of some memorable tableaux, traces bird evolution from the Jurassic Age. The upper floor is more concerned with the present day, getting you to 'fly' over the land like a bird and listen to the sounds of night and day. In a downstairs room, a camera allows you to zoom in on the wildlife of the lake.

From les Landes-Genusson it is only another 6 or 7 kilometres (4 miles) north to the town of **Tiffauges,** which, having come this far, must be visited. Perched on the banks of the Sèvre-Nantaise river on the northern boundary of the Vendée, Tiffauges' claim to fame is its castle, apparently once owned by the notorious Bluebeard (*Barbe Bleue*).

Although very little of the castle remains, its previous ownership by Bluebeard has made it a gift for the *animateurs* of today. They don't actually extract the blood of children here any more, but in a basement below the ramparts there is an alchemist's workshop conjuring up all manner of spells and potions in a most sinister atmosphere. Take that one or leave it, but out in the courtyard of the château, other more jolly performances are going on all day. Children joust on mock ponies, a primitive wooden crane lifts huge stones and in a side room a shadow theatre cheerfully relates an appalling story of Bluebeard's misdoings. Most popular is the display given by the medieval siege machines, which although here involved in a complicated bit of theatre, convincingly prove their worth by hurling apparent rocks at the distant château wall.

Amid all this revelry, serious seekers of medieval military architecture may find themselves a bit defeated at Tiffauges. Whatever remained of the original tweltfh-century building was effectively demolished by Richelieu in 1626. Only a small part of the curtain wall remains with the Round Tower and machicolated Vidame's Tower joined by a watchpath. Beside the entrance gate, the square keep is now filled with rubble and inaccessible, while the chapel is no more than a Romanesque archway, although guides do still take visitors down to the crypt.

Bluebeard

Gilles de Rais, who lived in the early part of the fifteenth century, was said to be the inspiration for Perrault's fairy-tale character 'Bluebeard'. A military man, he was a lieutenant in the army of Charles VII and fought alongside Joan of Arc in many battles. Her subsequent fate affected him deeply and he never fought again after her death.

Gilles de Rais was a wealthy man and his marriage brought him even more money, yet all was easily consumed by his love of the high life. Parties, feasts and elaborate pageants left him penniless, and in such dire straits he turned to alchemy. Among his many misdeeds in this field, he was said to have murdered hundreds of young children in the belief that their blood could be turned to gold. Eventually brought to justice, Gilles de Rais was condemned to death by hanging at Nantes in 1440.

Hills of the North

At Tiffauges you are at the very tip of the range of granite hills that runs across the north-east corner of the *département*. Known unimaginatively as the *Collines Vendéenes*, these hills are not particularly high – the highest point is just 290m (950ft) – but the relatively flat low-lying landscape on each side gives them their prominence. Many of the heights are crowned with windmills that can be seen from a distance away – in the Vendéan War the position of their sails at rest was a means of conveying messages across country. This very rural area is well off the beaten track, so it comes as a bit of a surprise to find that at the heart of it is one of the most celebrated tourist attractions in France. The Puy du Fou is so popular that it deserves a section to itself – see P62.

The presence of the Puy du Fou means that there is a lot of tourist accommodation in this area, and particularly in **Les Epesses**, where there are a couple of hotels and a first-class campsite, amenable to those who must keep the late hours of Cinéscénie. Surprisingly, only a few of the visitors stray into the local countryside, which remains remarkably peaceful and unexploited.

For a glimpse of perfect rural tranquillity, take the D752 north from Les Epesses to St Malo-du-Bois, and then turn right on the D72 to Mallièvre. A road on the left dips into the green bowl of the **Vallée du Poupet**. Here a picturesque old watermill beside the Sèvre-Nantaise has been converted into a restaurant, and beyond the little weir canoes can be hired to explore the rock-fringed river. A signed walk leads past a little campsite to the next watermill downstream, the Moulin de Chambon – and of course, there are the ubiquitous picnic tables. Since 1988, the Vallée du Poupet has hosted a popular summertime festival, with musicians and comedians performing outdoors.

From the Vallée du Poupet, the D72 will take you on to **Mallièvre**, a pretty former weaving town clinging to the rocky banks of the river. Mallièvre is proud of its past, and in a cottage at the top of the hill, a single room dubbed the *Cave du Tisserand* has been invested with a weaving loom. Pressing a button gives an interesting free show. From here you can follow the *Circuit de Fontaines*, passing the many springs of this village along streets with abundant floral displays. At each blue plaque a button can be pressed to deliver a slice of the village history (in French) – and all those water pumps still work.

Another short excursion from Les Epesses could be to the **Mont des Alouettes** on the N160, west of the Puy du Fou. At 231m (758ft), Alouettes is the highest point in the vicinity (although there are higher to the southeast – see below). Seven windmills once stood along the ridge here, and at the time of the Vendéan War, formed an important part of the local signalling network (see p64). Most of the mills were eventually destroyed by Republican forces, but of those that remain, one has been restored to produce flour. On the other side of the busy road stands a memorial chapel dating from 1823.

Just down the road from the Mont des Alouettes is the busy manufacturing

Take a walk

The Circuit des Fontaines is not the only marked walk at Mallièvre. If you walk down to the river beside the attractive road bridge hung with creeper, you can pick up the *sentier botanique*, a riverside path where certain plants and trees have been labelled. The *sentier botanique* actually forms the first section of the longer (2.5km/1.5 miles) *Sentier de la Genovette*, taking you into the countryside around Mallièvre and returning on a riverside path past the old weaving factory.

The riverside walk in the Vallée du Poupet can likewise be extended. Following yellow flashes from the Moulin de Chambon, you can climb out of the valley and through the village of St Malo-du-Bois, returning alongside another stream to Poupet – a total distance of 9.5km (6 miles). The well-signed route is shown on a board in the Vallée du Poupet, and local tourist offices should be able to find a leaflet about it.

town of **Les Herbiers**. Clothing and shoes are its chief products, with many factory outlets to be found in the industrial park on the N160 to la Roche.

To the north of Les Epesses and the Puy du Fou, the main attraction is the Train à Vapeur (steam train) based at **Mortagne-sur-Sèvre.** This enormously popular excursion comprises an hour's ride down the track to les Herbiers, half an hour at the station assisting with checks on the engine, and an hour's ride back again. Highlights are the viaducts – a long one over the Sèvre Nantaise and two lesser ones–but the countryside is otherwise pleasant in an undramatic sort of way. The company actually owns two trains, one steam and the other diesel, and it is not always possible to tell which one will come on which day. But it is the diesel that from time to time takes on the mantle of the Orient Express, pulling a sumptuously fitted-out dining car in which 6 or 7-course meals are served.

South of Les Epesses, the road dips and then climbs to the highest point of the Vendée, 290m (950ft), at the village of **St-Michel-Mont Mercure**. Naturally there is a church dedicated to St Michel (St Michael) on the summit. The church has a 42m (140ft) high bell tower, but not content with that, it has been topped by a huge red copper statue of St Michel, his cross pointing to the sky. From the rear of the church, a very narrow, half-lit stone staircase spirals up to two balcony viewing platforms, the highest just beneath St Michel's feet. The wind whips around this tower and you can feel it rocking as you climb. The only reassurance is that it has withstood all weather since it was built more than a hundred years ago. The same cannot be said of the statue, which took a severe battering in a winter storm of 1957 and needed to be replaced by helicopter. Stepping out on to the top balcony of the bell tower is breathtaking in every way. If you can bear to open your eyes, six *départements* are under your gaze, and you can clearly see the ridge of these hills stretching away north-west to the Mont des Alouettes.

Coming down from the dizzy heights, you might take the D755 west for a

The Puy du Fou

A thousand years ago there was a keep on a mound known as the Puy du Fou (local patois for Beech Hill), just outside the town of Les Epesses. That keep was demolished by the English in the Hundred Years War, but in the sixteenth-century a granite and brick Renaissance château was built beside a lake nearby. The château became a victim of the Vendéan War, but its ruins were 'discovered' by actor Philippe de Villiers in 1977 and a year later used as the backdrop for the very first evening spectacle on this site. 600 volunteer actors took part, and they were amazed to find that over the summer their performance had received 80,000 visitors.

From that point the Puy du Fou went from strength to strength. More and more people from local villages became *Puyfolais*, volunteering their time to act or serve as technicians. The first charity performance was put on in 1984, and the Puy du Fou has continued to make annual donations. In 1989 it was decided to organise daytime attractions as part of the Grand Parc du Puy du Fou. The scope and quality of these has increased enormously over the years, and the latest figures give the annual attendance at the Grand Parc as 740,000 and at the evening Cinéscénie as 375,000. These sort of numbers put it in 11th place among the tourist attractions of France (almost on a par with Futuroscope, or the Musée d'Orsay) – and yet many people in Britain have never heard of the Puy du Fou!

So what is it all about? Well, the Puy du Fou is not a theme park in the mould of Disneyland or Asterix – there are no fun rides of any sort. Instead it concentrates on history and spectacle, a series of shows, exhibitions and re-creations that are feast for the eyes and ears from the moment you step through the gate. Currently there are five main shows (les incontournables–the essentials), each of which lasts in the region of half an hour and is put on several times throughout the day. Most have a historical basis – the Gladiators tells the tale of Christian persecution in Roman times, the Vikings has good noisily triumphing over evil during the Nordic invasions, La Bataille du Donjon is a fiery siege from the Hundred Years War. The 2006 addition tells the swashbuckling story of 'Richelieu's musketeer' and is the only one to be held under cover. Oldest spectacle of all, the Bal des Oiseaux Fântomes grew from the falconry displays of the early days, and is sited in the remains of the original keep. Today it has birds being

released from a balloon tethered high above the park, and creatures as diverse as vultures and storks swooping over the spectators' heads. In 2009 the opening hours are being extended to include an additional evening spectacle of 'water and fire'. It requires an early arrival and careful planning to fit all this into your day. No wonder they sell two and even three-

Gladiators

day tickets! In addition to the major events there are a whole host of lesser spectacles taking place all over the park – and dotted around the grounds are a medieval city and an eighteenth century village, each with its craft stalls, a fort from the dark ages, a lively town from 1900, a sweet-smelling rose garden, a Chemin de la Mémoire with terrible scenes from the Vendéan War, a lake full of fountains and quite a lot more. For those wanting to dine in style with entertainment, there are two restaurants on the site that need to be booked on arrival. Everyone else must repair to one of the many fast-food outlets that truly are the only unimaginative thing about the Puy du Fou.

Cité Médiéval

Evening Cinéscénie performances generally take place on Friday and Saturday, since all the actors are volunteers from the local villages and have their lives to lead. As daylight fades, 15,000 people file into the terraces facing what comprises the 'stage' for this grand performance – the ruined castle with its lake, a rough-built village beside, and grassy swards to the front. The story is that of 'Jacques' – but then Jacques is the name always given to the oldest son of the Maupillier family, and so Jacques walks through the ages, and through him all the history of the Vendée is told. In point of fact, the storyline matters little, although you can get headphones that will give you an English translation, and the leaflet you are given as you enter supplies the background. It is the spectacular effect of a thousand actors all 'on stage' simultaneously, all playing out their own mini-scenes in a magical setting that will live in the memory. Horses gallop through the lake; dancers twirl and sway on the sidelines; whole families including babes in arms get on with their daily business; donkeys, geese and pigs play their part. Lighting effects are stupendous, allowing characters to melt away in a moment of darkness, and making flames leap as the château catches fire, searchlights pierce the air, and a last new dawn radiate over the sky.

On a practical note, tickets for July and August performances of Cinéscénie are generally sold out at the beginning of the year, and even performances outside high season will be fully booked well before the day. So you need to plan in advance and get in touch with the Parc either by phone or through the website. And note that the show goes on whatever the weather, with no refunds for anyone not wanting to brave particularly adverse conditions. In any case sitting still for a couple of hours after sundown is going to be colder than you think, so wrap up well.

Inclement weather of course reduces numbers in the Grand Parc. On a fine day in high season there will almost certainly be queuing for all the major spectacles, who open their doors half an hour before the performance, and close them when the seats are filled. An early arrival should give you more choice of seat (although of course you waste precious time standing around), but it doesn't always follow that the earliest get the best. A timetable covering both major and minor events is handed out when you arrive.

And finally, it is possible to hire English translation headsets for both the spectacles in the Parc and for Cinéscénie – at a price. For very little extra (if there are two of you) you can buy one with two connections, and so have a mini-FM radio to take home as a souvenir!

Windmill Semaphore

How many messages can you convey using the sails of a windmill? These were the crucial ones.

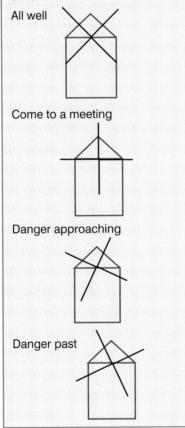

All well

Come to a meeting

Danger approaching

Danger past

is time to head east to the little village of **La Flocellière**. Interest centres on the Chapelle Notre-Dame, where a heavily ornate second chapel at the rear is a perfect replica of the Santa Casa de Lorette in Italy (said to be the early home of the Virgin Mary, carried from Nazareth by angels in the Middle Ages). Outside again, the village boasts some elegant nineteeth-century houses and a most attractive château with a thirteenth-century keep whose gardens can be visited.

From la Flocellière signs lead you to the Maison de la Vie Rurale (just south of St Michel-Mont-Mercure). This is an attractively-set ecomuseum concentrat-

St Michael

There are several references to St Michael in the scriptures, but he is particularly known for his fight in heaven against the powers of evil in the form of a dragon. He is said to be the 'prince of angels' or an Archangel.

Many institutions claim the patronage of St Michael, including soldiers, sailors, drivers, artists, bakers, grocers and police officers. He is patron saint of Germany, and of Cornwall among other places.

In the evangelisation of Europe, St Michael seems to have taken over from the pagan god Wotan, who being responsible for the weather, was often worshipped in high places. In France today there are many, many hilltop chapels dedicated to St Michel. Mont St Michel off the Normandy coast is a classic dedication because on that particular pinnacle, St Michel is also revered as patron saint of mariners.

couple of kilometres to take a look at the site of the **Moulin des Justices**. Built at the end of the nineteenth-century, this mill was a replacement for one that had been burned down by the Republicans. Several waymarked walks now start from the mill and there is a snack-bar on the site, open in summertime.

Back in St Michel-Mont-Mercure, it

ing on fruit, vegetables, poultry, sheep and pigs, but there are also summertime exhibitions on horticultural themes.

Still travelling south, the road leads to **Pouzauges**, passing two windmills in woodland on the left as you descend to the town. The windmills, enjoying a splendid view, can sometimes be visited – and the woods themselves, once the haunt of Druids, are now said to be inhabited by no less a person than the Fairy Mélusine (see P82). There are pleasant footpaths through the Bois de la Folie (and a fitness course) so you have every chance of getting a glimpse of her.

Pouzauges clings precariously to a hillside and a road climbs directly to its twelfth-century château, once owned by the infamous Gilles de Rais (see P59), at the top of the town. Little remains beside the grey solid keep, where wooden staircases have been installed to take you up a couple of floors for the view. Nevertheless, there is something very appealing about this unexploited château surrounded by chestnut trees.

Beneath the château, the steep, narrow streets of Pouzauges have been painted with a green line leading would-be admirers past all the most important sites of the town. This is strictly a walking route – the alleyways of this town are no place for cars. But a vehicle will be needed to visit Pouzauges' out-of-town viewpoint, the **Puy Crapaud**, which is signed from the bypass on the eastern side of the town. After St Michel-Mont-Mercure, the 270m (885ft) of this hill are not going to impress, but this time there is a windmill on top – or at least, half a windmill because the top part has been removed and a *table d'orientation*

installed. The base of the windmill is now a friendly restaurant (you access the staircase to the viewpoint via the bar) so this is a pleasant spot to hang around a while.

Back down on the bypass, the next roundabout south has signs to the Église Notre-Dame du Vieux-Pouzauges, a

On your bike – or look out for theirs!

Cycling is almost the national sport in France, and nowhere is it more popular than in the Vendée, where several major events are organised every year. You might want to give the Château of Pouzauges a miss on the first weekend of September when it becomes the focus of a hugely popular two-day race for all-terrain bikes known as the Vendée Verte VTT. With over a thousand competitors, bikes rule both roads and country tracks for miles around, and several hundred officials are scattered across the countryside to make sure it stays that way. Wherever you are in the *Collines* at that time, you won't miss the Vendée Verte.

church dating from as far back as the château. In 1948, a series of beautifully coloured frescoes was discovered on the north side of the church. Arranged in three layers, the lowest depicts events in the life of the Virgin Mary, while above are monsters and then some delightful cameos of the months of the year. Pressing a button delivers a French commentary with spotlighting of the most interesting features. More frescoes were found under the paint of the west wall in 1988 and have been superbly restored without the addition of colour.

l'Historial de la Vendée

A Drive from Pouzauges

Pouzauges could be the end of your trip south from Les Epesses, but if you would like to make a round tour of it, you could continue west on the D960 in the direction of Chantonnay. Now you are heading out of the hill country into fields of maize, sweetcorn and grazing Charolais. At the village of St Prouant (9km/5.5 Miles), a left turn will take you through some winding lanes to the French Protestant museum, housed in a château in the hamlet of **Bois Tiffrais**. Protestantism has always been strong in this western part of France where Calvin himself once preached. By means of documents, explanatory panels and a few memorabilia, the museum tells of the Wars of Religion, the placatory 1598 Edict of Nantes and the persecution and exodus of the Huguenots when it was revoked almost a century later.

Returning to the D960, a right turn a couple of kilometres further down will bring you to the lovely honey-stone **Prieuré de Chassay-Grammont**, set in open grassland. The priory here was founded by Richard the Lionheart in 1195 and was home to the Grandmontines, a strict order who permitted themselves no wealth or comforts, and subsisted on a near-vegan diet. Last inhabited by monks at the end of the seventeenth-century, the abbey was deconsecrated and used as a farm for some two hundred years before coming into the hands of the state. Now restored, its rooms can be seen gathered around a central square cloister. Most interesting are the vaulted refectory with its serving hatch and the elegant pillars and arches of the chapter house. One room houses a video of the monks' lives.

From Chassay-Grammont, the D113 heads west to **Mouchamps**, an attractive village on a hill above the leafy valley of the Petit Lay. In a park at the north end of the village is a memorial fashioned by the celebrated Martel Brothers (see P13). It commemorates brave local aviator René Guilbaud who died alongside explorer Roald Amundsen while attempting to rescue the crew of an Italian airship that had crashed near the North Pole in 1928.

Whether you leave Mouchamps heading north or heading east, you will soon pick up signs for the *Tombeau de Clemenceau*. Georges Clemenceau, fiery French politician of a century ago (see P42), is buried in the grounds of his father's small estate in the hamlet of le Colombier. He requested that his grave be totally unmarked – surrounded only by simple iron fencing, he lies under a cedar tree on a wooded slope above the Lay, with his father's grave beyond.

Minor roads to the north-west of Clemenceau's tomb will take you to another abbey, that of **Notre-Dame-de-la-Grainetière**. Founded by the

Vallée du Poupet

Benedictines in 1130, it withstood an English siege of the Hundred Years War, but fell under the combined effects of the Revolution and subsequent Vendéan War. Pillaged for its stone and pressed into service for the local farm, the abbey was in poor shape when taken over for restoration in 1963. Since then a community of monks has returned and the buildings are in use once more, although it is still possible to make a visit. Its most photographed feature is the one surviving side of the cloisters with its long line of graceful twin-columned arches.

From Notre-Dame-de-la-Grainetière you could make a quick return to les Epesses or Pouzauges , but there are two more fascinating places nearby. A few kilometres down the N160 is Ste Florence, home town of eccentric artist Gaston Chaissac (see P39). The primary school he once attended has become the **Espace Chaissac** with an exhibition as bizarre as the artist himself and outdoor lavatories that are the only such dedicated Historic Monuments in France (he left graffiti on their walls!).

North of the N160, more conventional wall painting can be found at **Mesnard-la-Barotière.** The squat 11th century church of St Christophe (on the edge of the village) has probably the most remarkable set of frescoes in the Vendée. In muted colours of red, blue and yellow, the walls of the chancel present some disturbing scenes – the beheading of John the Baptist and St Lawrence being burnt alive on a brazier – as well as a more tranquil Nativity, the Last Supper and a lot more. Among the biblical scenes are the painted coats of arms of local families. Church entry is free, there is a leaflet in three languages

St Michel-Mont-Mercure

Donjon de Bazoges

to explain all you see, and a French commentary is provided, with handsets (which may or may not be working) to do the same thing in English. Catering for whetted appetites, a film of other local frescoes is shown on an overhead screen. Opposite the church an attractive small park with water features has inviting-looking picnic tables.

No more than a stone's throw from Mesnard-la-Barotière (south–follow the signs) is the **Lac du Tricherie**, a lake with a sandy swimming beach, children's playground, crêperie overlooking the water, and pedalos and miniature electric boats for hire. Maybe this is not a suitable end to a busy day, but anyone staying in the area with a family would do well to take a look.

The Central Bocage

The *bocage* is the farming country of the interior, and it stretches right across the Vendée to the marshes of the coast in the west and the Marais Poitevin in the south. In summertime the fields glow brightly with sunflowers, in autumn they stand tall with maize or piled with *mogettes* (white haricot beans) and everywhere the cattle graze. Charolais seems the popular breed, but there are also rich brown Limousin and others. Through this rolling landscape the rivers gather strength as they drain south and west, carrying their water into the marshes. The River Lay, whose source is south of Pouzauges, passes through some particularly beautiful countryside, and around Mareuil its valley is home to the largest of the Vendée vineyards.

Travelling south from Pouzauges, you will first meet the Lay at the village of **Réaumur**, a name that should be ringing bells with scientists. René Antoine Ferchault de Réaumur, most remembered for the temperature scale that takes his name, was actually a native of La Rochelle, but spent holidays here in his family's country château. That château now welcomes visitors with rooms of scientific exhibits and explanatory panels. This visit is a very French experience, although you are offered a whimsical English account of the museum's contents. Most curious is a tiny theatre where the actors have been miraculously shrunk to maybe a twentieth of their size to fit in with the stage set – you may not understand what is going on, but the effect is fascinating. The carefully laid-out gardens contain an area for observing Réaumur's favourite creatures, the bees, and outbuildings house temporary exhibitions.

From the village of Réaumur there are some pleasant waymarked walks along the valley of the Lay. But leave that for a while and head south-west towards **Mouilleron-en-Pareds.** Just before reaching the town you will see signs pointing left to the Tassigny memorial and the Rochers de Mouilleron. High above you are three windmills on a draughty ridge and a rocky viewpoint with a statue of the Virgin on the highest point of the hill.

Take a walk

Why not reject the road and continue instead into the town of Mouilleron to reach the same point from a footpath (the *Sentier des Meuniers* – Millers' Path) that starts beside the *lavoir* below the town square. This is the route the millers and their donkeys would have taken, and yellow flashes will guide you all the way (6.5km/4 miles there and back).

Humble little town that it is, Mouilleron-en-Pareds has given birth to two of France's great men of not too distant times. Of Protestant stock, fiery left-wing politician Georges Clemenceau (see P42) was brought up in a terraced building at the top of the town. His finest hour came with the signing of the Treaty of Versailles in June 1919. Maréchal Jean de Lattre de Tassigny, of

René Antoine Ferchault de Réaumur (1683–1757)

Réaumur was a man with a plethora of interests. At the age of 16 he was sent to Bourges to study Civil Law and Mathematics. His first love was geometry, and aged only 24, he was elected a member of the *Académie des Sciences*. Next on his agenda was the investigation of industrial materials, the differences between iron and steel and the strengths of rope. From there he went on to meteorology, with the invention of the temperature scale that bears his name. Based on the expansion of alcohol rather than mercury, Réaumur took his freezing point to be 0 and his boiling point to be 80. The scale, at one time widely used, was gradually replaced by that of Celsius.

Réaumur's most enduring interest was natural history, including work on the digestion of birds and the composition of corals. Insects particularly fascinated him, and he wrote six volumes with illustrations detailing their appearances, lifestyles and habitats.

a Catholic landowning family, took a similar role in signing for France at the conclusion of World War II hostilities. His family home was a mansion beside the village square that now houses a museum detailing his military achievements. For more information on Lattre de Tassigny, see the box on p.70.

In addition to the photographs and family paraphernalia of the Lattre de Tassigny museum, you can also be taken across the square to another house that has become the **Musée Nationale des Deux Victoires**. Here the military careers of both men are celebrated. Most prized possessions are an eagle's head from the Reichstag in Berlin given to Lattre de Tassigny and a walking stick with a tiger head, carved for Clemenceau by soldiers in the First World War. The blotting paper under glass is a replica of that saved by Clemenceau after the signing of the Treaty of Versailles.

The house in which Clemenceau was born has recently been acquired by the museum, with the intention of extending their range of exhibits.

South-west of Mouilleron, **Bazoges-en-Pareds** is a pretty village quite dwarfed by the fourteenth-century *donjon* at its heart. This gigantic column of honey-coloured stone with a little pointed watch tower at one corner is all that remains of what must have been a most impressive château on this site. Although the rooms on various floors have now been appropriately furnished, the chief reason for visiting must remain the all-embracing view from the watchpath at the top. Beneath the keep, the courtyard is beautifully garlanded with flowers and a building has been taken over to house the Musée d'Arts et Traditions Populaires, a miscellany of objects associated with traditional country life. On the far side of the courtyard, the Medieval Garden was created by a former mayor in 1994. Aromatic plants, medicinal plants, herbs, fruit and vegetables are beautifully set out in a garden overlooked by an old circular dovecote.

Leaving Bazoges to the west, look for a sign to the **Ciste des Cous**, pointing you up a track to the right. In a couple of hundred yards you will come across the site of the oldest megalith in

Places to Visit

Offices de Tourisme

La Roche-sur-Yon

Rue Georges Clemenceau
85000 LA ROCHE-SUR-YON
☎ 02 51 36 00 85

Pouzauges

28, Place de l' Église
85700 POUZAUGES
☎ 02 51 91 82 46

Places of Interest

La Roche-sur-Yon

Haras National

☎ 02 51 46 14 47
Open Jul and Aug every day except Sun for guided visits at 10.45am and in afternoons 2–5pm. Sun visits 3pm only. Jun and Sept visits every day except Sun and public holidays at 3pm.

Le Poiré-sur-Vie

Moulin à Elise

☎ 02 51 31 61 38
Open Jul and Aug weekdays 10.30am–12.30pm, 2.30–6.30pm, Sun 3–6pm. Closed Sat.

Les Lucs-sur-Boulogne

Mémorial de la Vendée

☎ 02 51 42 81 00
Open daily Jul and Aug 10am–7pm; rest of year 9.30am–6pm (Sun 10am–7pm).

L'Historial de la Vendée

☎ 02 51 47 61 61
Open every day except Monday, April to September 10am-7pm; October to March 10am-6pm. Open Tuesdays until 10.30pm in July and August.

St Sulpice-le-Verdon

La Chabotterie

☎ 02 51 42 81 00
Open Jul and Aug 10am–7pm daily; Sept to Jun Mon to Sat 9.30am–6pm, Sun and public hols 10am–7pm (6pm Nov to Mar).

Les Brouzils

Refuge de Grasla

☎ 02 51 42 96 20
Open Jun to mid-Sept daily 11am–6pm; May Sun and bank holidays 2–6pm; latter part of Sept Sun 2–6pm. *Sur les Pas d'Amandine*, 2 performances every Sun afternoon (3.30 and 5.30) from Jul to mid-Sept. Also Thur evenings at 8pm in Jul and Aug.

the Vendée, a stone cairn dating from around 4000 BC. Although no longer covered over, the circular enclosure, entered by a corridor underneath a low arch, is remarkably well preserved. Excavations here a century ago revealed the bones of around 150 people and other artefacts.

From Bazoges the Lay continues west through Mareul, and the valleys of its many tributaries are home to the respected vineyards. While in this area you might also like to visit the **Moulin de Rambourg**, a picturesque restored watermill to the north in the valley of the Yon (at Nesmy). And moving west to Aubigny, the **Espace des Records** with its preposterously-sized household objects makes a fun visit for all the family.

St Georges-de-Montaigu

Maison de la Rivière

☎ 02 51 46 44 67

Open mid-Jun to end Aug daily 11am--7pm; Apr to mid-Jun and early Sept every day except Mon 2–6pm (Sun 7pm); mid-Sept to early Nov Sun and school holidays (except Mon) 2–6pm.

Tiffauges

Château de Barbe-Bleue

☎ 02 51 65 70 51

Open Jul and Aug daily 11am–7pm, Nocturnal Theatre Wed 10pm; Jun and Sept weekdays 10am–12.30pm, 2–6pm, weekends and holidays 2–7pm.

Mallièvre

La Cave du Tisserand

Open 10am–8pm May to mid-Sept every day; Apr, May and late Sept weekends.

Mont des Alouettes

Windmill

☎ 02 51 67 16 66

Open Jul and Aug daily 10am–7pm; Jun and early Sept daily except Tue 10am–12.30pm, 2–6pm; Apr and May weekends and holidays only 10am–12.30pm, 2–6pm.

Mortagne-sur-Sèvre

Le Train à Vapeur (Steam Train)

☎ 02 51 63 02 01

The train leaves Mortagne-sur-Sevre at 3.30pm and returns at 6pm. It is possible to make a one-way trip to Les Herbiers, but not one in the opposite direction. Trains leave every Wed, Fri and Sun in Jul and Aug; Sun only in Jun and the first two weeks in Sept.

St Michel-Mont-Mercure

Maison de la Vie Rurale

☎ 02 51 57 77 14

Open Jul and Aug daily 2–8pm; latter half of Jun and first half of Sept daily 2.30–6.30pm; May to mid-Jun, Sun and public holidays only 2.30–6.30pm.

Pouzauges

Château de Pouzauges

☎ 02 51 57 01 37

Open mid-Jun to mid-Sept daily except Mon 2–7pm.

Table d'orientation du Puy Crapaud

Access at any time except Wed afternoons.

Cont'd on the next page

Jean de Lattre de Tassigny (1889–1952)

After a distinguished career in the first World War, Lattre de Tassigny was made head of the French War College and then became a general in World War II. In 1943 he was imprisoned by the Vichy government, but escaped to Algiers, where he became head of the 'French Army B' (later called the French First Army). In August 1944 De Lattre's troops landed in Provence and began the liberation of the south. After marching through Alsace they crossed the Rhine into Germany. De Lattre accepted the German surrender in Berlin on 8 May 1945. After the war he commanded French troops in IndoChina, in which conflict his son Bernard was killed.

Places to Visit

Le Bois Tiffrais

Museé de la France Protestante de l'Ouest
☎ 02 51 66 41 03
Open mid-June to mid-September every day except Monday 2-6pm.

St Prouant

Prieuré de Chassay-Grammont
☎ 02 51 66 47 18
Open Jun to mid-Sept daily 10am–7pm.

Abbaye de Notre Dame-de-la-Grainetière
☎ 02 51 67 21 19
Open every day 7am–7pm.

Ste-Florence

Espace Gaston Chaissac
☎ 02 51 66 10 84
Guided visits Jul and Aug weekdays 10am–12noon, 2–6pm; rest of year weekdays 2–5pm, 1st and 3rd Sun in every month 3–6pm.

Cité des Oiseaux
☎ 02 51 91 72 25
Open Jul and Aug 11am–7pm every day; Jun and Sept 10.30am–12.30pm, 2–6pm weekdays, 2–7pm Sun, closed Sat; Apr and May 2–6pm every day except Sat.

Les Epesses

Le Puy du Fou

Grand Parc
Open 10am–10.30pm every day in Jul and Aug (9pm on nights of Cinéscénie); 10am–7pm most days in Jun and some days in Apr, May and Sept. The website www.puydufou.com will give you more details.

Cinéscénie
Performances every Fri and Sat at 10.30pm in Jul and 10pm in Aug. Other performances take place on some weekend days in Jun and the first weekends of Sept - the website above will fill you in on annual variations. Bookings are preferably made online (alternatively ☎ 02 51 64 11 11)

Mesnard-la-Barotière

Église St Christophe
☎ 02 51 66 02 74
Open all day every day in Jul and Aug and at most other times. If closed, apply to the mairie (open Mon to Sat 9am–12noon).

Réaumur

Manoir des Sciences de Réaumur
☎ 02 51 57 99 46
Open Jul and Aug every day 11am–7pm; Apr, latter half of Jun and first half of Sept every day 2–6pm; May to mid-Jun and mid-Sept to Nov, Sun, Bank Holidays and school holidays only 2–6pm.

Mouilleron-en-Pareds

Maison Natale du Maréchal de Lattre de Tassigny and Musée Nationale des Deux Victoires
☎ 02 51 00 31 49
These function as one museum, open every day throughout the year 10am–6pm (7pm in high season).

Bazoges-en-Pareds

Donjon
☎ 02 51 51 23 10
Open Easter to Sept every day 2.30–6pm; mid-Feb to Easter and Oct, Sun only 2.30–6pm.

Musée d'Arts et Traditions Populaires

Opening hours and telephone as Donjon

Nesmy

Moulin de Rambourg

☎ 02 51 06 03 15

Open Jul and Aug only, every day except Mon 1–7pm.

Aubigny

L'Espace des Records

☎ 02 28 15 50 63

Open Jul and Aug every day 10.30am-12noon, 1.30–6pm; Apr to Jun and Sept every day 2–6pm; Oct to mid-Nov Sun and Bank Holidays only 2–5.30pm.

For the family

Puy du Fou

To get the most out of it, arrive early and plan your day with care as soon as you get the programme (at the entrance). There just isn't time to see it all, and you will want to...

The Historial de la Vendée

Lots for the young here, and everything translated into English (except the helicopter ride and the special children's section). Another plus point is that you can go out for a break (play on the grass, picnic, etc.) and come back in. There is also a cafeteria for light meals.

Lac du Tricherie

For simpler pleasures, head for the Lac du Tricherie (off the road from Les Essarts to Les Herbiers). Swimming and playground are free, but you might get pressurised into those electric boats (although not for younger children).

A rainy day?

The Historial again

You could easily spend hours here.

La Chabotterie (at St Sulpice-le-Verdon)

Easily deserves a couple of hours of your time – and maybe the sun will come out for you to walk through the woods to the Croix de Charette. The restaurant at the gate is interesting, too.

Take the drive

Described from Pouzauges on P.66. You will get a good feel for the countryside (even though wet!) and there are many indoor museums, abbeys and the like to get you out of the car for a while.

A taste of the region

Mogettes

White haricot beans – are omnipresent. They are at their best when served with fresh Vendéan ham. If you are self-catering, it's probably best to buy the beans tinned or bottled – dried ones need long soaking and simmering, and fresh ones are hard to come by (late summer only).

Wines

Wines from the Fief-Vendéen vineyards. Favoured by Cardinal Richelieu, these are not 'great' wines but are very drinkable. Whites, reds and rosés are produced and have been accorded VDQS status.

Sweet Bread

Brioche Vendéen is a lovely light sweet bread, often flavoured with orange-water and maybe even something stronger.

3. The Marais Poitevin

The *départément* of Vendée meets that of Charente-Maritime in a vast low-lying plain known as the Marais Poitevin.

At its heart is the Sèvre–Niortaise river, and on either side innumerable water channels dissect the land. As recently as Roman times this whole area was under the sea and at Chaillé-les-Marais and Velluire in the north and Esnandes and Nuaillé-d'Aunis in the south you can still see the former cliffs. Over the centuries the rivers carried down their alluvium and the sea washed in its silt to fashion between them a foul-smelling marsh, punctuated by rocky outcrops that had once been islands in the sea. This swamp was first drained by the monks of the Middle Ages and later by Dutch engineers brought in by Henri IV.

The Marais Poitevin today is perceived to be in two distinct parts – to the west, the flat open grazing land of the Marais Désseché (Dry Marsh), and to the east, the attractive green labyrinth

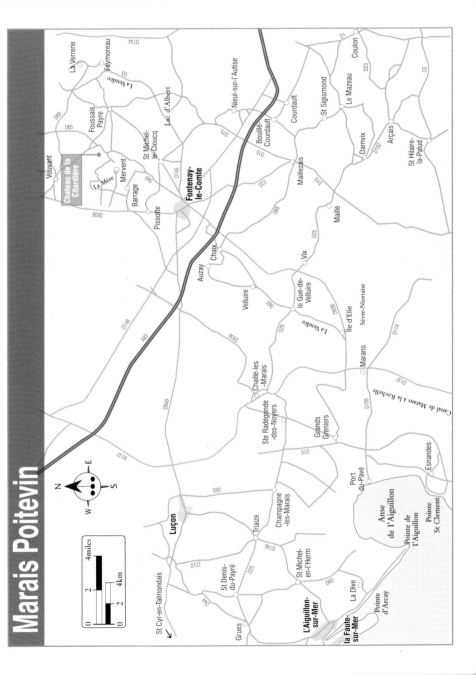

Marais Poitevin

of tree-fringed channels that form the Marais Mouillé (Wet Marsh). The whole area enjoys protected status as an 'Interregional Park', and is very well endowed with family-friendly cycle routes and walking trails.

There are no big towns in the Marais Poitevin, but on its northern border sits Fontenay-le-Comte, a time-warped place with an interesting history. Fontenay is usually considered as part of the Marais Poitevin — and along with it, the hilly Mervent-Vouvant Forest to the north, an area that is clearly neither *bocage* nor marsh.

Fontenay-le-Comte

Fontenay-le-Comte is a lovely old town in a splendid position — to the south lies the most attractive part of the Marais Poitevin, while immediately to the north are the leafy heights of the Mervant-Vouvant Forest. The town was the capital of the pre-Revolutionary province of Bas-Poitou, and takes its name from its fontaine, the Fontaine des Quatre Tias. Couched in a sixteenth-century façade, it bears a Latin inscription that translates as *The Fountain and Source of Fine Minds*. This grand motto was bestowed on the town by François I (his salamander emblem is on the fountain), and certainly there were many fine minds in Fontenay at the time (see box).

Fontenay had its heyday, and fortunately a few buildings from that time survived both the Wars of Religion, when the town was staunchly Protestant, and the Revolution. The Office de Tourisme offers a very comprehensive tour (aided by ceramic fountain logos let into the pavement), visiting these buildings and every other point of note in the town. For a much simpler circuit, you could keep east of the river and head for one of the car parks signed off the busy main street, the Rue de la République. On the opposite side of these two car parks runs the town's former main thoroughfare, the Rue des Loges. Although most of its houses are now shops, some have retained interesting façades — no. 26 (wrought

Of fine minds

Perhaps the best known of the fine minds was Rabelais, wordy satirist and creator of the giants Gargantua and Pantagruel, who spent three years in Fontenay studying Greek literature at the Franciscan monastery (1520–23) – he speedily defected to the Benedictines at Maillezais when Reformation literature was found in his possession. Another famous name was that of Francois Viète, said to be the 'father of algebra'. Viète was in reality an all-round mathematician who secured his position at the court of Henri IV by decoding messages meant for his enemy, Philip II of Spain. His greatest moment came when he solved a problem posed to the world by the greatly-esteemed Dutch mathematician Roomen, and so was seen to uphold the honour of French mathematics.

Others of note in sixteenth-century Fontenay were André Tiraqueau, learned lawyer and author of a treatise on matrimonial law, and poet and magistrate Nicholas Rapin, who lived in the magnificent Château de Terre Neuve on the edge of town.

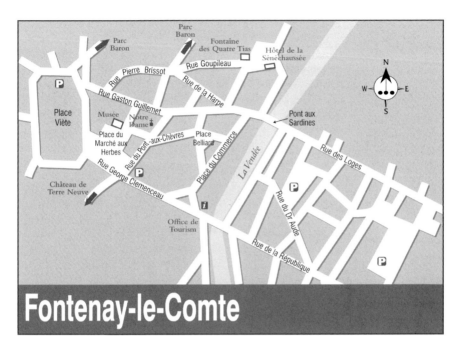

Fontenay-le-Comte

iron balconies) and no. 84 (the Maison Millepertuis - carvings) are the most notable. More recent additions to the scene are the loudspeakers supplying piped music!

The Rue des Loges ends at the river and the ancient Pont-aux-Sardines, so called because the quay alongside was where the fish was unloaded. Crossing the bridge here and then taking the second on the right will quickly bring you to one of the architectural gems of Fontenay, the Place Belliard. Fine arcaded Renaissance houses line one side of the square, but General Belliard on his central plinth determinedly looks the other way. He was born at no. 11 and achieved fame by saving Napoleon's life at the Battle of Arcole.

Leading from the Place Belliard, the narrow Rue du Pont-aux-Chèvres has the best display of Renaissance buildings in town – no. 9 (on the right) has a fine balustraded staircase and was once the home of the Bishops of Maillezais; no. 6 (on the left) has an imposing entrance gate topped by a rather time-worn statue of Laocoon; no.14 (the Hôtel de Rivaudeau) belonged to a one-time mayor of Fontenay and has a fine entrance porch, Doric columns and caryatids. The short street opens into the market square dominated by the seventeenth-century slender crocketted spire of the Église Notre-Dame. Carvings of the Wise and Foolish Virgins around the north door are worthy of attention, and it is sometimes possible to visit the eleventh-century crypt beneath the church.

At this point it is worth devoting a little time to the Musée de Fontenay, on the market square, and close to the church. All the region's history is proudly displayed on its three floors – Gallo-Roman glassware recovered

from a nearby sarcophagus, tradition-ally-carved furniture and a fine col-lection of paintings of local scenes by Vendéan artists. Look out for the one with the sardines being packed! The historical model of the town with its commentary is interesting.

After the museum, there is only one place missing on this whistlestop tour, the *fontaine* after which the town was named – or at least partially named, because the *Comte* in its title refers to the lord of the town, who in its early days was the Count (*Comte*) of Poitou. Since after the Revolution this was blatantly unacceptable, the town enjoyed a short spell as Fontenay-le-Peuple (Fontenay-the-People). But back to that fountain – from the market square turn right (the raised chestnut-tree-lined parking

Place Belliard

place on your left is the Place Viète with its own fountain), go right again on the Rue Gaston, and immediately left on the Rue Pierre Brissot. At its end, the Rue Goupilleau (slightly left) will bring you to the Fontaine des Quatre Tias (*tias* = pipes), in its Renaissance casing. When you have paid it sufficient homage–and found the salamander and the engraved names of the magistrates of Fontenay–the Rue Rochefoucault will quickly return you to the Pont-aux-Sardines. Take a quick glance at the Hôtel de la Sénéchausée (1590) on the corner as you turn.

On the outskirts of Fontenay (and signed from the Rue de la République), there is one more place that should not be missed. The **Château de Terre Neuve** was built for the sixteenth-century magistrate Nicholas Rapin by the architect Jean Morrison, who was also responsible for the houses on the Place Belliard. Although now a private home, the elegant L-shaped grey château, finished with pepper-pot turrets and fronted by statues of the

Fontaine des Quatre Tias

Muses, opens its doors to the public in summertime. Highlights of the visit are the stone 'Alchemist's fireplace' in the richly decorated sitting room, and the carved chimney breast supported by two griffons in an equally elegant dining room, but there are also the carved stone ceilings, period furniture, wood panelling from the Château de Chambord and a lot more. In latter years, the château was briefly (1940-43) home to the novelist Georges Simenon and it was here that he wrote *Maigret à peur* (Maigret Afraid).

Just outside the gates of the Château de Terre Neuve, Fontenay has yet one more curiosity. The concrete octagonal Tour Rivalland was erected here in 1880

Château de Terre Neuve

by a freemason determined that the spire of Notre-Dame should not rule alone on Fontenay's horizon. He cheated a little in taking advantage of the height of the land here, but was a good ten years ahead of his time in using poured concrete for his chosen medium.

The Mervent-Vouvant Forest

From Fontenay-le-Comte, a very short drive will take you into the forest to the north. The terrain is surprisingly hilly here, and the dense covering of deciduous trees plunges over outcrops of granite into the winding gorges cut by the rivers Vendée and Mère. On a spur above their mingling waters sits the attractive little village of Mervent, while Vouvant, one of the elite *plus beaux villages de France*, has its own hilltop location at the northern limit of the forest. The whole area is very popular with lovers of the outdoors – mountain bikers, walkers and canoeists.

Both the Mère and the Vendée have been dammed to give narrow snaking sections of lake, and it is this Lac de Mervent that you first meet when heading north from Fontenay on the D65. After crossing the tail end of the lake, the road climbs to a cross-roads beside an attractively laid out animal park known as the Natur'Zoo de Mervent. To the left is the forest, and going that way, you will quickly return to the lake shore at La Plage, an area of rough imported sand overlooked by a casual restaurant. Swimming is possible, pedalos and canoes are for hire nearby and there is a sailing school next door, making it a very popular location

on summer weekends. The village of **Mervent** looks down on all this from its vantage point on the opposite flank, and can be reached by another bridge a little further along, this time crossing not the Vendée, but the Mère.

Mervent is virtually perched on a rocky peninsula between the two rivers and the best place for a view of the waters is the Parc du Vieux Château, which is now the garden of the Hôtel de Ville. The village has a central square surrounded by all the essentials – a couple of shops, a bar, a squat red-tiled Vendéan church (look for the weight-driven clock inside) and a little Tourist Office, that though it keeps some unusual hours, is nevertheless crammed with literature on every aspect of the forest, including its walking and cycling trails. A recent addition is the Adventure Park in the woodland behind the village (next to the campsite), where those with simian inclinations can test nerve and agility on five graded circuits through the branches. There are bouncy castles for the tiniest, and an 18m (60ft) bungee-jumping tower for the craziest.

A forest drive

This short tour is a mere 20km (12.5 miles) or so, but it should give you a feel for the forest. From Mervent, return down the hill and cross the bridge over the Mère again. Take the next turn left, and the D99 will soon have you in the depths of the forest. At the **Pont du Déluge**, a high arched bridge over a tributary stream, you can walk down to the leafy glade beside the water's edge and perhaps be inspired by one of the walking trails that pass that way. If so, just wait a minute - the road soon crosses the route of the 4km (2.5 miles) *Sentier Sylvicole*, a nature trail marked by little blue arrows on sticks. You may not get much from the French text detailing the trees, but at least you will have a lovely forest walk.

Further on signs point you up the valley to the **Parc de Pierre Brune**. It is surprising to come across an amusement park in such an out-of-the-way spot as this, but it blends quite well and mostly concentrates on the unsophisticated attractions of a bygone age. Children will love its train, bumper-boats and enchanted valley of games–and it has a modest all-inclusive entry fee that shouldn't break the family bank.

In the steep cliffs up above the Parc de Pierre Brune is a cave known as the **Grotte de Père Montfort** – you can reach it by crossing the barrage and climbing the steep hill thereafter. From a parking area, steps descend to a hole in the cliffs that in 1715 offered shelter to a priest on a mission to convert the Protestant population to Catholicism. Louis-Marie Grignion de Montfort was later canonised and the cave became a place of pilgrimage.

On, on through the forest and signs are directing you left to the **Barrage de Mervent**. The dam is worth a look – white and gracefully curving, it is less forbidding than most – but note that this is a one-way road, you cannot simply turn round and come back. So maybe first you should continue out of the forest to the village of **Pissotte**, which is the centre of one of the four vineyards producing Fief Vendéen wines. There are *caves* (wine cellars) in the village to be visited. When you return across the Barrage of Mervent, the forest road takes you past interesting-looking clearings with picnic tables to arrive back on the D65 from Fontenay to Mervent again.

After that brief look at the forest it is time to go a little further north to visit the delightful village of Vouvant. On the way, at the hamlet of les Quillères, you might follow signs to get a glimpse of the **Château de la Citardière**. Picturesquely surrounded by its moat, this sixteenth-century château is now a popular crêperie and has incongruously decked its drawbridge entrance with a purple neon sign to tell you so. Exhibitions and other cultural events are added attractions in summertime. Just up the road at La Jamonière, the **Maison des Amis de la Forêt** may be worth a

The *Plus Beaux Villages de France*

Created in 1982, the Association of *Plus Beaux Villages de France* now has 151 members. Each village must satisfy 30 selection criteria – the simplest is that it must have no more than 2,000 inhabitants, while others depend on an assessment of its architectural, environmental and heritage value. These villages truly are the best of France. The award of such a prestigious title carries with it enormous tourist potential – and there are patriotic Frenchmen (and women) whose lifetime ambition is to visit every single *plus beau village*!

pause, particularly if you have children on board. Forest flora and fauna are on display (some unfortunately stuffed) and there is a video of forest life.

Beyond is the village of **Vouvant**, one of the more appealing of France's select *plus beaux villages,* with a fine location on a high bluff overlooking the River Mère.

At the highest point of Vouvant, the lonely building on the grassy swards is the Tour Mélusine, which is said to have been built (like many other edifices) by the fairy herself in a single night. It is always possible to climb the tower–if the door is not open you should be able to get the key from the café opposite. On the turreted top, a symbolic Mélusine spins in the wind and you can share her view over village, river and forest.

In reality, the Château at Vouvant, of which only the Tour Mélusine remains, is said to have been built by the Lusignan family in 1242–but at this point fact and fairy tale become confused because the Lusignan family actually claim descent from Mélusine and her husband Raimondin. At least one of their children, Geoffrey Longtooth, was real enough, a bloodthirsty character who plundered the Abbey of Maillezais in the thirteenth-century. Be all that as it may, the place where the château once stood is now used for local events (and for parking), and the Tourist Office alongside can offer yet more yarns of Mélusine in its basement rooms (the Maison de Mélusine).

Walking down from the château-site, another place with a story is the attractive Cour des Miracles, just across the

The Fairy Mélusine

Mélusine has been adopted as the Vendée's very own fairy. The story goes that in her youth she murdered her father, and for this she was condemned to have the lower half of her body changed to that of a serpent every Saturday evening. When in due course she met Raimondin, the young nephew of the Count of Poitiers, she would naturally only agree to marriage on the condition that he never saw her on a Saturday evening. All went well for many years, the couple lived in the château at Vouvant (which Mélusine built in one night) and ten children were born to them – although strangely, each child had a minor defect (a red eye, a small ear, a 'long tooth'...). Eventually curiosity overcame Raimondin and one Saturday evening he burst into his wife's room as she was taking a bath. While he recoiled in shock at the sight of her serpent's tail she flew out of the window, circled the castle three times and was never seen again. Since that day she has haunted Vouvant, and from time to time her high-pitched cry can be heard over the village. Mélusine is accredited with the building of many castles and, after her disappearance, each of these was said to crumble at the rate of a stone a year. Hence, the châteaux of Pouzauges and Tiffauges are little more than ruins, all that currently remains of the stronghold at Vouvant is the watchtower, while at Mervent there is nothing at all.

road. It is said that in the winter of 1715, Père de Montfort (of *Grotte* fame) was walking through this village when a dying child came out and asked him for cherries. The priest apparently told his

North door at Vouvant

Vouvant's Romanesque Church

The north façade of this church is a veritable exhibition of Romanesque art. Weird and wonderful creatures arch above the double doorway–monsters, cats' heads, birds and even possibly Mélusine herself (a woman with a fish's tail). Beneath them Samson is seen wrestling with the lion, and again with Delilah cutting his hair. Above all this, the Virgin Mary and John the Baptist have pride of place, and higher again are scenes of the Last Supper and the Ascension.

grandmother to go and pick some – and the tree at the centre of this courtyard was found to be laden with fruit.

From the Cour des Miracles it is only a couple of minutes walk to the centre of Vouvant, where elegant houses with tastefully-coloured shutters face the Romanesque church.

The inside is less remarkable than out, but it is worth going down into the restored eleventh-century crypt where various pieces of ancient sculpture found during excavation are kept. From the church, you could explore the ramparts, including the postern gate. A pleasant path runs beneath them, with views over the river and the thirteenth-century Vieux Pont.

Leaving Vouvant, there are a couple more places that are worth a visit before going south to the marshes. Just a few kilometres to the east (take the D31) is the village of **Foussais-Payré**. Here the doorway of the church displays even older carvings (eleventh-century). Although some do look their age and one or two heads have been removed in religious conflicts over time they still form a remarkable ensemble in which Christ and the apostles appear above the door between graphic representations of temptations and other mystic figures. Side panels display the Passion and later appearance of Christ to the apostles. Opposite the church are the seventeenth-century market hall and the Auberge St Catherine, one-time home of Viète (although there's nothing to tell you so), and another sixteenth-century house stands on a nearby corner.

From Foussais-Payré you could head on to **Faymoreau** and the Centre Minier (Mining Centre) at **la Ver-**

rerie. This hilly area on the border with Dèux-Sevres once boasted several thriving coal mines. The one at la Verrerie was last worked in 1958. Now the village has a new lease of life with one of its buildings (actually a glassworkers' hostel) converted to a 'virtual' mine. The simulated descent of the mine shaft is the most exciting part of the visit, with some fairly uninspired tableaux in the tunnels beyond. The final room uses video and sound and light effects to tell the miners' story (French only, but an English translation is offered). The village outside, being authentic, is at least as interesting as the mine. The houses are arranged in three long tiers around the hillside, with those for the lowest-grade workers at the top and those for the management at the bottom. Below them all, the rather grand Hôtel des Mines has been revived to serve meals to visitors, while on the far side, the chapel installed by the director's wife to cater for the workers' perceived spiritual needs has been given a new set of windows. The work of Carmelo Zagari, these nineteen works in vibrant colours have striking designs that link Christian themes with the work of the mines. A free brochure explains each window.

If from Faymoreau you turn south and head down the valley on the D3, you will come alongside the River Vendée at the **Lac d'Albert**, a particularly wide stretch formed by yet another dam on the river. Just past the village of Chassenon-le-Bourg, there is access to a beach complex with children's playground, canoes and supervised swimming.

Back in Chassenon-le-Bourg, a turn will take you south to **Nieul-sur-l'Autise**. The village has its own stretch of *marais*, but it also has a most splendid abbey, a working watermill, a botanical trail and a Neolithic site on the hillside above. Founded in 1068, the Abbaye Royale St Vincent stands at the heart of the village. Absurdly, your first impressions will be of state-of-the-art technology as you enter the abbey through a corridor of multi-lingual video screens describing the life of the monks. Further on there is a display of medieval instruments, each of which magically bursts into song as you approach. But you are back in the eleventh century in the beautiful pale-stone Romanesque cloisters, where you can look for the sculpted funeral niche of Aénor of Châtellerault, mother of Eleanor of Aquitaine (next to the chapterhouse). Eleanor herself was born in Nieul-sur-l'Autise. Alongside the abbey, the Romanesque church again has a wealth of interesting carving around its portal.

On the opposite side of the main

Take a walk

The botanical trail is a pleasant riverside walk whose length can be adapted to match the time available. The entire 24km (15 miles) waymarked circuit via St Hilaire-des-Loges would take a whole day – but just an hour would be enough to take you up to cross the river on the not-so-easily-handled *barque-à-chaîne* (boat-on-a-chain) and return. The Tourist Office at Maillezais stocks leaflets detailing the whole route.

Eleanor of Aquitaine (1122–1204)

Eleanor of Aquitaine, wife of two kings and mother of two more, was one of the most charismatic personalities of the Middle Ages. Intelligent, red-headed and reputedly very attractive, she was the oldest daughter of William X, Duke of Aquitaine, and from him inherited the lands of Guyenne and Gascony – a large slice of southwest France. At the age of 15 she was married to the future Louis VII of France – but there was a stipulation that she would retain her own lands, passing them on only to any son the couple might have. Pious Louis and lively Eleanor had little in common, and finally quarrelled while both were taking part in the Second Crusade. They returned in separate ships – and shortly afterwards were granted an annulment on grounds of consanguinity. There were no male heirs.

Eleanor promptly married Henry of Anjou, who was also known as Henry Plantagenet from his family emblem of a sprig of broom (*genêt*). Henry had much land in northern France, and two years later (1154), on the death of his mother's cousin King Stephen, he became Henry II of England. England now ruled all the territory 'from the Arctic Ocean and the Pyrenees'. Eight children were born to Henry and Eleanor, but over time they too had their differences (most notably over the murder of Thomas Becket). Eleanor joined with her oldest sons in a revolt against their father, but Henry had her captured and taken to England where she was held prisoner in various castles and manor houses for fifteen years. On Henry's death in 1189, the crown passed to their son Richard (the Lionheart) and he promptly released his mother. Eleanor stayed in England and ruled as regent, while Richard went off on the Third Crusade. Meanwhile Philip II of France had set his sights on recapturing territory. Richard returned to defend his lands, but suddenly died of gangrene in 1199, and brother John was on the throne.

Eleanor had by this time become a reformed and pious old lady, and had retired to her castle on Oléron. Here she set about tidying up the morals of the island with regard to the common practices of wrecking and looting. The success of her drastic remedies for this led to the Rôles d'Oléron (Rules of Oléron), the forerunner of all charters governing conduct on the high seas.

In her 78th year, Eleanor retired to Fontevraud Abbey on the Loire – but when war broke out between John and Philip, she immediately gathered her forces to join in again. Beseiged at Mirambeau and rescued by John, she returned to Fontevraud and announced her decision to take holy orders. Thus Eleanor's turbulent life ended peacefully at the age of 82, and she was buried beside Henry and Richard in Fontevraud Abbey, where it is possible to visit her tomb.

street from the abbey, the open grounds of le Vignaud host some unusual exhibitions, and on one side, sounds of trickling water lead you to the Maison de la Meunerie, the one-time home of the miller and his family. You can explore both their living quarters and the mill itself, which still grinds flour. On the nearby riverside, the trees bear plaques at the start of the botanical trail.

And when you finally leave Nieul-sur-l'Autise for the *marais*, it might be

Château de la Citardiére

worth taking a few minutes to look at the neolithic site of **Champ-Durand** – it is signed off the road to Oulmes. There is open access to this exposed place where excavations have revealed three concentric rings of earth and stone defences dating from around 2500BC. French-readers can learn all about it at the hut on the site.

The Wet Marsh (Marais Mouillé)

South of the road from Fontenay-le-Comte to Niort, the whole area is a green labyrinth of duckweed-covered water channels, often lined by pollarded ash trees to retain the banks, and thickly overhung by willow and alder. For inhabitants there are croaking frogs, scurrying coypu and silent herons. The wet marsh is best explored by the paddle boats that can be hired from the many tiny 'ports', but cycling and walking are popular here too – and even the car will take you to many fascinating corners.

Taking the D23 from Fontenay the first village on the marsh is **Maillezais** – you can see it as you approach because Maillezais stands on one of the former

Abbey of Nieul-sur-l'Autise

Mervent Plage

islands, and the gaunt ruins of its abbey rear up above the flat landscape. The Abbaye St-Pierre has had as eventful a life as any, having been founded early in the eleventh-century and sacked by the notorious Geoffrey Longtooth two hundred years later. Flourishing again in the sixteenth-century, it played host to the reactionary Rabelais, and then went on to become a Protestant stronghold under the control of the writer Agrippa d'Aubigné, who had the place fortified. The whole story is told in a sort of primitive *son et lumière*, using the bare stone walls of the refectory as a screen. Other rooms in the same monastery building can be visited (including the kitchen and dormitories), but of the abbey church itself, little more than its evocative skeleton remains.

The Abbey of Maillezais has its own port on the marshes, a most attractive spot from where you can hire one of the traditional flat-bottomed boats and

Tour Melusine

paddle off into the mysterious green channels. There are little signs to direct you at every junction, but if you still fear getting lost (or just want an easier life), guided tours are available. Maillezais has a second port outside the abbey and another tiny one closer to the town.

Before leaving Maillezais, don't miss taking a quick look at the church of St Nicholas in the centre of town – the doorway is ringed by a complete arch of acrobats and there are some other amusing sculptures on the façade.

From Maillezais it is only a few

kilometres south-west to **Maillé**, where silent electrically driven boats can be hired from the attractive port. Not far away (just off the road to Vix), the **Aqueduct of Maillé** is a remarkable feat of engineering that shunts one canal under the other. About 6km (4 miles) east of Maillé is **Damvix**, one of the larger ports on the banks of the arterial river of the *marais*, the Sèvre-Niortaise. Cycle hire, too, is on offer at the quayside here, and you can pedal west along the riverbank or south into the dense greenery of the area known as the *marais sauvage*.

To the east of Damvix, the road follows the river up to **Arçais**, one of the most photogenic ports with a nineteenth-century château looking down on all the activity. Arçais can be busy in summertime, although again it is possible to escape to that remote *marais sauvage* (though preferably not by car). On the edge of this wild marsh, and

signed from St Hilaire-la-Palud, **Les Oiseaux du Marais Poitevin** is an ornithological park where you can see some of the wildlife in its natural setting and take yourself off on footpaths into the swamps.

Arçais may not be exactly quiet, but you can find even more crowds upriver at **Coulon**. This is surely the most popular spot on the whole Marais Poitevin and maybe it should be reserved for weekdays out of season! Nevertheless, Coulon is attractive enough to merit its inclusion in France's list of *plus beaux villages* (see P81). Traditional cottages line its wharves, and it was surely the density of water transport here that, along with the duckweed, abundant vegetation and maze of channels, earned this whole area the epithet of *Venise Verte* – Green Venice. As befits such a watery Mecca, Coulon's quayside is home to the eco-museum of the Wet Marshes, the Maison des Marais Mouillés. Here

Paddle your own canoe

Well, you <u>can</u> hire canoes in the marsh, but it seems more in keeping to take one of the flat-bottomed *plates*. These boats travel 'back to front' – the wide end goes first, while from the narrow, pointed rear, a skilled handler can propel the boat using either a pole or a paddle. Inexperienced do-it-yourself visitors are thoughtfully issued with more than one paddle!

As well as paddles you should be given a 'life-saving-rope' and a map. The latter may be very difficult to work with (north could be anywhere, and there may be no landmarks), but many ports have marked out their 1-hour, 2-hour and 3-hour circuits using little coloured arrows on the watery junctions. This should be foolproof, but you need to remember where you joined the circuit or you could go round, and round, and round – Marshland vistas are all very similar!

If you want to take boating seriously, get hold of a boater's map (*Carte Nautique du Marais Poitevin* – IGN *Plein Air* series) from any stationers or Tourist Office. Every intersection on the *marais* carries a board marked with a letter (denoting the level) and a number, which together will identify it on the map. Success guaranteed!

On your bike

The Marais Poitevin is a cyclist's paradise with many well-marked routes and circuits, and maximum interest in the innumerable ports and waterside villages. Add to that the flat terrain and to the casual holiday cyclist it can all be very tempting. Just a word of caution – for those not used to cycling at home, hard saddles combined with bumpy towpaths can have devastating results. It might be as well to opt for a short circuit first time round!

Those who would like to try longer distances should ask any Office de Tourisme for the map *Le Marais Poitevin à Bicyclette*. OT can also advise on bike hire, which is available in just about every waterside village.

For a real long distance ride, it is possible to cycle all the way from Maillezais to Aiguillon (80km/50 miles) using designated waymarked tracks and minor roads. The route can be found in the informative brochure *Vendée – Les Sentiers Cyclables*.

the development of the marshlands is told using a relief model, and you can also see how the eels are caught and the traditional flat-bottomed boats (here called *batais*) are made.

Coulon's other family attraction is the aquarium that is strangely housed in one of the rather touristy shops that surround the church. Fish include some enormous ones found in the local canals along with more exotic species, and the visit incorporates a slide show about the flora and fauna of the marshes.

From Coulon the short canal circuit passes the village of **la Garette**, where the old houses have their back doors on the canal. In recent years artisans and craft shops have taken over restored premises, and a large car park has been provided on the main road (D1) for access. Once again there is a port offering boat hire.

Not far west of Coulon, one of the prettiest places on the *marais* is the port of **le Mazeau**, which is far less frequented than many others. Over a bridge from the port, a little campsite is tucked into the rich vegetation, and the narrow road continuing along the waterside makes a pleasant place from which to contemplate the marshland views. Following that road, you will once more find yourself in a very wild part of the marsh before returning along the opposite bank of the Sèvre-Niortaise to Damvix.

One other port on the marsh deserves a mention because it is so very different. North of le Mazeau (via St Sigismond, Liez and Bouillé-Courdault)

A slippery customer

Eel (*anguille*) is a very popular dish on the *marais*, and the creatures themselves are generally caught by baiting a wickerwork trap (a *boselle*) that is then placed at the bottom of the canal in a dark spot beneath the duckweed. These days eel-trapping is a strictly regulated activity. Even if you can't catch one yourself, try to gel a meal of eel while you are here – most restaurants have it on the menu!

Cycle routes and signs

Maillezais, Embarcadère de l'Abbaye

is the interesting **Port of Courdault**. This is not a traditional port like the others – instead the long channel with its bulbous end was constructed in 1840 specifically to tranship goods from the plains on to the marshland waterways. Today the port is a pleasant quiet corner, with an inviting looking auberge/restaurant that might make a fitting conclusion to anybody's tour of the *marais*.

Abbey of Maillezais

Port of Courdault

Arçais

The Dry Marsh (Marais Desséché)

The River Vendée, flowing through Fontenay-le-Comte, goes on to divide the Wet from the Dry Marsh. To the west of the river the landscape is flat open grassland where cattle graze and white egrets stalk, but with scarcely a tree in sight. Ditches, water channels and canals are everywhere and long lines of pylons march to the horizon giving an awe-inspiring sense of perspective. Views seem more about sky than land – this is not exactly beautiful countryside, and yet there is a certain magnetism about it. This was the land reclaimed from the swamp and the names of the larger canals bear witness to those who did the work. The central Canal des Cinq Abbés recalls the monks of five local monasteries, while the Canal de la Ceinture des Hollandais that spans the northern edge of the marsh was created later by Dutch experts.

Leaving Fontenay-le-Comte, the Vendée turns west and you can follow it through **Chaix** and **Auzay** to **Velluire**. Here the river has arrived on the plains. To the west of the village, the extensive grassland is communal grazing where local farmers turn out their marked animals at the end of the springtime floods, and bring them in again before the winter. South again, and just before **le Gué-de-Velluire** the D65 seems to be running along a clifftop. That is exactly what it is – or rather was – and an orientation table has been strategically placed to pick out all the features before you, most of which were once under the sea.

Le Gué-de-Velluire has a little port on the Vendée, and from there a narrow road runs beside the river all the way to l'Île d'Elle and its confluence with the Sevre-Niortaise. Leave that for the moment and continue west on the D25, which skirts the foot of the same cliff to reach **Chaillé-les-Marais**. Chaillé is the 'capital' of this area, and has a tiny eco-museum housed in a roadside farmhouse, just off the N137 (and should you be hunting for it, the Office de Tourisme is not far away). The Maison du Petit Poitou was once the home of the 'Keeper of the Dyke', who divided his time between farming the land and checking the water levels. One of the rooms offers a glimpse of the sort of life he might have enjoyed here a century ago. Next door the story of the draining of the marshes is told, and a relief map allows you to highlight the various canals dug out by the monks and everyone else since. Other showcases display the wildlife of the Dry Marsh.

West of Chaillé the D25 goes on through Ste Radégonde-des-Noyers and Champagné-les-Marais, crossing canals all the way. At **Triaze** (a village that rejoices in an annual cowpat festival) you have a choice, because there is interest in every direction.

To the north of Triaze, and very soon visible in the flat landscape, is the town of **Luçon**. Luçon owes much of its present day attraction to the young Richelieu's sojourn here as bishop (1606–1623) – not that he had any affection for the place, berating it with words like 'ugliest', 'filthiest' and 'mud-caked', all of which were true at the time. But today the sparkling white cathedral with its slender Gothic spire gives pride of place to Richelieu's finely-painted pulpit. Their other treasure is the nineteenth-century organ by Aristide Cavaillé-Coll on which there are frequent recitals. Cloisters on the south side of the cathedral give access to the Bishop's Palace.

The spire of the cathedral, visible for miles over the marshes, is surely Luçon's pride and joy, and it has recently been treated to 'progressive illumination' – it gets brighter as the evening wears on until it is positively radiant. But Luçon boasts another gem worth visiting, just 5 minutes, walk from the cathedral (up the Rue Charles de Gaulle). The Jardin Dumaine was given to the town by a benefactor back in 1872. Today there are lakes, fountains, waterfalls, green alleyways and a wealth of glorious colour compacted into its 4 hectares (10 acres). However taken you are with the waterside scenes, do not miss climbing up to the top of the garden where

Kamok

Just opposite the cathedral is the atmospheric shop of H. Vrignaud Fils who have been producing liqueurs here for almost 200 years. Kamok is their speciality, an ambrosial coffee-flavoured liqueur like no other, but there are also *digestifs* made from apples, pears, oranges and other fruit. All may be used in ways other than the most obvious, and with your purchases you will be offered some tempting suggestions.

figures from the fables of la Fontaine leap from flower beds around the lawns. These animals are not exactly topiary, rather created by vegetation climbing through a framework, but the effect is magical.

If you leave the Jardin Dumaine at its top end, you are very close (turn right) to the Chapel des Ursulines, a convent chapel with a 33-metre-long (108ft) wooden ceiling, covered in seventeenth-century paintings. It is well worth a visit.

West of Luçon the D949 skirts the north of the *marais* and crosses the River Lay on its way to the sea. If you have come this far, you must go on almost to **St Cyr-en-Talmondais**, where the gardens at the Court d'Aron are some of the most stunning of their kind. The Parc Floral et Tropical lives up to its name with an abundance of colour, and most memorably, a lake covered (from June to September) in delicate pink lotus flowers.

Back to Triaze on the marsh again, and the ornithologically-inclined will want to continue west to **St Denis-du-Payré** and its *Réserve Naturelle*. Although the entrance to the reserve is beside the main road, it is necessary to go first into the village to collect tickets at the Maison de la Réserve. Here they will also show you a film on the birdlife of the marsh (English possible) and take you up into the observatory on the top floor to peer out over the flat landscape. Back in the Réserve itself, screened boardwalks lead out to an observatory equipped with 18 telescopes, and manned by wardens at all times. Around 120 species come to St Denis every year, of which the majority

Mussels on the market at St Gilles-Croix-de-Vie

are seasonal migrators. The wardens are happy to point out everything to be seen, and there are large charts for added identification aids.

The road west from St Denis takes you right across the heart of the marsh, through Grues and past the Port of **Moricq** on the Lay, with views of the solid grey Tour Moricq that was built to defend it in its days of importance. Further on is the little town of **Angles**. The story goes that the community here was once menaced by a bear that was eventually caught by the local hermit. He had the animal petrified and flung it to the roof above the church door, from where it now peers down, still snarling.

But back to Triaze to take the road south now, to **St Michel-en-l'Herm**. Just before St Michel (at Les Chaux) you will pass on the left a farmhouse that sits on a bank composed entirely of oyster shells. In St Michel itself, interest centres on the Abbaye Royale, behind a high grey wall near the centre of the village. The abbey was founded in the seventh-century and the Benedictines who lived here played their part in draining the marshes. Subsequent conflicts, religious and otherwise, left the abbey devastated. Today a few rooms rebuilt in the seventeenth-century still stand, but most memorable are the gaunt skeletal arches of the ambulatory beneath the open sky.

Beyond St Michel-en-l'Herm, the road continues to **L'Aiguillon-sur-Mer** – a town not really on the sea but on the estuary of the Lay. A bridge spans the river to the resort of la Faute, but l'Aiguillon has created its own 'seaside' in the form of two huge lakes facing the estuary. One is used for sailing; the other, with fine imported sand, is the exclusive domain of bathers.

L'Aiguillon is a pleasant town but **la Faute-sur-Mer**, across the estuary, gets

A likely tale

The development of mussel-farming is apparently all down to one Patrick Walton, an Irishman who was the only survivor of a shipwreck off this coast in 1235. He settled where he had landed, and apparently set up a system of nets strung between stakes to trap certain birds. While tending his nets one day, he noticed that the mesh was covered in tiny mussels. These he decided to let grow – and they grew much bigger than the ones he casually found in the sand. The cultivation of mussels had begun.

the major share of the visitors. With low whitewashed buildings, a casino and plentiful shops selling the necessary buckets and spades, the little town of la Faute is a cheerful place. The 10km (6 miles) of sandy beach that stretch down its long peninsula with a nature reserve at the tip are superb for families. But the beaches of la Faute have a difference – out to sea are row upon row of dark *bouchots*, the stakes where mussels are grown. This makes no difference to the swimmers – even at low tide there is plenty of water – but it is a real bonus for those who like to indulge in a little shell fishing of their own along the beach. Mussels are the *raison d'être* not only of la Faute, but of l'Aiguillon and all the coast to the south. The shallow Bay of Aiguillon, all that remains of the Picton Gulf of the pre-Roman era, is particularly rich in nutrients beneficial for the growth of mussels.

Driving south from l'Aiguillon to the Point of Aiguillon, the road runs beneath a high dyke on the sea side, built by Dutch engineers. At times you can climb steps to surmount it, but the view is most easily taken in from the Point itself, where you can walk out across the dunes with the Île de Ré, La Rochelle and the bridge between them on the horizon. At low tide the ever-present *bouchots* of mussels run in a black band along the coast.

Coming back beside the long dyke, the only right turn leads to **La Dive**, a village that is very obvious, perched on its own cliff a kilometre or so inland. La Dive was an island until the seventeenth-century. Now it has installed a *table d'orientation* to impress you with its panorama, which includes the Pointe d'Arçay beyond La Faute as well as the Île de Ré and more.

From La Dive you must return to St Michel-en-l'Herm and Triaze – there are no other roads crossing the marsh.

Bouchots of mussels off the beach at la Faute

James Bond's favourite egg

The name of Marans is for ever associated with the breed of poultry that originated here – small dark chickens that lay reddish or chocolate-coloured eggs. Ian Fleming's hero James Bond was apparently a fastidious eater, and demanded a Marans egg for breakfast every morning he was at home, boiled for exactly 3⅓ minutes and served in a blue cup with a gold ring around the top. He was also rather partial to the same eggs scrambled.

But if you fancy a drive on the wild side, you could turn right towards Champagné-les-Marais and then turn right after the bridge (just before town). The road first follows the Canal de Champagné and is now well off the beaten track, but there is no fear of getting lost. Keep straight on where you can and turn left where you can't, and with very little to see on the way (only the Port de l'Épine with its couple of ramshackle boats) you will eventually reach the main D10A. Turn right here, and for more of the same, turn left in another half mile or so. Bear right now and you will cross the Grands Greniers lock, at least a variation in the terrain, and picturesque for this part of the world. From here you need only follow your nose to reach the main and very busy N137 just north of the town of **Marans**.

A surprisingly large town for the marsh, Marans achieved its stature on account of its position on the Sèvre-Niortaise and the canal that connects it to the sea. Once a major transhipment port for cereals from the plains, its harbour is now filled with ocean-going pleasure craft. Further along the quay-side, Marans offers a choice of super-vised and unaccompanied river trips. The town's most prominent feature is its modern church spire, glass with a skeleton of aluminium ships' mast. The gift of a local 'Dick Whittington' who left the town to find fame and fortune in Paris, it proved to be very difficult to install. Today it is possible to climb the church tower to admire the view – and you won't have any difficulty finding it!

A broad, straight canal connects Marans with la Rochelle, but the Sèvre-Niortaise wriggles its way across the flat plain to reach the mudflats of the Bay of Aiguillon, theoretically the 'sea'. The nearest you can get to the river's mouth is the tiny **Port du Pavé** (follow signs from Charron), which is no tourist attraction but rather a wide and very muddy slipway used by those tending the *bouchots* in the bay.

The Anse de l'Aiguillon has been a centre of mussel farming since the thirteenth-century and the eco-museum that tells you about it (the Maison de la Mytiliculture) has been given very smart new premises in the village of **Esnandes** to the south – coming from Charron, turn left at the entry to the town. This is one of the better eco-museums and gives an interesting insight into the life of a mussel-farmer. An English translation helps you understand all the detail and there is also

Mussel Farming

The Romans were particularly partial to mussels, and regarded them as food for special occasions. Roman recipes for cooking them are still in existence! Nevertheless it was not until the thirteenth-century that mussels began to be cultivated.

Today there are several methods of mussel culture. In the Netherlands, one of the biggest producers, they are mostly grown on the seabed, while in France they are grown under racks, on longlines (either on the surface of the sea or submerged) or on posts. The latter method is particularly popular in Normandy and on the coast of the Vendée.

The posts, known as *bouchots*, are huge stakes 6–8m (20–25ft) tall, arranged in lines with enough space between them to allow a flat-bottomed boat to pass. In early spring, when the sea temperature begins to rise, posts are driven in along the low-tide mark, and ropes are tied tightly between them to form a sort of grill. Mussels release their minuscule larvae in millions at this time of year, and they are carried in by the tides to attach themselves to the ropes. It takes a further six weeks or so before they are visible to the naked eye.

In early summer, with the young mussels just a centimetre or so across, the ropes are cut from the posts and wound around them instead. These young mussels are placed furthest from the shore, and are subsequently moved inland as they grow.

The mussels are finally harvested at around 18 months to 2 years of age. The work may be done either by hand or by machine. Strict health safety precautions are applied, after which the mussels may be kept under damp conditions for several days before eating, provided that they remain tightly closed and therefore alive.

Mussels may be served in many ways, but pride of place must go to the ubiquitous Moules Marinières, superb when eaten out of doors on a balmy evening – preferably with a view of the sea.

Moules Marinières for 4 people

Take 2 litres of mussels, discard any open ones, scrape and wash the rest thoroughly, and drain them. Transfer the mussels to a pan and add a bouquet garni, a little pepper, a finely chopped onion and a glass of dry white wine. Heat at first gently then rather more vigorously, shaking the pan from time to time. The mussels are ready when the shells are open and the mussel bodies detach easily (around 10 minutes).

Other mussel specialities from this region include Mouclade, where crème fraîche and egg yolk are added to the cooking, and Eclade, where the mussels are cooked on a bed of pine needles.

---

a twenty-minute film show about bird-life on the bay.

Right beside the mussel museum and also under the care of its staff, the solid grey fortified church of Esnandes seems firmly planted in the flat terrain.

Inside the church, there are model ships hanging from the rafters, ex-votos given by mariners in thanks for their deliverance from some particular peril of the sea. Others who were just as grateful but could not afford such extravagant offer-

Egrets on the Marsh

ings have simply scratched a picture of their boat in the stones of the church – look on the outside of the north wall for these, but if you cannot find them, someone from the museum will help. The museum will also give you access to the watchpath that encircles the church roof, from which the whole Bay of Aiguillon can be surveyed.

For more views of this grey *bouchot*-studded bay you could take the road along the coast from Esnandes. When it finally rises above the salt-meadows you have reached the **Pointe St Clément** with parking, picnic tables and a *table d'orientation*. Here you can look out over the muddy waters and take a long look at this strange landscape that was so recently the bed of the sea, and inland the little mounds that were once islands just lifting the horizon. You have already left the Vendée for Charente-Maritime here, and just to the south is the city of La Rochelle.

'Topiary' in the Jardin Dumaine

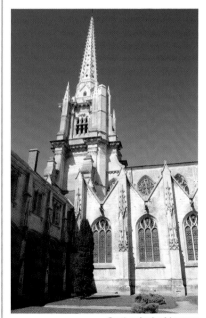

Cathedral of Luçon

Places to Visit

Offices de Tourisme

Fontenay-le-Comte
8, Rue de Grimouard
85200 FONTENAY-LE-COMTE
☎ 02 51 69 44 99

Luçon
Square Edouard Herriot
BP 269
85402 LUÇON cedex
☎ 02 51 56 36 52

Marans
62, rue d'Aligre
17230 MARANS
☎ 05 46 01 12 87

Places of interest

Fontenay-le-Comte

Musée de Fontenay
☎ 02 51 69 31 31
Open mid-Jun to mid-Sept 10am-12noon, 2–6pm daily except Mon (but closed Sat and Sun mornings); rest of year 2–6pm Wed to Sun.

Château de Terre Neuve
☎ 02 51 69 99 41
Open daily from May to Sept 9am-12noon, 2–7pm for guided visits.

Mervent

Natur'Zoo de Mervent
☎ 02 51 00 07 59
Open daily Apr to Sept 10am-7pm, Oct and Nov 2–6pm.

Mervent Adventures
☎ 02 51 00 20 63
Open Jul and Aug 11am-7pm daily; mid-April to July, Sept and Oct Sat 2–6pm, Sun and public holidays 11am-6pm.

Parc de Pierre Brune
☎ 02.51.00.20.18
Open from Easter to end Sept; Jul and Aug daily 10.30am-7.30pm; most days in Apr, May, Jun and Sept 11am-7pm.

Vouvant

Maison de Mélusine
☎ 02 51 00 86 80
Open (with Office de Tourisme) Jul and Aug only daily except Sun 10am-12.30pm, 1.30-6.30pm; Sundays and public holidays 10am-12noon, 3-6pm.

Faymoreau

Centre Minier
☎ 02 51 00 48 48
Open Jul and Aug daily 10am-7pm; Apr to Jun and Sept daily except Mon 2-7pm; rest of year Wed, Sat and Sun only 2–6pm.

Nieul-sur-l'Autise

Abbaye de St Vincent
☎ 02 51 50 43 03
Open May to Sept daily 10am-7pm, rest of year 9.30am-12.30pm, 1.30-6pm.

La Maison de la Meunerie
☎ 02 51 52 47 43
Open mid-Jun to mid-Sept daily except Sat 1-7pm.

Maillezais

Abbaye de Maillezais
☎ 02 51 87 22 80
Open Jun to Sept daily 10am-7pm; rest of year 9.30am-12.30pm, 1.30-6pm.

(Cont'd overleaf)

(Cont'd from previous page)

Places to Visit

Port of Maillezais

Boats can be hired from Apr to Oct from the Embarcadère de l'Abbaye ☎ 02 51 87 21 87), all year round from Le Petit Port Sauvage (T☎ 02 51 00 71 77) and from Jun to mid-Sept from the Port des Halles (☎ 02 51 87 14 00)

St-Hilaire-la-Palud

Les Oiseaux du Marais Poitevin

☎ 05 49 26 04 09
Open Easter to mid-Sept 10am–7.30pm; end of Mar to Easter and mid-Sept to early Nov 2–7pm (but closed Mon from mid-Sept).

Coulon

Maison des Marais Mouillés

☎ 05 49 35 81 04
Open: Jul and Aug daily 10am–7pm; Apr, May, Jun, Sept and Oct daily 10am–12noon, 2–6pm.

Aquarium

Open during shop opening hours in Jul and Aug only.

Le Mazeau

Embarcadère de la Venise Verte (boat hire)

☎ 02 51 52 90 73
Open from Apr to Oct.

Chaillé-les-Marais

Maison du Petit Poitou

☎ 02 51 56 77 30
Open Jul and Aug 10am–1pm, 2–7pm; June 2–7pm; Apr, May and Sept 2–6pm. Closed Sun mornings.

St Denis-de-Payré

Réserve Naturelle

☎ 02 51 27 23
Open Jul and Aug 9.30am–12.30pm, 3–7pm; Jun Sun only 3–7pm; Feb, April (approx) 9.30am–12.30pm, 2–6pm. May also be open during the week of All Saints' and between Christmas and New Year.

Luçon

La Chapelle Ste Ursule

Open Jul and Aug daily except Sun 2.30–6pm; rest of year by request at the Office de Tourisme.

H. Vrignaud Fils

☎ 02 51 56 11 48

St Michel-en-l'Herm

Abbey

☎ 02 51 30 21 89
3 morning and 3 afternoon visits on Tuesdays, Thursdays and Fridays in Jul and Aug only.

Esnandes

Maison de la Mytiliculture

☎ 05 46 01 34 64
Open mid-Jun to mid-Sept daily 10.30am–12.30pm, 2–7pm; Apr to mid-Jun and mid-Sept to early Nov, Wed, Sat and Sun only 2–6pm.

For the Family

Boating

Everyone will enjoy going in a traditional boat on the *marais*, and all bases have family-sized ones (up to 7 people). Even the littlest can take a turn with the paddling (but you can hire a guide to do the work for you if you prefer).

Cycling

Around Damvix and Arçais is excellent for cycling, with several circuits of suitable length clearly marked. Maps of these routes are available in tourist offices and bookshops in the vicinity, and bike hire bases are everywhere. For more ambitious cyclists, the Mervent-Vouvant Forest has mountain bike trails. Bike hire for these (if you haven't brought your own) is available from La Girouette at Vouvant.

☎ 02 51 50 10 60

Adventure Parks

Aspiring monkeys will enjoy swinging through the branches at the Mervent-Adventures arboreal park. Those who prefer to keep their feet on the ground might be happier in the Parc de Pierre Brune, again in the Mervent-Vouvant Forest.

A rainy day?

Nieulis-sur-l'Autise

The Marais Poitevin a very wet place on a rainy day and you will probably want to move out! For somewhere not too far away, you could try to the Abbey at Nieul-sur-l'Autise, where there is plenty of indoor interest – and if you want more, the miller nearby (at the Maison de la Meunerie) should still be grinding his flour.

Maison des Marais Mouillés

If you decide to stay on the marsh (hoping the sun comes out) you could take the opportunity to learn more about it at the Maison des Marais Mouillés in Coulon – and if still no sun, go round the corner to the aquarium in the shop (summer only).

Mytiliculture at Esnandes

Should you be near the coast (or be able get there), the Maison de la Mytiliculture at Esnandes is a fascinating insight into mussel culture – and you can always find somewhere to indulge in a large platter of *Moules-Frites* to complete the day.

A taste of the region

Eel

The marais is renowned for its eels (*anguilles*). With apologies to the eel, the texture and flavour put it somewhere between mackerel and chicken – and though not exactly a delicacy, it's a lot tastier than you might expect.

Mussels

You couldn't come to this part of the coast without sampling the mussels. Moules Marinières can be absolutely superb, but look out for Mouclade, made with crème fraîche, curry and white wine (among other things).

Others

Other local speciaities to look out for are derivatives of the wild marsh plant angelica (sweets, jams etc.), local goats' cheeses, and the liqueur Trouspinette (made from blackthorn).

La Rochelle, the *préfecture* (capital) of Charente-Maritime, is a fine old seafaring town whose narrow streets, half-timbered houses and fortified harbour have many a tale to tell.

To the west lies the sun-kissed holiday island of Ré, a narrow twisted ribbon of low-lying land stretching some 30km (19 miles) into the ocean. Going in the opposite direction, the hinterland of La Rochelle is known as the Aunis, off-the-beaten-track farming country that is renowned for its cereals and dairy products.

Together the three areas comprise the northern part of the *département* of Charente-Maritime.

La Rochelle

La Rochelle is without doubt the most fascinating place on the French Atlantic coast. Its colourful history goes back to 1199, when Eleanor of Aquitaine granted a charter to a little fishing village with an oversized harbour, and thus freed from its feudal constraints, the village began to develop trade. Local salt and wine were exported and wool and cloth brought in from Britain and Flanders.

By the sixteenthcentury La Rochelle had begun to think of itself as a 'Rebel Town', a Protestant stronghold in a Catholic region. In 1573 the Duke of Anjou was sent to besiege the town but it held out. With the help of a machine known as *l'Encensoir* delivering melted tar, 20,000 Royalists were slain and in a mere six months the siege was raised. Some fifty years later Louis XIII was on the throne and Richelieu was determined to take La Rochelle as a prime move in his Protestant purge. The English sent help in the form of the Duke of Buckingham, who, established on the Île de Ré, was promptly caught between the forces of the island's governor, Toiras, and the King's troops who were despatched from the mainland. Richelieu then built a 'dyke' of sunken boats across the mouth of the harbour, and no more help was forthcoming for La Rochelle. Even so, its fiery mayor, one Jean Guiton, declared that over his dead body would the city surrender, and banged a dagger into the marble table of the Town Hall to emphasise his words. Its blade made a notch there that is proudly displayed today. Fifteen long months passed and La Rochelle did surrender (October 1628), but only when its streets were strewn with dead and 5,000 starving residents remained of an original 28,000.

La Rochelle's privileges were withdrawn and its town walls and Protestant churches razed to the ground, but as peace returned to France it prospered again. With ships sailing all over the world, the wealthy merchants of La Rochelle soon owned sugar and coffee plantations in the West Indies. The city developed a 'triangular trade', taking cloth to the African coast, from there carrying slaves to the New World and then bringing home furs and other colonial products.

During the Revolution and subsequent Napoleonic Wars France lost many of her overseas colonies and the importance of La Rochelle diminished. It was, however, important to the German occupying forces in the Second World War, who established a submarine base at la Pallice, near the end of the bridge to Ré. The huge concrete structures that housed the submarines have proved too difficult to take down, and have been used in various film sets requiring U-boat scenes. La Rochelle was the last French city to be liberated.

That so much of this fine old city can be enjoyed today is thanks to its former mayor Michel Crépeau, who in 1974 resisted 'modernisation' and instead came up with the pioneering idea of a pedestrian zone. More forward thinking provided the town with a fleet of yellow bikes, housed at various stations around the city, with absolutely free use for all.

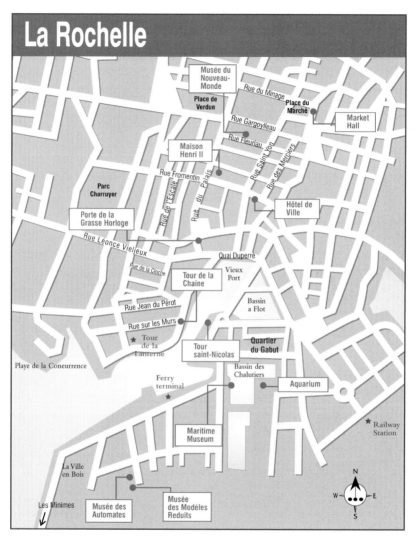

A tour of the city

Though that idea has needed modification, you can still pick up a free bike (in exchange for a piece of ID) in La Rochelle, and even electric cars are on offer for a more-than-reasonable sum.

A tour of the city

Reserve the bike (or car) for later, because the old town of la Rochelle is best explored on foot. Its classic scenes, the ones that grace every book and brochure, are of the **Old Port**, bristling with the masts of modern yachts, beyond which three very different ancient towers guard the exit to the sea. This is the hub of things, a very good place to start, and out of season you can even find parking alongside the inner basin (the Bassin à Flot) or nearby just beyond the aquarium. From here

105

Electric cars for hire, La Rochelle

Above: Place du Marché, La Rochelle

Right: Quay Duperré in La Rochelle

Below: Colourful buildings in the Gabut, La Rochelle

Entrance to the harbour

you can reach the **Gabut** district to the south of the port. It stands on the site of yet another defensive bastion, pulled down in 1858. The brightly-coloured wooden façades of the present day buildings recall those of the fishermen's huts and workshops that once com-prised the **Ville en Bois** district across the Bassin des Chalutiers to the south. On the edge of the Gabut is the Office de Tourisme, and it might be worth popping in before going any further because they offer a 'Passport' for 2, 3 or 7 days with free public transport and

Yellow bikes

reduced museum entrance fees. This has to be a bargain if you are spending any time here, because La Rochelle has such an exceptional range of museums – see P112 for all the details.

Forget the museums for the moment (although you can already glimpse the aquarium across the Bassin des Chalutiers and the huge boats that comprise the Musée Maritime nearby) and walk on through the Gabut district to where the not-quite-vertical **Tour St Nicholas** stands on the end of the harbour wall. It was built in the fourteenth-century on a raft of floating logs and you wonder if anyone today is checking its list. The tower can be explored and houses models, plans and a maze of staircases leading to the parapet, but if you think you might make a habit of tower-visiting, check out the possibility of a combined ticket including the Tour de la Chaîne opposite and the Tour de la Lanterne just behind.

From St Nicholas you can take a long walk around the Vieux Port or instead walk south (crossing the entrance to the Bassin des Chalutiers), and take a quick trip on the ferry to reach the **Tour de la Chaîne**. Its name derives from the chain that was once slung across at night to keep out those of evil intent. The tower houses a new family-friendly exhibition on the founding of Quebec, with audioguide tour following two of the emigrants.

Behind la Chaîne (walk out along the raised Rue-sur-les-Murs), the **Tour de la Lanterne** is the most fascinating of the three, because although it was built as a lighthouse, it was also used as a prison, and those who were confined here left a multitude of engravings in

its soft-stone walls. English, Dutch and Spanish names can be identified, with dates, messages and some painstakingly executed carvings of the ships in which they had once served. Some of the last prisoners were les Quatre Sergents, four hapless army officers who dared to oppose the post-Napoleonic restoration of the monarchy, and so were held here before being sent to Paris for execution. The view from the (sometimes windy) balcony extends seawards to include the remains of Richelieu's dyke at low tide. The red tower (Tour Balise Richelieu) marks the present deep water channel, which was formerly the dyke's weakest point.

After the Lantern Tower it is time to take a look at the old town, entered through the **Porte de la Grosse-Horloge** (bell tower) on the quayside. If you don't want to retrace your steps to get there, take the next road inland, the Rue St Jean-du-Pérot. It is lined with upmarket eating places, among them the curious cruise-ship-like façade of André's, one of the most famous fish restaurants in France.

Beyond the archway of the Grosse Horloge (it too can be climbed for the view in summertime), the **Rue du Palais** divides the residential district from the commercial. Arcaded on both sides, among the fascinating shops are glimpses of the fine old buildings of another age. On the left, the mellow-stoned **Hôtel de la Bourse** is the Chamber of Commerce and its fine old eighteenth-century courtyard is ringed by balconies and decked with carvings of half galleons above the entrance. Next on the left, the Rue Fromentin leads through to the **Rue** d'Escale, and on its corner is the **Maison Venette**. Nicholas Venette was a doctor who clearly did so well treating the local wealthy merchants' families (and writing books) that he was able to have his house adorned with statues of some of the most famous men in medicine - Hippocrates naturally has a place, and Galen stands beside him. Other houses in the Rue d'Escale, and in the other streets of this area, were the homes of wealthy eightennth-century merchants, tall narrow buildings discreetly concealed behind high walls. The Rue d'Escale itself is paved with shiny coloured pebbles that were once ballast in ships returning with a light cargo of furs from the New World.

Back on the Rue du Palais, you could cross the road to take a look down the Rue des Augustins, where the sixteenth-century **Maison Henri II** stands set back behind wrought iron gates. Coming back again, the cathedral stands on your left, a rather solid uninspiring building for such an otherwise remarkable town. It dates from the eightennth-century and you may think that its only unusual features are the ex-voto paintings off the north aisle, simple works given by sailors in gratitude for some special deliverance at sea.

Beyond the cathedral you are in the **Place du Verdon**, a vast empty space only occupied by a bus terminus and a few hundred yellow bikes waiting their turn for an outing. If that is not for you, keep along the right-hand side of the square, where the Café de la Paix, all gilt, painted woodwork, mirrors and dripping chandeliers, recalls its clientele of former days. The great and the good, the avant-garde and the simply unconventional came here – Georges Simenon (creator of Maigret), a regular customer in the 30s, was renowned for clattering in on his horse and tying it outside while he took a glass or two.

The next road on the right is the **Rue du Minage**, flanked on both sides by low arcades. The street ends at the Fontaine de Pilori, but take a few steps to the right and you are in the little market square with its nineteenth-century market hall, all overlooked by a rather prominent half-timbered building. Much of old La Rochelle is half-timbered, but the wood has in most places been covered with slates to protect it from the salt-laden breezes. Leading from the market square, the Rue des Merciers has more of these *colombages*, but take instead the parallel Rue St Yon, from where you can make a quick right into the Rue Fleuriau. Here on the right you will find the sevententh-century Hôtel Fleuriau, elegant home of a family who prospered through the triangular trade.

Les Francofolies

For a glimpse of the livelier (and noisier) side of La Rochelle, come here in mid-July, at the time of the Francofolies. Inaugurated in 1985 by radio broadcaster Jean-Louis Foulquier, it is a celebration of all modern French music, including rock, jazz, hip-hop, reggae and more. An open-air stage is set up on the Esplanade St Jean d'Acre, various other venues are pressed into service for more intimate performances, and a fringe festival encourages young talent.

The building now houses the Musée du Nouveau-Monde.

Back heading south on the Rue St Yon again, you soon reach the **Hôtel de Ville** – dating from around 1600, it is as impressive an edifice as you might expect in this most remarkable of cities. Entered through a walled courtyard, the pale-stoned building is hugely ornate, arcaded at the lower level, with a richly decorated ceiling to the gallery behind the arcades. The elaborate carvings and sculptures on the façade above include statues of the Four Virtues (Prudence, Justice, Power and Temperance), while perched on high in a tower of his own, Henri IV clutches the cherished Edict of Nantes. The elegant rooms of the upper floor are reached by a balustraded stone staircase. Hung with paintings, they lead to the smallest chamber, which was the office of the good Mayor Guiton. Surrounded by Aubusson tapestries, pride of place is given to the marble-topped desk on which he famously brought down his dagger.

Leaving the Hôtel de Ville, take the opportunity to walk around to the back, where in the Rue des Gentilshommes you will find the Porte des Gentilshommes, a heavy door surmounted by the three-masted galleon of La Rochelle. This was the door reserved strictly for the *gentilshommes*, the elders of the city, and to enter this way was a privilege. Continuing down the Rue des Gentilshommes, you will very soon reach the Quai Duperré beside the Vieux Port again, and can return to your starting point.

Out of town

There is of course a lot more to La Rochelle. To the south of the city is the modern suburb of **Les Minimes**, boasting Europe's largest marina for pleasure boats and a carefully-managed sandy beach. There is plenty of parking in Les Minimes and a frequent ferry service connects it with the Vieux Port – an alternative to battling with the traffic in the centre. In the other direction, the city is flanked on the western side by the Parc Charruyer, a corridor of vegetation with paths, flower beds and even an animal park. On the waterfront here, the little Plage de la Concurrence marks the start of the **Mail,** an esplanade that runs west to the place where Richelieu built his dyke. All this is merely a 30 minutes or so walk out of town, but to go on you may well feel you need one of those yellow bikes. A further 3 km (2 miles) will bring you to another beach, the Plage de Chef de Baie, and beyond it, the fishing port. You might want to turn tail there, because next comes the commercial port of **La Pallice**, but an extension of the two hours' free bike hire will get you well beyond La Pallice and over the bridge to the Île de Ré, a veritable cyclists' paradise.

The Île de Ré

No one seems to know for certain where the name Ré came from, but the most appealing suggestion is that it derived from that of Ra, the Egyptian sun-god. Ré enjoys around 2,600 sun-hours a year, a figure in line with that of the Mediterranean, making it one of the sunniest places on an already sunny

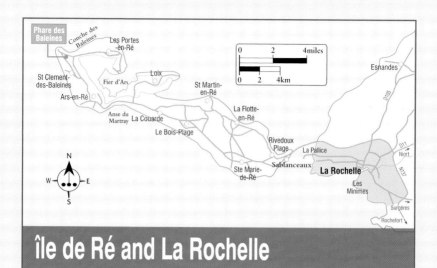

Île de Ré and La Rochelle

coast. Its evocative epithet 'the white island' was acquired perhaps on account of its beautiful silver-sand beaches, or maybe because of the shimmering strong light in which the whole island is bathed. In truth this long thin strip of land was until the Middle Ages not actually one island at all, but rather three islets, that silting and man's efforts

(Cont'd on p116)

Museé des Automates: Pierrot (left) and Juggler (Right)see P.112

Museums of La Rochelle

The term museum hardly does justice to some of the attractions of La Rochelle. From the fun of the 'Family Four' (The Aquarium, the Musée Maritime, the Musée des Automates and the Musée des Modèles Réduits) to the esoteric pleasures of the Musée des Beaux Arts, there has to be something for everyone.

The Aquarium

Housed in an appropriately glassy building, the new Aquarium (opened 2001) stands beside the Bassin des Chalutiers. 'Go down' in a diving bell, walk through a tunnel of jellyfish, touch the tentacles of sea-anemones, admire the brilliant colours of exotic specimens, watch the activity on the lagoon or walk under huge sharks – it's all a memorable experience. A tropical rainforest inhabited by piranhas ends the day.

Open every day of the year – July and August 9am-11pm; April to June and September 9am-8pm; October to March 10am-8pm. Last entries 90 minutes before closing time. ☎ 05 46 34 00 00

Musée Maritime

Moored in the Bassin des Chalutiers are *France 1*, a former weather ship, and *l'Angoumois*, a fishing vessel. You can ramble over them freely, climbing up to the bridge, descending steep ladders to the engine room, peering into the crew's quarters, the galleys and the dining rooms – and even getting a look at the operating theatre on board *France 1*, equipped to deal with emergencies in the fishing fleet of its area. Both vessels have exhibitions on board – videos of fishing on *l'Angoumois*, and most notably on *France 1*, film of the life and exploits of single-handed round-world navigator Bernard Moitessier. His ketch, the *Joshua*, is moored on the quayside behind *l'Angoumois*.

Open every day July and August 10am-7pm; April to June and September 10am-6.30pm. Last tickets an hour before closing. ☎ 05 46 28 03 00

Le Musée des Automates

This museum and the Musée des Modèles Réduits stand side by side in the Ville en Bois district, not far from the *embarcadère* for the ferry to La Chaîne. The *Automates* are mechanical toys, dozens of them performing the most complex and ingenious sequences of movements. Part of the museum has been evocatively set out as a turn-of-the-century street in Montmartre, with street musicians and working models in every shop window. Do not miss the delightful doll that carefully signs her name Pierrot, and then dots the 'i' and crosses the 't' with amazing precision.

Open every day throughout the year – July and August 9.30am-7pm; rest of year 10am-12noon, 2-6pm. ☎ 05 46 41 68 08

Musée des Modèles Réduits

Hundreds of scale models of cars, boats and trains are packed into this museum. The centrepiece is a huge railway layout that includes a tunnelled mountain on one side and a precise re-creation of La Rochelle's famously stylish station on the other. The naval section has miniature vessels of all kinds in a panelled corridor reminiscent of below decks, and stages a sea battle between sailing ships, with lots of noise and smoke.

Hours are as those for the Musée des Automates. It is also possible to reduce costs by purchasing a joint ticket. ☎ 05 46 41 64 51

Musée du Flacon à Parfum

Above a perfume shop in the Rue du Temple (behind the Quai Duperré), this private collection of perfume bottles is surprisingly fascinating. The twenty glass cases each have a different theme from the utilitarian containers of Russia to the erotic ensemble and the exhibits from the great perfume houses.

Open every day throughout the year 10am-12noon, 2.30-7pm. ☎ 05 46 41 32 40

Musée du Nouveau-Monde

Housed in the wood-panelled rooms of an eighteenth-century mansion are prints, photos, paintings, sketches and a few artefacts, all relating to the trade with New World. Portraits of American Indian chiefs with their solemn deeply-lined faces are quite moving.

Open every day except Tuesday throughout the year – April to September 10am-12.30pm, 2-6pm (Sunday 2.30-6pm only), October to March 9.30am-12.30pm, 1.30-5pm (Saturday and Sunday 2.30-6pm only). ☎ 05 46 41 46 50

Musée d'Orbigny-Bernon

A town house on the Rue St Côme (near the Rue d'Escale) displays archaeological items, furniture, ceramics (especially from China) and memorabilia from La Rochelle's eventful past. Look out for the famous picture of Richelieu on his dyke, by Henri Motte.

Opening times as for the Musée du Nouveau-Monde. ☎ 05 46 41 18 83

Musée des Beaux-Arts

On the second floor of the former bishop's palace, this is a small collection of European paintings from the fifteenth to the twentieth century.

Open every day except Tuesday throughout the year – April to September 2-6pm (Sunday 2.30-6pm); October to March 1.30-5pm (Saturday and Sunday 2.30-6pm). ☎ 05 46 41 64 65

Muséum d'Histoire Naturelle

Housed in a fine 18th century building, this long-established museum has recently been given a facelift to bring it into line with 21st century expectations. Exhibits range from creatures of the sea shore to fossils, butterflies, large mammals and a wealth of specimens brought back from remote civilisations by 19th century explorers.

Open every day except Monday, April to September 10am-7pm; rest of year 10am-6pm (but open until 9pm on Saturdays throughout the year). ☎ 05 46 41 18 25

Musée Protestant

Beside the Protestant Temple, this collection of memorabilia (portable altar and pulpit, 'secret sign' badges) bears witness to the past difficulties of Protestantism in La Rochelle.

Open July to mid-September only, 2.30-6pm every day except Sunday (other times by appointment). ☎ 05 46 50 88 03

Salt from the marshes

Salt worker at La Guittière

Three things are necessary to extract salt from the marshes: clay soil, sun and wind – and the Île de Ré has them all in abundance. Salt has been harvested here since the monks from the Abbaye des Châteliers put their minds to the business in the twelth-century. In the mid-1800s there were more than a thousand salt-workers on the island – today there are barely a tenth of that number, but this even so represents a revival of interest. In recent years young men have returned to take over the pans – and since the work is largely confined to the summer season, it combines very well with the winter-orientated toil of the neighbouring vineyards.

A base of workable clay on the island facilitates the creation of a system of basins of different sizes at different levels, each connected to the next by a channel, yet separated from it by low walls. The largest of these basins, the one at the highest level, acts as a reservoir and is filled only by the highest tides every fifteen days. From there the sea-water flows under controlled conditions into basins of ever decreasing size and depth. Salt production is a summer business because sun and wind are needed to evaporate water so that the brine becomes ever saltier as it goes. In the final basins (known as the *oeillets*) white crystals of salt begin to appear on the surface and are scooped off using a special implement. These are the *fleurs de sel*, the very finest quality salt. The coarse salt that remains then crystallises at the bottom, and is raked out to form piles at the corners of the pan. Rather grey in colour, it is left to drain and dry out overnight before collection.

In July and August salt is harvested like this every day and the *saulniers* labour from dawn to dusk, but as the temperature begins to fall in September, collections become less frequent. Heavy rain at any time is a problem, because it dilutes the salt water in the pans, so ruining the production. To understand the work of a salt farm, it is best to visit after a few days good weather.

At the end of the season, all the salt pans are cleaned out and the whole marsh is flooded to preserve it from the adverse effects of winter frost and rain. In early spring the cycle starts all over again. The basin walls are built up, the channels are cleared, and the marsh is drained so that cracks on the floors of the basins can be repaired. All this can take time, but around the beginning of June water is let into the system again and production begins immediately.

A single *oeillet* of 25sq m (30 sq yd) may render up to 50kg (110lb) of salt a day, and 1 ton in a season. All depends on the weather – the whole island produces nearly 5,000 tons in a good year, a figure that can be reduced to 500 tons in a bad one.

The Île de Ré is by no means alone in its salt production from the marshes in this way. In the Vendée, Beauvoir-sur-Mer, St Gilles-Croix-de-Vie, Olonne-sur-Mer and the island of Noirmoutier all have significant areas of salt extraction, as does the Île d'Oléron in Charente-Maritime.

Salt pans on the Île de Ré

have subsequently joined together. The nearest of these islets to the mainland is that of St Martin, home to the capital town, where the landscape is one of agricultural fields and far-spreading vineyards. Loix, the little islet to the north-west of St Martin, is by contrast low-lying *marais*, the scene of past and present salt-farming. Furthest west, and joined to St Martin by only a narrow causeway, is the islet of Ars, a crescent-shaped piece of land curving tightly around the saltpans and wildfowl reserve of the Fier d'Ars (Bay of Ars). The whole amounts to something like 30km (19 miles) in length, and yet nowhere is the land more than 19m (60ft) above sea-level.

Sitting just off the west coast, the Île de Ré was naturally keenly coveted by the English in both the Hundred Years War and the later Wars of Religion, and as a consequence it changed hands several times. Prosperity returned with peace. Strangely, the people (known as the *Rétais*) were not seafaring by nature, and preferred to gain their living from the land and the shore. Wine and salt were their source of income, and in the mid-1800s, the population numbered around 18,000 souls, more than are on the island today. The 1880s phylloxera crisis in the vineyards and the decline in the use of sea-salt resulted in an all-time low in its economy, with many families leaving for the mainland.

Today Ré is thriving again as a holiday island, its accessibility having been greatly increased when the road bridge from La Pallice was opened in 1988. 2.9 km (1.8 miles) in length and rising to 32m above the highest tide, someone thought to make it curved rather than straight, and so created something even attractive. Despite a fairly stiff toll, it now carries more than 100,000 visitors to the island every summer. But Ré has taken care to preserve its essential character. In its ten villages, the low houses remain whitewashed, and owners are encouraged to paint their shutters the traditional green and to look after the hollyhocks that spring from every crevice in the streets. Campsites and holiday chalets on the island are well camouflaged with vegetation, beautiful beaches remain undeveloped, there is no nightlife – and, provided with one hundred kilometres (60 miles) of carefully maintained cycle track, many holiday-makers choose, like the original islanders, to move around on two wheels rather than four. Along with all this, traditional industries flourish again. Early vegetables, especially asparagus, are grown, the vineyards produce interesting wines (and even cognac and Pineau des Charentes), and some of the salt pans are taken over by oyster-farmers, while others are stacked with glistening piles of salt once more.

A tour of the island

The bridge to Ré has plenty to distract the driver, and the feast for the eyes continues when you reach the island. First on the right is the long golden sweep of **Rivedoux Plage**. Then come the stark ruins of the Cistercian **Abbaye des Châteliers** that can be seen across a bare field – long ago its stone was pillaged for the building of the Fort de la Prée on the promontory behind. A little further on, you will have to leave the main road to reach **La-Flotte-**

en-Ré, which is one of the esteemed *plus beaux villages* of France (see P81), and therefore not to be missed on any account. The green shutter rule seems to be applied strictly in La Flotte, and the hollyhocks in its narrow streets must surely be very carefully nurtured to achieve such fine blooms. The heart of the village is its harbour surrounded by elegant houses and seafood restaurants that beckon irresistibly on a warm summer's evening. Don't forget also to take a walk along the seafront and perhaps to call in at the Maison du Platin, where the exhibits tell of seafaring, fishing and oyster-farming.

La Flotte is a beautiful village, but next along the coast **St–Martin–en–Ré** is scarcely less appealing. St Martin is the island's capital and has the same magical ingredient of a restaurant-flanked harbour, (a much bigger 'two-pronged' one this time, as befits a town that once traded with the West Indies and the New World), but there are added extras in St Martin. First of these is the church at the top of the town, where you can climb up the tower past its noisy bells to a rooftop with a splendid view of the harbour. Then there is St Martin's history, which has left it with a fine citadel and a complete ring of

fortifications. This was the town held by the island governor Toiras against the besieging Duke of Buckingham, and after all that was resolved, Vauban moved in to augment its defences. The town of St Martin is still entirely contained within high grey walls pierced by only two impressive gateways (Porte Toiras, Porte des Campani) that can be clearly seen from the main road by-passing the town. Vauban's seafront citadel was subsequently used to house prisoners waiting to be deported to penal colonies in Devil's Island or New Caledonia, places of no return. Famous among these was the wrongly-accused Captain Dreyfus in 1894, and screen hero Papillon (alias Henri Charrière), one who did escape. The little harbour from which they left their homeland can still be seen below the citadel's main gate.

From St Martin the main road leads west past vast acres of vineyards and skirts the village of la Couarde. A little farther on, a right turn takes you out to the village of **Loix** – and you have no difficulty believing this was once a separate island. Loix itself boasts a restored tide mill, but well before you get there, you must allow yourself to be diverted by the **Maison du Marais Salant**, an unobtrusive white building at a bend in

---

Donkeys in trousers

On the seafront at St Martin, near the citadel, is the Parc de la Barbette, where on a summer afternoon you may see a very curious phenomenon – donkeys in gingham trousers! These beasts who come to delight the children today are the reincarnation of the many donkeys who worked on the mosquito-ridden salt flats in years gone by. The thoughtful Rétais kitted them out with trousers to protect their legs, and even sometimes with straw hats. Nowadays postcards of the scene abound, and every souvenir shop carries its quota of bloomered, soft-toy donkeys.

Cycle tracks on Ré

the road. Salt has been the *raison d'être* of Loix for centuries, and there is no better place than this ecomuseum to hear the story of its production. Guides (some speaking excellent English) use a relief model of the salt pans to explain the comings and goings of seawater in the various basins, after which you are taken outside to see the saltpans, and watch whatever work is going on. This is a commercial venture as well as a tourist attraction, and you will be amazed at the hard physical work required of a *saunier*.

Plage des Prises

La-Flotte-en-Ré

You may like to continue from the ecomuseum to the village of Loix and then on the little road to the **Pointe du Grouin**, to take in the splendid view of St Martin across the bay and, further afield, the south coast of the Vendée. After that it will be time to return to the main road and turn west again. At Martray the isthmus between the two one-time islands is no thicker than the road itself and the dyke above it. The village of **Ars-en-Ré** is just beyond, and from a distance you can pick out its white steeple with a black tip, so painted to make it easily distinguishable by boats at sea. Ars has a large yachting harbour, and an attractive tangle of the narrowest streets behind.

Cycles there are in plenty on the Île de Ré, but somehow they seem to

Donkeys in bloomers

On your bike

The Île de Ré is 'as flat as a pancake', and it boasts 100km (60 miles) of dedicated cycle track. By bike even the most amateur of cyclists can easily reach every village, beach and place of interest – and there is even a vélo-bus (pulling a cart for the bikes) to get you home should you have strayed too far. Naturally there are intersections with roads, and occasionally even some piece of tarmac that is shared, but there is no doubt that bikes rule on Ré. Hire is available in just about every village, with some companies offering AA-like breakdown service and roadside repairs. If all that makes you immediately dream of a green totally car-free holiday, go ahead – but just give a little thought to that part of you that sits on the saddle and maybe give it a little practice at home first!

An overloaded ark

This corner of the island also has what is possibly its main tourist attraction, the **Parc de l'Arche de Noë** (Noah's Ark), now also called **Parc Amazonia**. The animal life you might well expect (free-flying parrots, monkeys, tortoises and the rest), but extras include shells and butterflies, a Museum of the Oceans, a 'music room' with 16 organs and synthesisers, Inca ruins and a historical section with waxwork tableaux spelling out the story of the island's convicts. Enough time should be reserved!

increase in number as you approach the northern tip of the island. Maybe the **Phare des Baleines** (lighthouse) represents the most appealing destination for a day's outing – who knows? – but there they are in their hundreds.

It is not only the cyclists that find this far-flung point of the island attractive – visitors arrive here by the coachload. Fortunately they don't all go up the lighthouse at the same time – or even up the lighthouse at all – because there are 250 on-the-narrow-side spiral steps to be negotiated to reach its viewing platform. For those who make it, there are wide sea views from the coast of the Vendée in the north to the Île d'Oléron in the south, while behind stretches the whole low-lying island with the marshlands of the Fier d'Ars nearby. On the shore some 55m (180ft) below, you can distinguish the fish locks (see P165), and also the former lighthouse tower, built here in 1682. And before going down, there is one more fascinating view reserved for the very brave. Lean over the banister of the staircase (the further the better for the effect!) and you will see that the spiralling railed steps look strangely like the inside of a snail shell.

East of the lighthouse, woodland backs a wild sweeping bay known as the **Conche des Baleines** (the *Baleines* were the whales, of which there were hundreds off these shores in Roman times). Beyond is **Les-Portes-en-Ré**, a fashionable village by Ré standards, and perhaps the best place to spot some of the (mostly French) celebrities who have homes on the island.

Now you are almost at the end of the island. All that remains is the **Pointe de Fier**, with the lovely pine forest of Trousse Chemise on the dunes behind its sandy beaches. The land now has almost completely enclosed a huge bay of mudflats used for salt farming and more lately for oysters. An old salt hangar in the marshes has become an ecomuseum, (the Maison du Fier), and attractively presents information on the thousands of birds that call in annually on their migrations, and others that come here to nest. See P165 for more details about the reserve, known as the Lilleau de Niges.

There is only really one road on which to return from the tip of the island by car – although by bike there is an exhilarating track around the marshes of the Fier d'Ars. Both bikes and cars must cross the isthmus at Martray, after which a signed turn through the woods will take you down to the south-facing **Plage des Prises**. This curving beach of white sand, backed by pines and holm oaks, is totally unexploited, and said to be the finest on the island.

From the Plage des Prises it is only a short step to **la Couarde**. This was the first village on the island to be developed as a resort, although it has now been convincingly overtaken in that role. It still boasts a long family-friendly sandy beach, which continues past the next village in line, **le Bois Plage**. These little holiday retreats are backed by acres of vineyards and in Le Bois Plage the local wine cooperative

can be found on the road to Ste-Marie. The Rosé-des-Dunes with its slight hint of iodine is the one to look out for, but there are other reds and whites, and a Pineau des Charentes that is heaven when poured into the bowl of half a Charentaise melon.

Coast, vineyards and agricultural fields stretch on to **Ste-Marie-de-Ré**, after which the land turns a corner. The last beach, that of Sablanceaux, faces all the industry of La Pallice, and yet its sands are still as perfect, if now golden rather than white.

The Aunis

When the Aunis was created in the tenth-century it reached just from the Sèvre-Niortaise to the Charente, and was the smallest province in the kingdom of France. A thousand years on, the administrative district of Aunis is even smaller, comprising mostly the northern part of the original area. Writing about it here is something of a deception, because much of it has been described elsewhere – Aiguillon Bay, Marans, the southern part of the Marais Poitevin and much-prized Maillezais with its abbey are all technically within the Aunis. What remains is the south-ern agricultural plain, the land that no holidaymaker ever visits, the untram-melled domain of the farmer, and none the less appealing for that.

Courçon is the town in the north, not a remarkable place, but you might like to call into its remodelled tenth-century church, where there is a copy of Raphael's Holy Family. To the south stretches the **Forest of Benon**, remnant of a much larger woodland continuing in a band as far east as

The Tower of the Fools

Benon is a village with a curious tall clock tower. The story goes that in the nineteenth-century, the new owners of the Château of Benon took it upon themselves to exclude villagers from parts of the forest they had customarily used for themselves. Legal proceedings ensued, and the château owners were asked to pay damages. With funds so raised, the villagers set their hearts on a clock. The local curate decided he didn't want it on the church, and so the village council were left to vote on a motion that a special tower should be built for it. Just six votes carried the day, and so the tower became known as the *Tour des Six Sots* (Tower of the Six Fools). The clock face itself was carefully positioned to face away from both church and château!

Tower of the Six Fools

St Martin-en-Ré

Chizé. Benon is now the only forest in the Aunis and nature trails and picnic tables have been provided.

South of the forest the plains stretch down to the *marais* of Rochefort. Cereal crops, maize and sunflowers are grown, along with melons and the *mogettes* (white haricot beans) that are popular right up into the Vendée. Also present are the vineyards that belong to the Bois Ordinaire division of the Cognac region. These vineyards were once much more widely spread, but after phylloxera destroyed the vines in the 1870s, dairy farming began to take over. Now the town of Surgères in the east is famous throughout France for its butter, which has achieved AOC status.

The one place you are likely to visit in the Aunis is **Surgères** because it is on a main road (the D911) to Rochefort. If you do pass that way, don't leave without the butter for which it is famous (there are several sorts) – but also make sure you walk to the bottom of the town to visit the château site and the fine Romanesque church. The original château at Surgères dated from the twelfth-century, but the fortifications you can see today are the relics of sixteenth-century restoration. One tower still stands alone, and has more recently been named the Tour Hélène in homage to the local heroine Hélène de Fonsèque (also called Hélène de Surgères).

On the far side of the château site, flanked by a park with ancient chestnut trees, the church of Notre Dame de Surgères cuts a fine figure with its octagonal arcaded tower. The church is in best Romanesque tradition, with blind arcades, door vaults carved into signs of the zodiac and various grotesque figures, and lateral niches occupied by horsemen whose identity is unknown. The capitals inside the church are worthy of inspection and must have left medieval congregations with little doubt of the glories of heaven and even less of the torments of hell.

Hélène of Surgères (1546–1618)

Hélène, a maid of honour at the dissolute court of Catherine de Medici, was very beautiful yet rejected all her suitors. Chief among these was the poet Ronsard, who immortalised her in his *Sonnets à Hélène*. Hélène, however, remained unmarried, finally returning to Surgères to live quietly in the château which her brother had restored, devoting herself to a life of good works.

Not quite vegetarian!

The people of the Aunis are particularly long-lived, and they put it all down to their penchant for eating lumas. Lumas (their other name is cagouilles) are small stripy snails with thin shells, and a good shower brings everyone out into the fields and hedgerows to look for them. There's nothing new about this – the Romans loved snails, and in the Middle Ages they were always eaten on fast days because the church did not consider them to be meat.

Places to Visit

Offices de Tourisme

La Rochelle

2, quai Georges Simenon
Le Gabut
17025 LA ROCHELLE Cedex 01
☎ 05 46 41 14 68

Île de Ré

BP 28
17580 LE BOIS-PLAGE-EN-RÉ
☎ 05 46 09 00 55

Surgères

5, Rue Bersot
17700 SURGÈRES
☎ 05 46 07 20 02

Places of Interest

La Rochelle

Hôtel de Ville

☎ 05 46 41 14 68
Jul and Aug, tours at 3pm and 4pm every day; Jun, Sept and school holidays, tours at 3pm every day; Oct to May, tours at 3pm Saturdays and Sundays only. Tickets from the Tourist Office.

Yellow bike hire

☎ 05 46 34 02 22
All year round from the Place de Verdun, every day except Sun, 9.15am–12.15pm, 1.50–6pm; May to Sept from the Quai Valin, every day 9am–12.30pm, 1.30–7pm (no lunch break Jul and Aug). First 2 hours free.

Museums

All opening hours and telephone nos. given on Page 112.

Île de Ré

Maison du Platin (La-Flotte-en-Ré)

☎ 05 46 09 61 39
Open Easter to early Nov Mon to Fri 10.30am–12.30pm, 2–6pm.

Maison du Marais-Salant (Loix)

Tel 05 46 29 06 77
Open Jun to Sept 10am–12.30pm, 2–7pm (6pm Sept); Apr and May 2–6pm; Oct and early Nov 2–5.30pm; mid-Feb to Apr 2.30–5.30pm.

Le Phare des Baleines

☎ 05 46 29 18 23
Open Jul and Aug 9.30am–7.30pm; Apr to Jun 10am–7pm; Sept 10am–6.30pm; Oct to Mar 10.30am–5.30pm.

Parc de l'Arche de Noë (Parc Amazonia)

☎ 05 46 29 23 23
Open Jun to Aug 10.30am–7pm; Apr, May, Sept, Oct and early Nov 2–6.30pm. Last entries 1½ hours before closing.

Maison du Fier

☎ 05 46 29 50 74
Open every day Apr to mid-Sept 10am–12.30pm, 2.30–6pm (but closed Sat mornings); autumn half-term 2.30–6pm.

For the family

Cycling

Hire bikes and enjoy the freedom of the dedicated tracks. You will be able to get all the child seats, trailing carriages, 'tandem' bikes, etc. needed to accommodate the whole family whatever their ages. In La Rochelle bike hire is free (for 2 hours) but some traffic negotiation is required.

The beaches

Those on the south coast of Ré are perfectly safe, sandy, and gently shelving. Children's 'beach clubs' with swings, trampolines etc. can be found at le Bois-Plage, la Flotte, La Couarde and les Portes in season. At La Rochelle, the supervised beach at Les Minimes is best, and there is lots of nearby parking.

Museums

The 'family four' in La Rochelle will keep everybody happy. See P 112 for details.

Arche de Noë

This multi-facetted zoo must have something for everyone (children particularly love the animals' feeding times).

A rainy day?

La Rochelle

The city seems tailor-made for rainy days. Work your way through the multitude of museums (costly, but get a 'passport' from OT), or window shop under the arcades (only costly if you succumb).

Île de Ré

There's not much to do on the Île de Ré if it rains – fortunately it doesn't very often! Retreat to a harbourside café or head for one of the ecomuseums (but not the salt one).

Aunis

In the Aunis, you could always try collecting *lumas*!

A taste of the region

Wines

Make sure you sample wines from the Ré vineyard – especially the Rosé des Dunes. It's unusual to find vines growing this close to the sea, but you can't really taste the salt! Pineau des Charentes (red and white) is excellent, too.

Sea salt

Try the Fleurs de Sel on a salad dressing.

The Aunis has lots to offer

Butter from Surgères has a big reputation – but the people of the Aunis are also partial to rabbit (known as orylag or Rex), and, of course, those *lumas*.

This central area of Charente-Maritime is focused on the River Charente itself, and on the valleys of its tributaries. Rochefort, near the mouth of the Charente, was Louis XIV's purpose-built military port, his fortified arsenal intended to combat the naval incursions of the English. Saintes, some 30 km (20 miles) upstream, is essentially a Roman town, with some remarkable remains to be seen. And the Saintonge, the extensive area around Saintes that includes the valleys of the Boutonne and the Seugne, is particularly renowned for its wealth of splendid Romanesque architecture. The eastern part of the Saintonge is also home to some of the vineyards producing Cognac – and although the town of Cognac itself is just outside the bounds of Charente-Maritime (it is actually in the *département* of Charente), it had to be included to complete the picture.

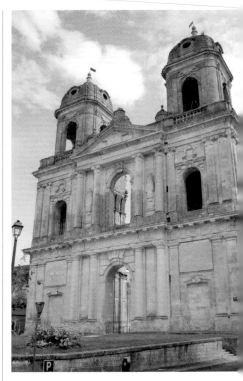

Rochefort

The mid-seventeenth-century was a time when England, Holland and France were vying with each other for dominion over the seas, with many skirmishes and changes of alliance on all sides. In France Louis XIV was determined to find himself a secure port on the Atlantic coast, a place where he could build his warships and suitably equip them without fear of attack from his maritime rivals. Jean-Baptiste Colbert, his chief naval minister, was despatched to the area we now know as Charente-Maritime, and found himself weighing up the relative merits of the estuaries of the Seudre and the Charente. The latter won the day – its mouth was protected by a long peninsula and a couple of offshore islands where forts could be positioned, while to north and south, the huge islands of Ré and Oléron gave added protection. Moreover, the Charente had a large kink in its course just 15km from the sea. Within the confines of this loop, on the site of the village of Rochefort, he decided to establish his new military base.

Building started in 1666, originally

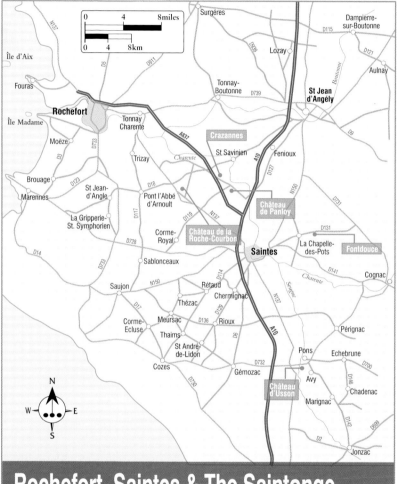

Rochefort, Saintes & The Saintonge

in wood, and very quickly the new town went into the production of the required men-of-war. Twenty years later it was deemed necessary to rebuild in stone, but by then the Rochefort arsenal was by far the finest in France, employing more than 5,000 men and turning out two or three completely fitted out warships every year, while repairing others. Over the next 200 years it went from strength to strength and many famous ships were built in Rochefort. By 1830, Rochefort was so proud of itself that a 'triumphal arch' (Porte du

Soleil) was erected at the entrance to the arsenal complex – which itself housed 11 shipbuilding yards, 4 refitting basins, a huge wood store and workshops producing rope, iron, gunpowder and everything else a good warship might require. Although France's first steam-powered warship was built here, the needs of twentieth-century warfare proved too much for Rochefort and the arsenal was closed in 1926.

Rochefort today is a handsome town, with elegant seventeenth-century houses lining wide palm-tree-lined streets that cross each other with the right-angled military precision you might expect. The town's centre is the Place Colbert, an attractive place graced with a fountain and ringed with shops and restaurants, but naturally enough, tourist interest is focused on the riverside arsenal. Here you are immediately greeted by the huge white marquee that covers the dry dock – where since 1997 a handful of carpenters have been striving to produce an exact reproduction of the *Hermione*, the ship in which Lafayette sailed for the New World in 1780. For a small sum you are invited to inspect this enormous ship from every angle. It makes a fascinating visit, with spice added by the witty comments (French, but sometimes easy to guess) of the seagull on the information panels. The *Hermione* is scheduled to be completed in 2011 (although it is a date that has been extended before), after which she will be floated out into the Charente. And it is claimed that 'one day the *Hermione* will sail over to Boston'. It is interesting to note that the original *Hermione* was completed in just six months!

Beyond the impromptu canvas, the next edifice on the quayside has in contrast been there for more than 300 years. The long low **Corderie Royale** (Royal Ropeworks) is Rochefort's most famous (and certainly most photographed) building. The Ropeworks was founded by Colbert and is built on a floating raft of oak logs since the land here was too marshy for normal foundations. Ship's rope is long and the Corderie is long too – 374m (1,227ft) to be exact – a classic clean-cut building of pale stone under a grey slate mansard roof. Unfortunately the original building here was a casualty of the retreating German forces at the end of the last war, but every stone has been faithfully replaced. The visit to the ropeworks comprises only two small rooms relating to the manufacture of rope for ships' rigging accompanied by an area of temporary exhibitions, but you are free to admire the building from outside and to explore the gardens. These include a little maze of sculptured yew hedges grandly entitled the Labyrinthe des Batailles Navales and a long stretch of well-tended beds between the Corderie and the riverside. A path here leads you beside the Jardin des Retours, whose exotic species may well be descendants of those brought back by Rochefort seafarers of a bygone age.

Leaving the arsenal through the Porte du Soleil again, the fine old building on your left is the Hôtel des Cheusses, one time residence of Rochefort's naval officers, and, since 1936, home to the **Musée National de la Marine**. Many of the model boats inside have been used for training in shipbuilding. Associated with this museum (joint tickets issued) is the **Naval Medical School**,

Begonias

The name of this popular little flower derives from that of Michel Bégon, naval governor of Rochefort at the end of the seventeenth-century, and a keen botanist. It was Bégon who suggested sending the priest Charles Plumier to study the vegetation of the West Indies. There, in 1689, Plumier described a plant with 'fat leaves and round flowers', which he verbosely named *Begonia roseo flore, folio orbiculare* in honour of his mentor. Over the next 200 years many more foreign species were brought back to Rochefort, but it is the begonias that have remained centre stage. Today you can visit *la Serre Conservatoire* (south of the town, near the Pont Transbordeur), a complex of greenhouses that houses the world's most important collection of begonias, and is particularly devoted to rare and little known species. Naturally you have the opportunity to make purchases.

housed in the old naval hospital on the opposite side of the town. Inaugurated in 1722, its anatomical exhibits, surgical instruments and medical library are shown off on guided tours.

Within walking distance of the arsenal, a couple of other museums offer diversions for a rainy day, or indeed any other. The **Musée des Commerces d'Autrefois** (just south of the Place Colbert – follow the signs) is prime browsing ground – on four floors it

Pierre Loti

Pierre Loti, whose real name was Louis Marie Julien Viaud, was born in Rochefort in 1850. He left the town at the age of 17 to enter the naval school of Brest where he rose to the rank of captain. In this role he was able to travel the world, and fellow naval officers soon began persuading him to record some of his experiences. The works he produced revealed a great sensitivity and Loti became considered the finest descriptive writer of his day. He was elected to the prestigious Académie Française in 1891.

You will find mention of Pierre Loti at other sites in Charente-Maritime – his bust adorns a corner of St Pierre-d'Oléron where he used to spend family holidays, and the splendid Château of Roche-Courbon owes its restoration to the passion he felt for its lonely setting. But it is in Rochefort, in the home he bought in later life (his own birthplace and the house next door), that his eccentric nature is laid bare. His bedroom is a monastic cell, strangely flanked by a Damascan Mosque and an elaborately tiled Turkish Salon, while downstairs there is a medieval banqueting hall. Other rooms are equally bizarre, and taking one of the guided tours (English possible in summertime) of Loti's house is guaranteed to be a memorable experience.

Pont Transbordeur

houses more than twenty 'shops' decked out as they might have been at the turn of the century. The museum is privately owned, and the chemist's, the dentist's, the milliner's, the grocer's, the bistro and all the rest are manifestly the work of a passionate collector. The other not too distant museum (again you can follow the signs) is the **Maison Pierre Loti**. The French writer Pierre Loti is not that well known outside his own country and you might wonder what interest his former home could possibly offer. See the box on p129!

Rochefort does not make a lot of its riverside, but immediately to the south of the town there is one site that is particularly worth visiting. Here the **Pont Transbordeur**, a massive transporter bridge built in 1900, still

Musée des Commerces d'Autrefois

Corderie Royale

shuttles traffic (or at least passengers and cycles) across the Charente on its platform a few metres above the water. There is a perfectly good road bridge of course, but the visit here is purely for the experience – for a most modest sum, all that wonderful machinery is sent clanking and creaking into motion. And once on the other side you can entertain yourself with a free exhibition on unusual bridges before climbing on board for the return.

From the Pont Transbordeur, riverside paths connect with both the Corderie site and the Station de Lagunage (Water Treatment Station) a couple of kilometres distant. This would seem an uninviting destination for a walk, but the water in the basins here is so pure that it attracts a wide variety of wildfowl, particularly those passing on migration, and a hide has been specially provided for their observation. See P165 for more details on the site.

Around Rochefort

From the Pont Transbordeur south of Rochefort you can turn west, where the Charente slips to the sea past the fishing village of Port des Barques and the tiny island of Île Madame. **Port des Barques** is not too remarkable, being renowned only for its natural seawater pool to the north of the village, but getting to the **Île Madame** can be something of an adventure. The island is connected to the mainland only by a low shingly causeway known as the Passe aux Boeufs. To reach it you need to drive west past Port-des-Barques as far as possible, and then go down on to the beach itself – and though the causeway is only passable at low tide, this is well off the beaten track and there are no posted tide tables to tell you the hours of safety. Nevertheless you can get these from any Office de Tourisme and most days the tide allows several hours for visiting.

The highest point of the island is

crowned by a rather ugly and inaccessible fort built here in the eighteenth-century to augment the defence of Rochefort. Rather more attractive are the sea views from the 3km (2 miles) signed path that takes walkers all around the coast (driving is just possible, but best out of season). The peninsula of Fouras, the Île d'Aix, Fort Boyard and Oléron can be picked out across a turquoise sea dotted with boats. Taking the signed route, the first field on the left after leaving the causeway contains a gigantic cross of pebbles, a memorial to 254 priests who died here in 1794. Being shipped to the penal colonies by the post-Revolutionary Republicans, they became ill with typhus and, dead or dying, were deposited on the island. Their appalling story is told on the plaque beside the cross. Further on

there are cliffs, a freshwater well arising from the sea, former salt pans and an attractive row of the curious spindly-legged fishing ensembles known as *pêcheries*. Refreshment on the island can be obtained from an oyster farm-cum-restaurant, *the Ferme-auberge Marine* – but with anything more than a snack in mind, it might be as well to reserve, as this out-of-the-way place surprisingly enjoys a widespread reputation for its seafood.

South of the Charente, the drained marshlands extend all the way to the mouth of the Seudre. Grazed by cattle, this *marais* is also the domain of sea-birds, wildfowl and storks, who have their own designated sanctuary west of the village of **Moëze**. From the Île Madame causeway, you can head south past a viewpoint and a long line of *pêcheries* to the village of St Froult, from where the road to the beach leads directly to the reserve (see P165 for details) – but you might want first to head for Moëze itself, where the church boasts a very different example of a Hosanna Cross (*Croix Hosannière*).

South-west of Moëze (via the D5) the only other settlement on the marsh is **Brouage**. Once much closer to the sea, the well-preserved ramparts of this town rise now above an empty but green landscape, and it is clearly a place with a history. An important trading post in medieval times, its position on the marshes made it the centre of Europe's salt industry. It later became the site of the Royalist arsenal during the siege of La Rochelle (1628). At this time Cardinal Richelieu ordered the reinforcement of its fortifications and – with a little later help from Vauban

Hosanna Crosses

Usually a pillar of stone sited outside the church, the Hosanna Cross was effectively a pulpit with a stone lectern from which, on Palm Sunday, the priest would read the gospel describing Christ's entry into Jerusalem. The people would then process from the cross to the church waving branches of box or laurel in lieu of palm leaves and shouting 'Hosanna!' Hosanna Crosses are a particular feature of Charente-Maritime and other examples can be found at Chermignac and Aulnay. The one at Moëze is distinctive in that it is strangely ringed with Doric columns. It is thought to have been moved to the cemetery from a position closer to the church.

- they have remained impressive to this day. The ramparts, with watchpath, form a perfect square with sides of 400m (1,200ft); there are two entrance gates (the Porte Royale and the Porte d'Hiers) and seven projecting bastions. The northern Porte Royale was once the gateway to the quays where salt was transhipped. Inside the ramparts, several of the old military buildings have survived – the Halle aux Vivres, once a food store, now houses the Museum of European Military Architecture (a miscellany of maps and models with appropriate descriptions – French only), while other historic buildings like the powder stores shelter temporary exhibitions. With the silting up of the salt pans and the establishment of the arsenal at Rochefort, all Brouage's importance declined. Today its isolation gives it a strange haunted feel out of season, while summer dispels the ghosts with crowds of visitors.

Brouage's other claim to fame is that in the mid-fifteenth-century it was the birthplace of Samuel Champlain, the founder of Quebec. Loving the sea from his youth, he became a proficient navigator and sailed up the St Lawrence River to establish the fur trade there. Links with Canada are made much of – the Maple Leaf flutters before Champlain's birthplace which offers his life story in a state-of-the-art 'museum' (actually seven video enclaves with English commentary beamed down on designated seating). Also interesting are the three stained glass windows in the church, given by the provinces of Quebec and Ontario, and depicting the lives of the settlers.

'A pair of star-crossed lovers'

The other story of Brouage concerns the young Louis XIV and his equally youthful sweetheart Marie Mancini, the niece of Cardinal Mazarin. With the recently-signed peace treaty with Spain in mind, the Cardinal thought it propitious that Louis should marry the Spanish infanta instead. This was duly arranged and as Louis headed for Spain, Marie was sent to stay with her cousins in Brouage – 'the most boring place in the world'. Here, with nothing more to occupy her thoughts, she would daily climb to the watchpath, look out over the marshes, and think of Louis. In time the Cardinal had his niece moved elsewhere. She was never to know that returning from Spain, Louis escaped his entourage and, hoping to catch a glimpse of Marie, hurried to Brouage. She had gone, and all he could do was to stay in the room she had once occupied and share with his absent beloved that view of the empty marsh. Today the stone staircase climbed by Marie Mancini still gives access to the watchpath.

Fouras and the Île d'Aix

Sitting astride a narrow peninsula at the mouth of the Charente is the town of Fouras, the departure point for the island of Aix. Although in summertime Aix can also be reached by boat from both La Rochelle and Oléron, most people opt to take this short 25-minute crossing. Aix has all the attractions of an island (and more), but Fouras is a fascinating place too, so if you are coming this way, it is worth leaving time to explore.

Fouras is a resort rooted in the days of the Belle Époque, when sea bathing was becoming fashionable and the new railway delivered seasonal crowds of pale-skinned Parisians keen to try this new venture. The villas they built are scattered throughout the town, and particularly along the north coast promenade, where the golden sweep of sand has views across the bay of Yves to the similarly dated resort of Châtelaillon-Plage. But being on a peninsula, Fouras has its bread buttered on both sides, so to speak. On the southern shore there are more beaches, and between them, one of Vauban's military exuberances in tawny local stone. Fort Vauban dates from 1689, and was one of the first in a line of defences designed to protect the precious arsenal at Rochefort. Bare and almost windowless, its sheer bulk hangs heavily over the sun-seekers on the Grande Plage below – and yet, caught in the long rays of evening light, it is almost attractive. Housed in the keep is a museum displaying items ranging from Gallo-Roman remains to souvenirs of the Belle Époque, while on the terrace overlooking the bay, orientation tables identify every headland and island.

From Fouras, a long finger of land extends seawards, culminating in the jetties of the Pointe de la Fumée. Here the shores are strewn with all the paraphernalia of oyster-farming – the warm waters off the point are particularly favourable for the spawning of oysters and Fouras even exports the spats (larvae) to other areas. From the jetty, boats regularly set out past the oyster beds and island Fort Enet (a later fortification, built 1812) to the almost-Mediterranean **Île d'Aix**.

Aix is a tiny crescent-shaped island, 3km (2 miles) long and no more than 700m (756yrds) wide. With palm trees and tamarisk, sandy beaches, meandering footpaths, forest cycle tracks (no cars allowed) and a couple of appealing sea-

Napoleon on Aix

After his defeat at Waterloo in June 1815, Napoleon remained in France, finally coming to Rochefort in July hoping to escape to the New World. At Fouras he was cheered and carried triumphantly to a boat taking him to Aix. On the island he stayed at the governor's house, which he himself had commissioned in 1808. His frigate was moored off Enet, but the English warship *Bellerophon* blocked its exit from the bay. Negotiations were refused, and on 14 July Napoleon wrote the famous letter in which he threw himself on the mercy of Britain. One General Gourgaud was commissioned to take the epistle to the Prince Regent in England, but he was refused permission to land at Plymouth. Napoleon later surrendered to the crew of the *Bellerophon*, and was taken to Plymouth and then to exile on the remote island of St Helena in the south Atlantic. He died there in 1821.

Boat landing on the Île d'Aix

view restaurants, this should be an idyllic holiday isle – and yet Vauban's Fort de la Rade (at its tip) and the various other military installations scattered around mean that it doesn't quite fit the bill. It makes a pleasant day's outing though, and interest is added by the Napoleon museum housed in the only two-story building in town.

The Napoleon museum on Aix was founded by the great-grandson of General Gourgaud. Its ten rooms contain a wealth of Napoleon memorabilia (his effigy appears on various unlikely items like clocks) but pride of place is given to a copy of the surrender letter, set on a table in the Emperor's bedroom, where it was written. An elm

Napoleon museum, Île d'Aix

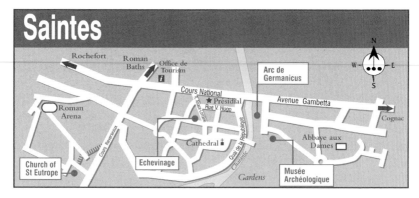

tree in the garden bears an ash grafted by Napoleon himself.

On the opposite side of the road, the other Gourgaud museum on Aix bears witness to the General's sojourn in Africa. The entire contents of an African safari park seem to have been stuffed and crammed into two rooms with a lot more besides. The centrepiece is Napoleon's white dromedary from his campaign in Egypt.

Saintes

Leaving Rochefort for Saintes you might for once choose to go by autoroute! The A837 is owned by Autoroutes du Sud de la France, who are well known for their policy of providing rest areas with added distractions to divert road-weary drivers. In this case the distractions are both designated Pôles Natures (centres of regional interest). About 15km (10 miles) from Rochefort, the rest area termed the Aire des Oiseaux is set alongside a fine old farmhouse (the **Ferme des Oiseaux**) with courtyard. The honey-stone buildings are filled with exhibitions on the birdlife of the Charente valley, and indeed of all Charente-Maritime. Videos, tableaux of habitats and superb

recordings of birdsong by day and night leave you amazed that this could be offered entirely free. For those who have longer to spend (and those who can return – there is a 'back door' via the D128 to Geay) there are regular guided bird-spotting walks.

Travellers in the opposite direction (Saintes to Rochefort) cannot access this rest area. Instead they are treated to another *pièce de résistance* in the form of the **Aire de la Pierre de Crazannes**, set in an old limestone quarry. Pergolas and shaded walkways lead you to a building housing an exhibition on the quarry's former life including waxwork figures of the workforce and displays of their tools. You are told that this stone was used for Fort Boyard, the Cordouan Lighthouse, Cologne Cathedral and even (well, possibly) the base of the Statue of Liberty, and an artistic film shows the foxes and badgers who inhabit the deserted quarry today. Again all is free; the added extra is in the form of tours of the quarry, and the back door to this one is off the D128 to Crazannes.

When eventually you make your way to the heart of **Saintes,** you are immediately reminded that it is a town of Roman origin when your eye catches the classic **Arc de Germanicus** standing alongside the river. The grey twin-arched edifice seems out of place here, and that is just what it is – due to the wisdom of Prosper Merimée, famed Inspector of Historic Monuments, it was re-located from its original site at the entrance to the Roman river bridge when the latter was demolished in 1843. The Arc dates from AD18–19, with an inscription dedicating it to Germanicus, the Emperor Tiberius and his son Drusus – and Caius Julius Rufus, the blatantly generous donor of the arch, is given a mention. There is parking space in the vicinity of the Arc de Germanicus, and it will probably be easier to leave the car on this side of the river away from the main town in summertime.

A tour of Saintes

From the Arc de Germanicus it is just a few paces along the riverside to another site of Roman interest, the **Musée Archéoligique**. The stylish building that was once an abattoir houses a jumble of Roman masonry retrieved from various sites around the town. The assorted segments of statues, monuments, coving, capitals and friezes all thrown together is impressive, and it is said that there is a lot more of the same still lying beneath the buildings of the town. This is just the free annexe, so to speak – the more valuable finds are kept behind glass in a nearby building which you will need a couple of euros to enter. The museum's pride and joy is part of a Roman chariot wheel showing its metal bands and spokes, kept under glass on the floor.

Beside the Musée Archaeologique a footbridge spans the river giving access to the town itself, but before heading that way, take the opportunity to visit the **Abbaye aux Dames**, a few streets away and still on this side of the river. More free parking space can be found around the abbey. The first abbey was founded here in 1047 and was run by an order of Benedictine nuns. The abbess was generally appointed from among the most eminent families in France – known as 'Madame de Saintes', she was responsible for the education of some of the most well-connected young ladies of the time. The abbey was finally a casualty of the Revolution, and reached its lowest ebb after being used as a barracks in World War I. Restoration has since taken place and the abbey you see today is a handsome pale-stone edifice flanked by the seventeenth-century buildings of the convent. Above it stands a classically Romanesque circular-on-square bell tower, pierced by arcades on all sides and finally topped with a scaly-looking dome, the 'pine-cone' of Poitou.

The interior of the abbey is less ornate than outside, its solid pillars and high roof giving an impression of space and light. The otherwise bare walls are hung with 13 modern tapestries by J F Favre, an exciting depiction of the creation. The convent buildings often have exhibitions of modern art, and a music festival is held here every summer.

Back to the footbridge over the river now, and the first building of note you will meet on the far side is the **Cathedral**. On the site of a much earlier church, it is a solid, largely fifteenth-century building in the style known as Flamboyant Gothic. The entrance

Anse du Saillant, Île d'Aix

porch at the foot of the bell tower is graced with angels, prophets and former bishops of Saintes.

From the cathedral narrow streets lead up into the old town with its pedestrianised area. In the centre (Place de l'Echevinage – beside the library) there is a free permanent exhibition known as the Architecture and Heritage Interpretation Centre. In other streets architectural gems are mixed with modern shops. On the Rue Victor Hugo look out for the fine seventeenth-century house known as

Arc de Grmanicus, Saintes

Tapestries at Abbaye aux Dames

A Romanesque Treasure

The Abbaye aux Dames is one of the designated *Trésors de Saintonge* (see P141) on account of its magnificent Romanesque façade. Flanking the main entrance, the capitals are richly sculpted with men and beasts and surmounted by four distinctly-fashioned arches separated by patterns of birds and foliage. The inner arch shows angels worshipping the hand of God; next comes an arch where the evangelistic symbols sit on either side of the Lamb; gruesome scenes of the torture of the martyrs decorate the third arch, while the fourth is packed with old men wearing crowns, sitting in pairs and playing musical instruments. The coving of the blind arcades on either side of the doorway also merits inspection – the Last Supper on the left, and Christ himself, possibly with apostles, on the right.

the **Présidial**, now home to the Musée des Beaux Arts comprising Flemish, Dutch and French paintings from the fifteenth to the eighteenth-century. Later art works can be found in the elegant belfry-topped **Echevinage** on Rue Alsace-Lorraine.

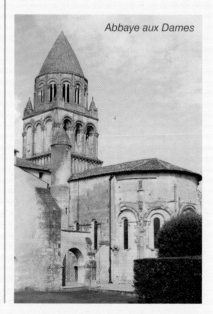

Abbaye aux Dames

What price fame?

Both museums display work by one of Saintes' most famous sons, Bernard Palissy (1510-90). Originally a surveyor by profession, he endured a long period of penury while labouring to discover the process of enamelling. Eventually he succeeded and found favour and fortune at the French court in Paris. Sadly he died in the Bastille at the age of 80, held there for refusing to renounce his Protestant faith. The new road bridge is named after Palissy, a trip boat and nearby restaurant bear his name and there is a statue of him in flowing robes near the river.

The other renowned son of Saintes is one Dr Joseph Guillotin (1738–1814). At the time of the Revolution he set his mind to inventing a more humane means of cutting off heads – but was said to be less than pleased when he was told that in his honour the device was to be named the Guillotine. He has no memorial!

The Rue Alsace-Lorraine leads out of the old town on to the main thoroughfare for traffic, the Cours National. Here, just beyond the imposing colonnaded Law Courts, you will find the Office de Tourisme, who can offer you a more extensive town trail than that here. One place you would not wish to miss is the **Roman Amphitheatre** (*Les Arènes*) and from the Tourist Office signs direct you along the Cours Reverseaux (opposite) and then right on to the Rue St-Macoult, a walk of just a few minutes. The Amphitheatre is small by Roman standards (although it could accommodate 15,000, the whole population of Saintes), and is set in its own natural valley. With its ancient terraces now grassed over and the silhouette of St Eutrope's church gracing the hill behind it makes an attractive scene. It is possible to tour the site and learn more with the aid of an audio-guide.

A path alongside the Amphitheatre soon leads you to the **Church of St Eutrope**. The relics of the saint, a bishop of Saintes martyred in the second-century, are housed in the eleventh-century vaulted crypt beneath. This crypt was the original church, which had the choir and transept of a second church then built above it. The common nave was demolished in the nineteenth-century, but both crypt and present-day nave (the first transept) reveal early finely-wrought capitals (look out for Daniel in the Lions Den). The handsome fifteenth-century spire was given to the church by Louis XI. He had a particular affection for Saint Eutrope, whom he claimed had healed him of dropsy. Saintes is on the main pilgrim route from Paris to Santiago de Compostela (the Via Turonensis) and pilgrims of the Middle Ages would stop here to do homage to St Eutrope. Latter-day pilgrims, ever increasing in number, have their own hostel in the old buildings behind the church.

From St Eutrope, signs lead you back to the old town – although strangely they disappear before you actually get there. For the return to your car, just remember that downhill leads to the river!

Other visits are possible in Saintes. The ruins of the Roman baths stand on a hill behind the Tourist Office, although they are not that impressive.

Access is tricky by car because of the one-way systems, but it is only a short walk. The Tourist Office could also direct you to the remains of the Roman aqueduct, a car ride away to the north-west of the town. And forgetting the Roman connections, Saintes is home to one of the 23 **Haras Nationaux** – the National Studs. On the outskirts of Saintes (follow signs to Cognac), the stud offers regular tours during the summer months. Along with the thoroughbreds and arabs, you can meet the delightful *Baudets de Poitou* (shaggy donkeys) and draught horses of the breed known as the Trait Poitevin.

The Saintonge

Saintes was the main town in a fairly extensive pre-Revolutionary prov-ince known as the Saintonge. Today the area is divided for administrative purposes into three parts – the rural agricultural land to the north and east is known as the Vals de Saintonge, the central area around Saintes is the Saintonge Romane on account of its wealth of Romanesque architecture, while the long finger of land pointing south along the valley of the Seugne is Haute Saintonge.

Vals de Saintonge

At the heart of the Vals de Saintonge region is the rather quaint town of **St Jean d'Angély**. The story goes that in 817, Pépin, Duke of Aquitaine received the head of John the Baptist, brought to him from Alexandria by the Monk Felix. To house the relic, he founded an abbey in the town of Angeriacum (later to become St Jean d'Angély). In

Treasures of the Saintonge

France is fond of its *Routes Historiques* (Historic Routes) and the *département* of Charente-Maritime has nominated its 20 top architectural 'treasures' – châteaux, abbeys, and other buildings of note – to be included in one of these under the title of *Trésors de Saintonge*. Perhaps diplomatically, these gems are scattered the length and breadth of the Saintonge (one or two are even outside its boundaries) and it would be a very long drive indeed if you were to see them all. So although this is termed a 'route', if you pick up a leaflet at a Tourist Office you will see that there are no directions, and you must just dip into these treasures as you please. And with the abundance of fine architecture in the Saintonge, you may wonder why the list is not longer!

the ninth-century marauding Vikings set fire to the abbey and the precious skull was lost. The abbey was later re-established and given to the Benedic-tines of Cluny. It became a staging post on one of the main pilgrim routes to Santiago de Compostela.

The fine abbey you can see today is the result of rebuilding in the seven-teenth and eighteenth-centuries and is one of the declared *Treasures of the Saintonge*. It houses a library, a school of music and the Centre of European Culture. Of the abbey church (*abbatiale*) begun in 1741, only the façade was

The legend of the Head of John the Baptist

The head of John the Baptist (originally given by King Herod to the dancer Salome) was naturally one of the most valued relics of the Middle Ages. St Jean d'Angély was not the only abbey to claim to have it in their possession! In the years after its loss in the Viking raids, it is said that Duke Guillaume le Grand was inconsolable, and that the unfortunate Abbot Hilduin (appointed in 989) was frequently at the receiving end of his bouts of temper. So it was most fortunate that on a pilgrimage to Rome in 1010, Hilduin miraculously 'found' the saint's head in a ruined wall. The Duke was delighted and organised great festivities, during which the king himself gave a golden cup on which the relic was displayed. The head remained at St Jean d'Angély for more than 500 years before being lost again in the pillages of the Wars of Religion. And although the town now features the relic on its coat of arms, so far there have been no more miracle recoveries!

completed. Its remnants – two towers and a few other pieces of masonry – stand enclosed beside the 'modern' nineteenth-century church. Both abbey and towers can be visited at certain times in summer. The town itself comprises a few characterful streets of shops, gathered around a central square with its carved stone Fontaine de Pilori. Worth a wander is the Rue de la Tour de l'Horloge, a cobbled thoroughfare passing under the arch of the medieval bell tower, flanked by half-timbered buildings.

South-west of St Jean d'Angély, take time to visit the pretty hillside hamlet of **Fenioux**, where a well-preserved twelfth-century Lanterne des Morts looks out over the valley. The tower was built over the ossuary in the churchyard and every night someone would have climbed its incredibly narrow dark spiral staircase to light the lantern that kept watch over the dead. The nearby Romanesque church has an interesting west façade, displaying among other things the signs of the zodiac.

North of St Jean d'Angély, two more *Trésors de Saintonge* are to be found close to the *départemental* border. Both the Château of Dampierre and the Church at Aulnay are more than worth seeing, but before you head that way, spare just a few moments for the *autoroute* – or at least for one of its rest areas! The A10 autoroute to Poitiers is owned by the lateral-thinking Autoroutes du Sud, and at **Lozay** they have created a **Garden of Romanesque Art in the Saintonge** to introduce the resting driver to the glories of the region he is about to enter. With reproductions of the carvings on arches and capitals in churches all over the region (and explanatory texts in English as well as French), this is the best place to find out what you would most like to see. And at the same time you can even pick up free leaflets recommending itineraries. Happily you do not need to be on the *autoroute* to benefit from all this – the Aire de Lozay can be accessed by following signs from the village of Lozay, approximately 10 km (6 miles) north of

St Jean d'Angély, then parking outside the gate and entering on foot.

Once you have been to Lozay you will be keen to visit the finest of all Romanesque churches at Aulnay, but on the way you could stop off in the village of **Dampierre-sur-Boutonne**. Its château, one of the Saintonge Treasures, has a splendid setting on an island in the river. Its most notable feature is the two-tiered gallery façade, in which the ceiling of the upper gallery is an assembly of stone panels, each carved with an allegorical symbol, some of them with added text. The originator of this ceiling is not known, but it dates from about 1545, a time when François I had banned the publication of books on alchemy, and it seems that the 93 panels of this ceiling essentially form an alchemist's textbook in stone.

Tragically and mysteriously, the **Château of Dampierre** suffered a serious fire in 2002. All its fine interior

Lanterne des Morts, Fenioux

Baudets de Poitou

furnishings were lost and most of the stone ceiling panels were cracked or worse. Each has been carefully taken away for repair and replaced, a costly enterprise justified by the uniqueness of these carvings. The current (fifth generation) owners of the château, Jean-Louis and Marine Hédelin, now live largely on the site to supervise its restoration – and if you are fortunate enough to be taken round by one of them, you are guaranteed a very interesting lesson in alchemy. They have also spent ten years creating 'a garden dedicated to Diktynna' centred on an allegorical maze and scattered with curious statues with obscure meanings. Fulcanelli featured the château in his definitive work on alchemy in the 1930s, and Salvador Dali became interested in it when he, too, began to study alchemy. One of the outbuildings houses an exhibition of Dali's horses among other paintings and explanations of alchemy, while an attic has a less complicated display of the seven most important families owning the château, in the costume of their times.

After all that, switching the thoughts to humble donkeys requires some mental agility! Nevertheless, just up the road (3km/2 miles east), Dampierre has another attraction worth visiting – the donkey farm of **la Tillaudière**, where the beautiful shaggy-coated local donkeys known as *Baudets de Poitou* are bred. Just driving up to the farm you will see plenty of these in the fields on either side, but if you can spare longer, you can join a guided tour to hear all about their history and breeding.

Finally, it's south again to **Aulnay**. The church greets you at the entrance

The Baudet de Poitou

The Baudet de Poitou is a big donkey with large ears, and most characteristically, a long brown or black shaggy coat that hangs in matted coils, and can look almost moth-eaten. It is not a good working donkey – and not a good riding donkey either. The sole reason for keeping the Baudet was to breed the males (jacks) with mares of the Poitevin or Mulassier breed, who were used as draught horses on the Poitou marshes. The offspring of this cross was the sterile Poitou Mule, a very powerful and willing workhorse that was in demand all over Europe.

With increasing mechanisation, the need for working mules declined and so did the numbers of both the Baudet and the Mulassier. In 1977, the number of registered Baudets de Poitou was a mere 44. Since that time careful breeding programmes have raised the number to almost 400. At the Ferme de la Tillaudière, you can meet not only the endearing Baudets, but also the attractively-coloured Poitevin draught horses, who give carriage rides in summertime.

to the town (on the D129E) and you can find parking opposite. The Saintonge has many fine Romanesque churches but the church of St Pierre at Aulnay, once a major halt on the road to Santiago de Compostela, stands in a league of its own. All the classic themes of Romanesque church carving are here. The west door is arched by signs of the Zodiac, Wise and Foolish Virgins, Virtues and Vices and Angels worshipping the Lamb. To the right Christ is attended by Saints Peter and Paul, while to the left St Peter is crucified (upside down). The south transept door is even more ornate – kneeling figures hold up Christ and his Apostles and then the Old Men of the Apocalypse, while above them all range a host of weird and wonderful mythological creatures. Inside the church, make sure you take a close look at the capitals, particularly those around the transept. Among them you will find one decorated with elephants with tiny ears – and to clear up any mistaken identity, the words *Hi sunte elephantes* were engraved above! Outside in the churchyard, the Hosanna Cross with its obvious lectern bears engravings of Saints Peter, Paul, James and John.

The Saintonge Romane

In the area known as the Saintonge Romane you will find a particular concentration of both Romanesque churches and of buildings in the *Trésors de Saintonge* list. In Saintes itself, the Abbaye aux Dames and the Musée Dupuy-Méstreau are included in the latter prestigious roll, while to the north and west, four similarly-honoured châteaux and an abbey are each within half an hour's drive of the town. You won't visit them all in a day, but just getting a glimpse makes a good introduction to this part of the Saintonge – and on the way home you can call in at a couple of possibly equally meritorious sites that didn't get a mention.

Bike it or hike it – the Chemin de la Pierre

Starting from Crazannes, the 10km (6 miles) circular Chemin de la Pierre (Route of Stone) passes through the depths of the Quarry of Crazannes (see P137), visits a rock face where modern-day sculptors are working (you can even have a go yourself) and calls in at two ancient ports on the riverside, one with restaurant facilities (Port d'Envaux). Free adult bike hire is available from the Maison de Pierreux at Crazannes – open June to September, every day except Mondays and Tuesdays, 2.30-6.30pm

---

A tour of the Treasures of the Saintonge

Starting from Saintes, just 12km (2.5 miles) to the north (reached via the D114 and D128), two very different treasure-list châteaux sit almost side-by-side. The large pale-stoned **Château de Panloy** was rebuilt in 1770 and is a classic example of Louis XV architecture. Since then it has been in the ownership of the same family and you are permitted to see just a few rooms decked with tapestries and furnishings of a former age.

A kilometre up the road, grey-stoned turretted **Crazannes** is a smaller, much older château (twelfth – fifteenth-century). The carvings on its façade indicate that in its earliest days it welcomed pilgrims en route to Santiago de Compostela. In addition to guided

Romanesque Churches in the Saintonge

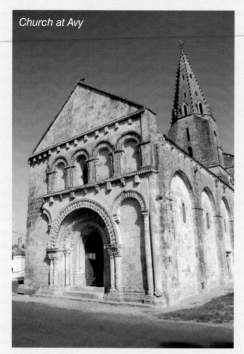
Church at Avy

Romanesque art belongs to the eleventh and twelfth-centuries, the period known as Norman in Britain. At this time pilgrims from all over Europe were pouring through Charente-Maritime on their way to and from Santiago de Compostela and many new churches were built in consequence. The churches are renowned for the intricacy of their exterior carvings, which clearly drew inspiration from the East (Armenia, the Byzantine Empire) as well as from Celtic, Spanish and other foreign cultures. The area known as the Saintonge has a veritable exhibition of these churches, especially south of a line from Saintes to Rochefort, where the churches belonged to the Clunisians of Saintes.

The sculptors of Romanesque churches particularly concentrated their efforts on the arches above the entrance door and on blind arcades on either side. The chevet (the east end of the church) seems to have excited particular enthusiasm, and modillions under the eaves gave scope for some of the most amusing characters. Certain themes recur – Christ with saints and apostles, angels, good and evil, wise and foolish virgins, the weighing of souls, virtues conquering vices, monsters devouring the

tours, both châteaux welcome paying guests.

From Crazannes head west to St Porchaire and then turn north on the D122 signposted to Geay. A kilometre or so up this road, deep in oak woods, you will pass possibly the loveliest château in all Charente-Maritime, that of **Roche-Courbon**. It is all the more endearing because it has a story. The original château here was fifteenth-century, and its beauty was much enhanced in the seventeenth-century when the de Courbons added arcades and a balcony to their château. When the estate was sold in 1817 all was in order, but its next owners neglected it seriously. In the 1860s, the French writer Pierre Loti (see P129) spent the holidays of his youth at nearby St Porchaire, and on wandering through these overgrown woods was charmed by the ivy-covered fairy-tale château he discovered at their heart. In 1908 the forest was to be sold for its wood and the château for its stone when Loti heard of its intended fate. In an article in *Le Figaro* in which he pleaded for funds, he termed the château 'Sleeping Beauty's Castle', and so caught the imagination of wealthy

Corme-Royal

damned, lovers embracing, acrobats contorting their bodies into grotesque poses and musicians playing curious instruments. Among and between them weave designs of antique leaves, birds and animals.

While some of these themes seem secular, it is possible that all have an underlying spiritual or biblical meaning. What that meaning might have been is a matter for speculation – and there is plenty. Romantic minds have postulated that, for example, the birds of which there are so many represent spirituality on account of their soaring flight. They are often seen drinking from a cup (sometimes even one held by Christ) and in doing so are taking in the Word which they then spread to the world. Acrobats twist their bodies to point to heaven and so represent final spiritualisation. Old men with beards are to be replaced by the 'new man', men putting out their tongues are rejecting the faith, musicians represent heaven with their lyres or corruption with more bawdy instruments. It is thought that every detail was put there for a purpose – yet sadly the language of Romanesque art can no longer be fully understood. There is likewise no record of who produced all this fine artwork. The only signature left is one 'Robert' on a capital in Thézac.

St Fort-sur-Gironde

Paul Chenereau. In the succeeding years both woodland and château were restored and the gardens returned to their former French-style glory.

Today the glistening white Château of Roche-Courbon stands above a formal lake in which it is perfectly reflected. Neat paths and geometric lawns are offset by conically-clipped box and classical statues. Flowers, carefully segregated by colour, stay within the confines of their beds, fearful of disturbing the symmetry. The best view of all this is from the terrace at the top of the steps at the far end of the gardens – and when

you have taken it in, you can escape formality by wandering off on woodland paths leading to the gorge of the River Bruant and exploring (as Loti once did) caves in its steep sides that were once home to prehistoric man.

After a disastrous winter flood in which statues toppled over, the gardens of Roche-Courbon are now dependent on wooden staging lifting them above the marshy ground beneath. While entry to these remarkable gardens is possible at virtually any time, entry to the château itself is by conducted tour only. On these you are taken by

Kiss-me-not

Note the white bonnet on the table in the bedroom at the Chateau of Roche-Courbon. Women in both the Vendée and Charente-Maritime traditionally wore such a headdress and it was known as a *quichenotte*. Since the bonnet was starched and projected over the sides of the face, invading Englishmen were wont to refer to it as a *Kiss-me-not*, for obvious reasons.

way of a painted oak-panelled room (curiously with a bath on one side) through a drawing room to a dining room furnished in Louis XIII style. A traditional kitchen (not in its original position) and a *Santogeaise* bedroom with a short 'sitting-up' bed complete the tour.

10km (6 miles) or so north-west of Roche-Courbon, the next Treasure, the **Abbey of Trizay,** sits in lonely isolation amid empty fields above the valley of the Arnoult. A thousand years ago the Benedictines first came to this silent place. In recent years the ruins of their abbey have been given a substantial facelift and now house an exhibition of modern art. The abbey church with its large chevet boasts eight modern stained glass windows in surprising designs.

South-west of Trizay (by the most winding of roads), the **Château of St Jean d'Angle** is the last of the five treasures in this area. This fortified little château belongs to the twelfth-century when its builder, Guillaume de Lusignan, was owner of an extensive area of salt marsh and needed to defend his valuable land. In a long series of attacks and sieges the château changed hands many times until peace was restored to the area in the seventeenth-century. In 1995 a new owner began his own restoration of the château, for which he has since won several awards.

And now it is time to return to Saintes – but you are just a couple of kilometres away from the village of **la Gripperie St Symphorien.** The church here is simple but classically Romanesque, its doorway arched over with carvings of people, birds and foliage. A foretaste of greater things to come!

Back on the main road, you will need to turn left on to the D728 to return to Saintes – and in the village of Nancras you will see signs to the **Abbey of Sablonceaux** just to the south. Established here in 1136, extensive restorations enable you to admire the handsome bell tower and red-roofed conventual buildings today. Inside, the abbey church is typically Cistercian in its plainness, retaining Romanesque cupolas in its nave and a Gothic choir lit by modern windows.

Finally you must get back on the D728 to Saintes – but one last tiny diversion is mandatory. Just off the road, the church at **Corme-Royal** has some of the finest Romanesque decoration to be found in the Saintonge. Above the door, the layers of carving show angels, Christ proclaiming the Gospel to the apostles, fine foliage and a host of the faithful. Vaulting the blind arcades around the door are other classic elements of Romanesque design – the Wise and Foolish Virgins, Virtues and Vices, Saints and Martyrs. A brochure to be found inside the church can be carried outside to help identify every detail.

The area to the south-west of Saintes is particularly rich in Romanesque churches. The only printed itineraries to guide you round seem to be those you can get from the Aire de Lozay (see P142) – apart from a walking route of 36km (22 miles) visiting 8 churches, described in the Topoguide *La Charente-Maritime et ses Îles* (Ref. 171). But whatever tour you plan, make sure you include **Chermignac** (for its Hosanna Cross), **Rioux** (superb chevet), **Rétaud** (carving all round) and **Corme-Écluse** (for its very delicate west front). Then you could add **Meursac** for the adventure of exploring its low dark fifth-century crypt (stairs by the altar – take a torch!), and **Thaims** where there are vestiges of a ninth-century edifice in its walls.

While making a tour of the churches, you might well think it worthwhile to stop for a lighter diversion at the village of **St André-de-Lidon**. This is the fringe of cognac country, and the Deau family who own the Domaine de Chaillaud offer you the chance to explore their beautiful botanical gardens and maybe even picnic there before going on to visit their distillery. The bilingual tour and easy-to-understand French film take place in an atmosphere heavily laden with evaporating cognac (said to be the angels' share) – and the tasting session at the end is more than generous.

In Cognac country

More cognac vineyards are to be found to the east of Saintes. The town of Cognac itself lies in this direction (actually in the *department* of Charente) and you would certainly not want to miss it out. Nevertheless, a couple of places on the way are worth a visit, or at the very least a passing glance.

Immediately east of Saintes (on the D131) **la Chapelle-des-Pots** has been a village of potters since the Middle Ages. Fine ceramics are still produced here today – you may have seen their outlets in several of the nearby towns. The factory stands beside the road, and allows visitors to wander around its workshops freely to see how the products are moulded, fired, painted and glazed. Naturally you will feel inclined to purchase afterwards!

From la Chapelle the D131 leads east to the ruins of the pale-stoned **Abbey of Fontdouce**, tucked deep in a lonely valley. A Benedictine establishment built in the twelfth and thirteenth-centuries, the last monks left it some 200 years ago. Of what remains, the most impressive is the Gothic chapter house with its ribbed vaulting resting on slender pillars.

Cognac is a mere 10km (6 miles) to the south of Fontdouce – although you might first want to prepare yourself with a visit to the little Museum of Cognac at nearby **Migron**. A family-run museum on a private estate, this is not only informative but good fun. Ranged around other exhibits are columns of scents for you to identify – and it's no use being waffly about it, because you are given an 'exam sheet' that will be marked at the end of the day. By that time you will have sampled some cognac and/or pineau,

Cont'd on p 152

Cognac

Still at the Ecomusée du Cognac

In the sixteenth-century, Dutch and English merchants carrying wine from the Charente found that if the wine was concentrated it would keep better and they could carry more of it. When a slump in the industry ensued, thousands of barrels of this distilled wine were left to languish in the cellars – and when opened many years later were found to contain an ambrosial liquor. So Cognac was born!

The town of Cognac is now the centre of a vast area of vineyards whose grapes, mostly of the Ugni Blanc variety, are dedicated to producing the double-distillate Cognac. The area has six subdivisions, according to the quality of the grapes grown – central and best are the Grande Champagne, then come Petite Champagne, Borderies, Fins Bois, Bons Bois and Bois Ordinaires. Great Cognac naturally comes from the best grapes – a cognac labelled *fine champagne* means that the grapes have only come from the Grand and Petite Champagne regions.

Grapes picked at the end of October are rapidly fermented and then put into a copper *alambic* in which the liquid is boiled and its vapour condensed and collected. The first distillation produces an eau-de-vie that is around 30% proof. A second distillation then increases this to around 70%, after which the liquid is put into barrels. Barrel-making is an art in itself – only oak from the Limousin region must be used and its quality contributes significantly to that of the liquid inside. The cognac must stay maturing – and evaporating – in the barrels for at least two and a half years. When taken out it has distilled water added to reduce it to acceptable alcoholic strength. The final act is all down to the *Maître de Chais* who needs a very fine 'nose' for blending the different vintage cognacs. Cognacs are classified according to the age of the youngest ingredient – less than 2½ years and it has a VS label, then come VSOP, VO and finally XO or 'Napoleon' for the most aged.

Five great cognac houses are based in and around the town of Cognac. Each offers an explanation of the distilling process, a tour of their *chais* (wine stores) and *dégustation* at the end, but each visit has something different about it – make your choice from below.

Hennessy

With headquarters on one side of the river and *chais* on the other side you get a boat trip in between (extended to about 5 minutes by going down to the bridge to turn). Hennessy headquarters are 'state-of-the-art' and there is a museum section for browsing at the end. English visits possible. Open mid-April to October and end December every day 10am-5.30pm; March to mid-April and November to mid-December Monday to Friday only, 9.30am-4.30pm. ☎ 05 45 35 72 68

Otard

Based in the château where François I was born, the added extras are a tour of some of the rooms (inhabited by waxwork figures) and guides dressed in period costume. Otard owns no vineyards, but simply buys and ages the spirits. Open April to October every day, and weekdays only November and December 11am-12noon, 2–5pm ☎ 05 45 36 88 86

Martell

Less immediately glamorous in that it is not on the riverside, it includes a trip round the founder's eighteenth-century house (Martell is the oldest of the producers) and a life-size replica of a barge that once carried the cognac down the Charente.
Open April to October weekdays 10am-5pm, Saturdays and Sundays 12noon-5pm. ☎ 05 45 36 33 33

Rémy-Martin

3km out of town (south-west, off road to Pons), you get a trip round the vineyards with this one – and a little train to take you round. Fingerfoods are included with the tasting. A higher quality visit offers more secrets of blending and 'gastronomic dishes' at the tasting. Open every day from April to October 10am-5.30pm (lunchbreak 11.15am–1.30pm outside high season). ☎ 05 45 35 76 66

Camus

Just out of the centre of Cognac, a little train is put on to take you there, with a mini town tour on the way. Camus is a family business and concentrates on showing you the skills of distillation and coopering with no added frills. Visits can be bi-lingual if desired. Open June to September 10.30am–12.30pm, 2–6pm (but closed Monday morning and Sunday.
☎ 0545 32 72 96

so the blow will be a little softened. Elsewhere, you can wander through five rooms telling of the life of a nineteenth-century vigneron, examine an *alambic* from all angles, watch a cine-projection in the 'theatre' and even learn an awful lot about coffee and cigars (the natural accoutrements to cognac) in a new outhouse display.

Armed with such profound knowledge, you may think it time to head straight for one of the great **Cognac** houses in town – see P150 for details

François I and the salamander

François was a contemporary of Henry VIII in England, with whom he negotiated at the Field of the Cloth of Gold (1520). He was primarily a man of learning who strove to push forward the boundaries of knowledge on all fronts. With the Renaissance sweeping across Europe he became a great patron of the Arts, encouraging his friend Leonardo da Vinci to spend his latter years on the Loire.

The salamander was a mythological beast living in fire, therefore representing thriving in adversity. On his tenth birthday, François was given a medallion engraved with a salamander and adopted it as his own emblem from that moment. His châteaux at Blois and Chambord are liberally decorated with salamanders, as are many other buildings with which he was associated including the Château at Cognac.

of their visits. But if you can spare the time, park first on the wide road beside the river and from there take a look around the old town. Beside the road bridge the grey château now blackened by mould from cognac fumes belongs to the house of Otard. It claimed its place in history when King François I was born here in 1494 and lived at the château throughout his childhood. The supports of the King's Balcony overlooking the river are carved with François' own emblem, the salamander, which can also be seen on various other buildings in the town.

Beside the château, the tower-flanked Porte St Jacques opens into the narrow winding streets of the medieval town. Fifteenth-century houses are on every side, some half-timbered and some with upper stories overhanging. The main street is the Rue Grande, leading up to the Romanesque Église St Leger, but side streets and alleyways cry out to be explored. This part of the town is very different from that at the far end of the wharf, where the elegant mansions date from a more prosperous era two hundred years later. If you take a left turn here (past the Hennessy building and the handsome Rue Saulnier) you will find yourself in the Place de la Salle Verte, with a glass-fronted building on your left. Concealed in all this splendour is the *Espace découverte* – actually a 'free show', a rather arty introduction to some of the splendours of the Charente valley and Cognac country with a browse upstairs afterwards. For the Musée des Arts de Cognac next door you will have to pay, but it lives up to its external promise, spelling out the story of cognac by leading you through a dazzling maze of tableaux, film theatres, video screens and lighting effects, with just a little conventional material besides. English headsets are available.

The Haute Saintonge

To the south of Saintes the long wedge of land that is the Haute Saintonge seems almost an outpost of Charente-Maritime. Its central artery is the River Seugne, a tributary of the Charente, and on the banks of this have developed its two major towns, Pons and Jonzac.

Pons cannot be missed, a hilltop town with an enormous twelfth-century square *donjon* (keep) looking out over the River Seugne and the plains below. The keep is even more impressive at close quarters, its 30m (100ft) height dwarfing the handsome administrative buildings and gardens at its feet. This entire hilltop area was once the fortress of the Lords of Pons, who were the mighty rulers of a very large domain in these parts. Their motto *Si roi de France ne puis être, sire de Pons voudrais être* (What the king of France cannot be, the Lord of Pons will) gives some insight into their grandiose ambitions. Today you can climb to the summit watchpath and look out as they must have done on the lands they once owned.

Back at ground level, the chestnut trees in the park shelter the statue of Émile Combes, a son of Pons who became Prime Minister of France in 1902. He is best known for his part in dissociating the church from the state.

From the heights of the *donjon*, a narrow maze of streets leads down to the bypass road at the foot of the hill. If you can make your way through it, you

The Pilgrimage to Santiago de Compostela

After the crucifixion, it was said that James the Great went to spread the gospel in Spain. Returning to the Holy Land some years later, he was promptly beheaded for his faith by King Herod Agrippa. Two of James' own disciples apparently put his body into a boat (in some versions a stone one!) and returned to bury him in Spain. In AD844 the mortal remains of St James the Great were miraculously 'found' on a hillside in north-west Spain. Recognising the importance of this, a cathedral was soon built to house them, and pilgrims began to pour from all corners of Europe to worship at the shrine. Four main routes developed in France, starting from (or passing through) Paris, Vézelay, Le Puy-en-Velay and Arles, routes that eventually joined together to cross northern Spain. Along these *Chemins de St Jacques,* hostels, chapels, monasteries and hospitals were built to offer shelter to the pilgrims, who carried the scallop-shell emblem of St James to identify themselves. The four routes and the buildings associated with them have now been given UNESCO World Heritage status.

Do not think pilgrimage is a thing of the past! The last 40 years has seen a revival of interest in Santiago, and in 2007 more than 114,000 pilgrims from all over the world claimed a *compostela* (a certificate given for completing the journey). The route passing through Aulnay, Saintes and Pons (the Paris route) is not the most popular, but there are still pilgrims on the trail.

Pilgrims on the roundabout, Pons

must arrive at a roundabout on which five pilgrims seem to be having trouble finding their way to Santiago. Pons was a staging post on one of the major

Pilgrim Hospital, Pons

pilgrim routes across France. Beside the roundabout the Romanesque Église St Vivien must have seen its share of pilgrims, but just up the road opposite, the **Hôpital des Pèlerins** is one of the finest surviving relics of the time and has recently been restored. A vaulted passage across a cobbled road connects the hospital with the church the pilgrims once attended, now the burial place of the Lords of Pons and a historical museum. The hospital room itself was entered through a richly carved Romanesque doorway on the opposite side. It has a fine beamed ceiling and now houses a permanent exhibition on the various pilgrim routes through Poitou-Charente. Outside its doors, a medieval garden has been planted. Most evocative of times past are the stone seats under the passageway where the pilgrims once sat and waited – perhaps for the hospital to open or perhaps to enter the town itself, since the hospital was outside its walls. The graffiti they left behind are still clearly seen. Other

Romanesque carvings decorate the passageway beside the doors. If you fancy a challenge, try looking for the eel, a legendary character of Pons who was too wily and slippery ever to be caught. You need to look carefully but he is there, entwined in the vegetation on one of the capitals.

Champagne region

To the east of Pons, vineyards of the Petite Champagne region clothe the rolling chalk hills. The villages tucked between them boast some of the finest Romanesque churches in the region. **Pérignac**, austere in its setting but richly decorated, **Echebrune**, whose façade with its glorious portal is reproduced in the Aire de Lozay, and **Chadenac**, the most impressive of all, could each claim a little of your time.

Porte de Ville, Jonzac

Château d'Usson

The Writing on the Wall

Another curious feature of the Romanesque churches in this area is that many of them bear graffiti dating from goodness knows how many hundred years ago. People, birds, ships, horses, geometric patterns and a lot more have been engraved into walls both inside and out. If you want to see a real exhibition of these, go along to Moings (north-east of Jonzac), but Echebrune has quite a number, and on most churches you can find one or two if you hunt around. Pick up the free booklet *Carnet de route des Graffiti* from any Tourist Office in this area (there is also a special leaflet on the graffiti of Moings) and you are sure to be inspired!

The latter is truly a masterpiece, assembling on its façade Christ in majesty, saints, monsters, Virtues and Vices, Wise and Foolish Virgins, St Michael with his dragon and nasty-looking scenes with dogs chasing a lamb.

South of Pons, the bristly-spired church of **Avy** is another worth investigating – and if you get that far, there is an interesting château nearby. The **Château d'Usson** is now known as the Château des Enigmes and is totally given over to a game solving a series of 'riddles' scattered throughout both grounds and interior. The equipment for the game seems a little run down, but the château itself is still an exuberant example of Renaissance architecture (and it is amazing to think that it was carried here piecemeal from its original home in Lonzac, 10km away).

South again now, and the last church you must visit is at **Marignac**. At the east end of the church the carved capitals and friezes still display their original polychromy. Look for two classics – the Woman taken in Adultery and the Lion Hunt.

South of Marignac, **Jonzac** is dominated by its fifteenth-century château in which its administrative buildings are housed. A handsome arched gateway to the town survives as do some medieval alleyways in the vicinity of the château. Below it all winds the River Seugne and it is possible to hire boats from a jetty near the stone bridge over the river. Jonzac's other notable building, the sixteenth-century Cloître des Carmes, stands nearby and today serves as a cultural centre.

New life was breathed into **Jonzac** when in 1979 a warm spring was discovered on the outskirts of town. Now there is a thriving thermal establishment, with so much warm water that an overflow stream runs under the railway to fill a small bathing lake with sandy beach on the opposite side. A children's playground and adventure park are nearby. Not content with these watery diversions, Jonzac has more recently opened Les Antilles, a magnificent swimming complex including wavepool, waterfall and beach with shops and restaurant beside. Nearby a working windmill turns its sails to entertain the visitors and a casino adds glamour to the scene.

Places to Visit

Offices de Tourisme

Rochefort
Avenue Sadi-Carnot
17300 ROCHEFORT
☎ 05 46 99 08 60

Saintes
Villa Musso
62, Cours National
17100 SAINTES
☎ 05 46 74 23 82

St Jean d'Angély
Bureau de St Jean d'Angély
8, Rue de la Grosse Horloge
Place du Pilori – Bp 117
17416 ST JEAN d'ANGÉLY Cedex
☎ 05 46 32 04 72

Pons
Place de la République
17800 PONS
☎ 05 46 96 13 31

Places of Interest

Rochefort

Le Chantier de l'Hermione
☎ 05 46 82 07 07
Open daily, Apr to Sept 9am–7pm (8pm Jul and Aug); Oct to Mar 10am–12.30pm, 2–6pm. Note last entry ½ hour before closing. Guided tours also possible throughout the year (at least 3/day).

La Corderie Royale
☎ 05 46 87 01 90
Opening times as for Hermione. Guided tours again available throughout the year.

Le Conservatoire du Begonia
☎ 05 46 99 33 20
Guided tours May to Sept, Tue to Fri 2.30, 3.30 and 4.30pm, Sat 3.30 and 4.30pm; Feb to Apr, Oct and Nov, Tue to Fri 3.30 and 4.30pm.

Le Musée National de la Marine (possible joint ticket with École de Médecine Navale)
☎ 05 46 99 86 57
Open daily May to Sept 10am–8pm; rest of year 1.30–6.30pm. Closed Jan.

École de Médecine Navale (possible joint ticket with Musée National de la Marine)
☎ 05 46 99 59 57
Guided tours only – Jul and Aug daily 10.30am, 2.30 and 4.30pm; Jun and Sept daily 2.30 and 4.30pm; Feb to May and Oct to Dec, daily 2.30pm.

Le Musée des Commerces d'Autrefois
☎ 05 46 83 91 50
Open Jul and Aug daily 10am–8pm; Apr to Jun, Sept and Oct 10am–12noon, 2–7pm; Nov, Dec, Feb and Mar 10am–12noon, 2–6pm. Closed Sun mornings throughout year.

La Maison Pierre Loti
☎ 05 46 99 16 88
Guided visits only. Jul and Aug daily except Tue 10am–6.30pm; Jun and Sept daily except Tue 10.30am–5pm: Feb to May and Oct to Dec daily except Tue and Sun morning 10.30–4pm. No tours over lunchtime throughout the year. Reservation strongly advised.

(cont'd overleaf)

Places to Visit

Le Pont Transbordeur

☎ 05 46 83 30 86

In operation Apr to Sept daily 9.30am–7pm approx. (but closed Mon mornings); Feb to Mar and Oct 9.30am–5pm approx. (but closed Mon afternoons). Lunchbreak taken throughout the year.

Brouage

Maison Champlain

☎ 05 46 85 80 60

Open daily 10.30am–12.30pm, 2–6pm.

Fouras

Musée Régional du Donjon

☎ 05 46 84 15 23

Open Jun to mid-Sept daily 10am–12noon, 3–6.30pm (but closed Mon mornings); rest of year, school holidays every day 2.30–5pm, otherwise weekends only 2.30–5pm.

Île d'Aix

Musée Napoléonien

☎ 05 46 84 66 40

Open throughout year daily except Tue 9.30am–12.30pm, 2-6pm (5pm Nov to Mar). Last admission 1 hour before closing.

Musée Africain

☎ as above

Opening times as for Musée Napoléonien. Joint tickets for both museums available.

A837 autoroute

Ferme des Oiseaux

☎ 05 46 95 06 92

Open Jun to Sept daily 10.30am–12.30pm, 2–7pm; Apr and May daily except Mon 10am–12noon, 2–5.30pm; Oct, Nov, Feb and Mar Wed, Sat and Sun 10am–12noon, 2–5pm.

Pierre de Crazannes

☎ 05 46 91 48 92

Open Jun to Sept 10.30am–12noon, 2–7pm; Apr and May daily except Mon 10am–12noon, 2–5.30pm; Oct, Nov, Feb and Mar Wed, Sat and Sun 10.30am–12noon, 2–5pm.

Saintes

Musée Archéologique

☎ 05 46 74 20 97

Open Apr to Sept Tue to Sat 10am–12.30pm, 1.30–6pm, Sun 1.30–6pm; Oct to May Tue to Sun 2–5pm.

Abbaye aux Dames

☎ 05 46 97 48 48

Visits to conventual buildings including bell tower Apr to Sept 10am–12.30pm, 2–7pm; rest of year 2–6pm. Guided visits in afternoons in high season.

Présidial (Musée des Beaux Arts)

☎ 05 46 93 04 94

Open Jun to Sept daily 10am–12.30pm, 1.30–6pm; rest of year 2–5pm. Closed Mon.

Échevinage (Musée des Beaux Arts)

☎ 05 46 93 52 39

Opening times as for Présidial.

Roman amphitheatre (Les Arènes)

☎ 05 46 97 73 85

Open Jun to Sept daily 10am–8pm; Oct to May, Monto Sat 10am–5pm, Sun 1.30–5pm.

Haras National

☎ 05 46 74 35 91

Guided visits at 3 and 4.30pm. Jul and Aug daily; Jun, Sat and Sun only.

St Jean d'Angély

Abbaye Royale

☎ 05 46 32 04 72

Guided visits daily in Jun and Jul at 3, 4 and 5pm.

Dampierre-sur-Boutonne

Château de Dampierre

☎ 05 46 24 02 24

Open daily Jul and Aug 10am–7pm, Jun and Sept 10am–6pm. Also Sun afternoons from mid-Mar to May and Oct to mid-Nov.

L' Asinerie du Baudet du Poitou

☎ 05 46 24 68 94

Guided visits. Open Jun to Sept daily 10am–12noon, 2–6pm; Apr and May every day except Mon 10am–12noon, 2–5.30pm; Feb, Mar, Oct and Nov 10am–12noon, 2–5pm.

Château de Panloy

☎ 05 46 91 73 23

Guided visits. Open daily, Jul and Aug 10am–7pm; May, Jun and Sept 10am–12noon, 2–6pm.

Château de Crazannes

☎ 06 80 65 40 96

Guided visits. Open 2–7pm daily in Jul and Aug; weekends and holidays from Mar to Jun, Sept and Oct.

Château de la Roche-Courbon

☎ 05 46 95 60 10

Gardens, Park and Caves open daily 10am–12noon, 2–6.30pm (5.30pm in winter). Closed Sun mornings and weekdays in January.

Château and keep open every day except Thur from mid-May to mid-Sept.

Abbaye de Trizay

☎ 05 46 82 34 25

Open daily except Mon, mid-Jun to mid-Sept 10am–12noon, 2–7pm; rest of year 2–6pm. Closed Sun mornings.

Abbaye de Sablonceaux

☎ 05 46 94 41 62

Church open daily but visits to 'whole site' possible 1st Sun in each month 3–6pm, and daily in July and Aug 3–6.30pm.

St André-de-Lidon

Domaine du Chaillaud (Deau)

☎ 05 46 90 08 10

Open Apr to Sept daily 9am–7pm; rest of year weekdays 9am–6pm.

La Chapelle-des-Pots

Poterie de La Chapelle

☎ 05 46 91 51 04

Open Mon to Fri all year 8.30am–12.30pm, 2–6pm.

Abbaye de Fontdouce

☎ 05 46 74 77 08

Open Jul and Aug daily 10.30am–7.30pm; May, Jun, Sept and Oct daily 2.30–6.30pm (Sun and holidays 10.30am–6.30pm); Apr Sun and holidays 10.30am–6pm.

Cognac

Espace découverte

☎ 05 45 36 03 65

(cont'd overleaf)

(cont'd from previous page)

Places to Visit

Open Jun to Sept 10am–6.30pm; Apr, May and Oct 10.30am–6pm; Mar and Nov 2–6pm. Closed Tue except in Jul and Aug.

Musée des Arts du Cognac

☎ 05 45 32 07 25

Open Jul and Aug daily 10am–6.30pm; Apr to Jun, Sept and Oct 11am–6pm except Mon, rest of year 2–5.30pm except Mon.

Pons

Donjon de Pons

☎ 05 46 96 13 31 (OT)

Opendaily from May to mid-Sept and weekdays only from mid-Feb to Apr and mid-Sept to end Oct. No times given.

Hôpital des Pèlerins (Hôpital Neuf)

☎ 05 46 96 13 31 (OT)

Open Jul and Aug daily 10am–12.30pm, 2.30–7pm; mid-Apr to Jun and Sept to mid-Oct 10am–12noon, 3–5.30pm. Last admission half an hour before closing.

Château d'Usson (Château d' Énigmes)

☎ 05 46 91 09 19

Open daily from Easter to All Saints' 10am–7pm (8pm Jul and Aug). Last admission 2 hours before closing.

Jonzac

Les Antilles

☎ 05 46 86 48 00

Open every day, but times vary and are published only a little in advance. Call for current details.

For the family

Water

There's a lot of it at Jonzac. Choose the under-cover Antilles or the open-air *base de loisirs* with its warm bathing lake and other activities alongside.

Looking into the past

Older children might enjoy an 'interactive voyage' from the Big Bang to Neanderthal times at the new high-tech Paléosite at St Césaire (8km/5 miles due east of Saintes).

Donkeys

At the Asinerie at Dampierre-sur-Boutonne, where the donkeys are like big shaggy teddy bears. Very appealing!

Cycling

The peaceful cycle tracks on the Île d'Aix are ideal for families, and the kids can't really get lost if they go off by themselves. The downside is the double cost – boat tickets and bike hire.

A rainy day?

Go to Cognac

Visit the museum, the Espace Découverte, and as many cognac houses as you can fit into the day (or before it stops raining). Get a *passeport* from any one of them to reduce entrance fees in the others.

Rochefort Museums

Think museums and make your way to Rochefort. The Corderie Royale, the *Hermione*, and the Musée Maritime will keep you dry for a while, after which you could dash up to Pierre Loti's house, or the Musée des Commerces d'Autrefois.

Bird reserve at Moëze

Face it down and head for somewhere really wet like the bird reserve at Moëze. You can spend as long as you like in the observatory and the birds won't be put off by the weather.

A taste of the region

Cognac

You could do a variation on Shirley Valentine and 'drink a glass of cognac in a country where the grape is grown'. Don't miss out on the cognac-cum-grape juice Pineau des Charentes either – it tastes superb on the local Charentaise melons.

Goat's cheese

There are quite a lot of different ones from this area, and it seems that each has a peculiar name. Look out for Chabichou and when you've found that you might go on to Bougon...

Mussels,clams and oysters

All the finest produce of the sea can be harvested along the coasts around Fouras and Brouage.

Oléron, Marennes and the Seudre estuary, and the long strip of land along the banks of the Gironde, together form the south-western boundary of Charente-Maritime. Oysters are the *raison d'être* of most of this area – although the waters of the Gironde harbour other gourmet treasures in the form of lamprey, shad, megrest and eels. With pleasant light wines from the Île d'Oléron, cognac from the banks of the Gironde, and some of the great Médoc wines finding their way across the estuary, gastronomes are well served here. But aside from all this, sunny Oléron offers all the classic ingredients of a family holiday, and the estuary of the Gironde is one of the most fascinating corners of this whole region.

The Île d'Oléron

The Île d'Oléron is the largest French island with the exception of Corsica. 35 km long and 8km (22 x 5 miles) wide, it is substantial enough to support the growing of fruit, vegetables and vines inland, and on the coast, a flourishing oyster-culture industry in the south-east and sea-fishing at La Cotinière on the west. While in the nineteenth-century salt and wine were the mainstays of its economy, in recent years oysters and, above all, tourism have taken over the

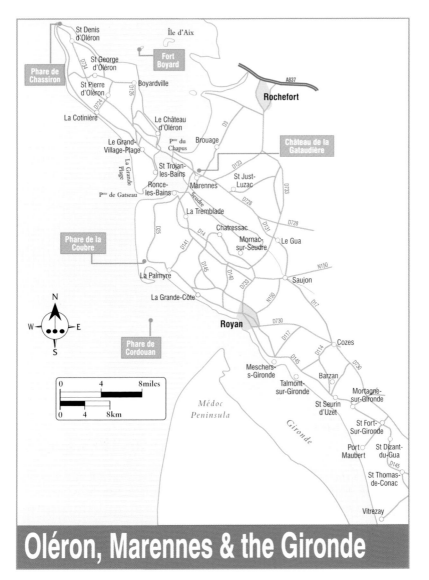

Oléron, Marennes & the Gironde

role. And Oléron has a lot to offer its visitors – wide sandy beaches with forested dunes in the south-west, dramatic rocky shores in the north, cycle tracks to reach every remote corner, and an exotic air lent by plants like oleander, tamarisk, yucca and agave that thrive in the almost-Mediterranean climate.

Oléron is connected with the mainland by a 3km (2 miles)long toll-free concrete roadbridge, built in 1966. Beyond it the D734 continues to the tip of the island, bypassing a string of small towns on the way. In the middle of the island sits the capital, St Pierre, with marshes on one side and vineyards on the other.

St Pierre d'Oléron is a pleasant enough town, but very busy in high season, when it can seem the whole island population has come to do its shopping at the same time. A generous car park is provided in the Place Gambetta, and alongside it you can find both the Office de Tourisme and the newly-housed **Musée de l'Île d'Oléron**. In the latter, items relating to salt, fishing and oysters are crammed into one main room, with a little overspill for sea-bathing and a special room for a video visiting every place of note on the island. The contents are all very French, but some English translation is offered.

Surrounded by pedestrianised shopping streets, the eighteenth-century church of St Pierre is most notable for its belfry, from the top of which the prospect includes the islands of Ré, Madame, Aix and more. Walking away from the church, an alley on the other side leads to the Place Camille-Memain (parking here too) in which the centre-piece is an impressive thirteenth-century Lanterne des Morts. This lantern that once watched over the souls of the departed looks a little lost surrounded by twenty-first-century cars and shoppers, but the cars rather than the lantern are out of place, because the square has been built over the former cemetery.

While in St Pierre, devotees of

Pierre Loti (see P129) might like to seek out his bust outside the house where he once spent family holidays (the Maison des Aïeules). The writer himself is buried in its garden, along with his childhood bucket and spade as he requested

A tour of the island

Oléron's central main road is busy, and best avoided if you want to get a real feel for the island. Turn right on the first possible road over the bridge and you will find yourself heading for **le Château** – in this case not a castle, but rather a town that stands within the walls of a seventeenth-century stronghold conceived by Louis XIII and Richelieu. If you have strictly taken the first road, you will not actually arrive at the town, but at its port, which, being the heart of the oyster-culture industry, is the most fascinating part. Huts of brilliant but blending colours line the roadside and extend along the banks of the muddy channels on either side. In some you can purchase oysters, others have been converted to craft shops or restaurants, one houses an excellent wine co-operative, but most retain their original purpose as workplaces for the oystermen. From the jetty at the end of the road you can watch the oysters being unloaded, and then walk along to the harbour where the flat-bottomed boats moor beneath the walls of the citadel itself.

After the port, a short walk (via a footbridge) or a drive will take you to this citadel, which was built after the siege of La Rochelle to protect the arsenal at Rochefort, and later reinforced by Vauban. Although much of the

Birdwatching in Charente-Maritime

The western coast of France is directly on the flightpath of the hundreds of millions of birds that travel annually between Siberia and northern Europe and the warmer shores of Africa. Mudflats and coastal marshes between the Bay of Bourgneuf in the north and the Gironde in the south are teeming with worms, shellfish and other suitable food. While birds such as heron, little egret and shelduck are resident here, others like the avocet, turnstone, redshank and ringed plover find this coast a comfortable place to spend the winter. For a few more it is simply a welcome hotel-restaurant, a place to recover before continuing with the journey. It follows then that spring and autumn are the best times for birdwatching, and while you can see interesting birdlife all along the coast, Charente-Maritime has several designated sites open to visitors – for more details than those below, get the booklet *Découvrez la nature en Charente-Maritime* from any Tourist Office.

La Réserve naturelle de Lilleau de Niges, Île de Ré

The reserve has an interesting permanent exhibition in an old salt hangar called the Maison du Fier, near les Portes-en-Ré. Free access path on to the marsh and guided visits both on foot and by bike. Open April to mid-September 10am–12.30pm, 2.30–6pm (7pm July and August). Autumn half-term 2.30–6.30pm. Closed Saturday mornings. ☎ 05 46 29 50 74

La Réserve naturelle du Marais d'Yves

(Accessed from a lay-by on the southbound carriageway of the N137, mid-way between La Rochelle and Rochefort). There is a small Nature Centre with a model of the reserve. Guided visits only (foot and bike). Open designated days throughout the year – see booklet. ☎ 05 46 56 41 76

La Station de Lagunage, Rochefort

A water treatment station situated beside the Charente, south of the city of Rochefort. Footpath and observatory (sometimes with guide present) are freely accessible at all times. Guided visits on foot and by bike. Open throughout the year. For dates of visits see booklet. ☎ 05 46 82 12 44

La Réserve naturelle des marais de Moëze-Oléron

North of Brouage. The reserve has a 'welcome centre' (La Ferme de Plaisance) open only during Easter and summer holidays. Guided visits on foot possible. The *Sentier des Polders* (1.4km/1 mile circuit) leads out to an observatory on the marsh.
Sentier des Polders accessible September to January 12noon–6pm; February to August 8.30am–6.30pm. The 2.4km (1.5 miles) *Chemin des Tannes* alongside the reserve has two observation points and is always accessible. ☎ 05 46 83 17 07

Le Marais aux Oiseaux, Île d'Oléron

This is a different reserve (more like a family animal park) that also has a role in treating birds found injured in the wild. Among the appealing residents are a turkey that seems to guard the entrance and a pig won in a lottery by someone too kindly to eat it. You can walk around the whole site in about an hour, and visit the treetop observation platform that looks over the marshes. Open July and August 10am-7pm; April, May, June and September 10am–1pm, 2–6pm (but closed Sat and Sun mornings); rest of year - every day except Sat in school holidays 10am–1pm. 2–6pm, otherwise Wednesday and Sunday only 2–6pm.

Fort Boyard

In 1988, Fort Boyard was purchased by French Television Channel 2 to be the setting for a newly-devised game show. The first series went on air two years later. In each game a team of friends would enter the fort and take timed challenges and solve riddles in order to gain its keys. More challenges requiring courage would then reveal a password that released treasure. With certain enigmatic characters needed to complete every production, it was all very complicated – and yet *Fort Boyard* caught on right across the world, with more than 20 countries (as far away as Korea and Canada) producing a version of it. The UK ran a series of *Fort Boyard* from 1998 to 2001, and then the variation *Challenge* in 2003.

Fort Boyard

citadel was destroyed in a bombing raid in 1945, you can still admire its design, and visit various rooms that now house exhibitions and craftsmen's workshops.

Beyond the citadel, ramparts stretch around the town, and are most imposing on the sea side where the archway *portes* were once used by oyster farmers and fishermen coming and going from their work. If you follow the ramparts around to the north, you can continue on a narrow road skirting the ramshackle huts of the oyster farmers on the shore side. The road eventually bends away and reaches a junction at les Allards where the road opposite leads to the Marais aux Oiseaux bird reserve (see P165 for details).

Turning right at this junction, a few more bends on a road across the marshes will bring you to the colourful leisure port at **Boyardville**. If you cross the channel here and continue to the seafront, you can pick up a road into

Fish locks

Fish locks are an old-fashioned and simple way of shore fishing. They are crescent-shaped walled enclosures into the top end of which the fish can swim at high tide. As the tide recedes the entrance is left high and dry and the water itself drains through a grill at the lowest point. At low tide, the fisherman wades out to the lock and catches the trapped fish with a harpoon or something similar.

The lighthouse organises trips to see the working of the fish locks, and there is a small museum at la Noue on the Île de Ré.

Oyster boats on the east coast

Huts at La Cité de l'Huître

the Saumonard Forest, where there is parking with access to a fine beach. Just offshore the dark bulk of Fort Boyard emerges from the ocean. It, too, was once part of the defences of the mouth of the Charente, but has achieved fame in recent years thanks to its television appearances. It is not possible to land at the fort but boat trips encircling it leave from Boyardville and St Denis.

The road through the Saumonards Forest is for bikes only; car-bound souls must return inland before heading out for the coast again at **la Brée-les-Bains**. A scenic road then follows the fine sandy beaches that stretch from here to **St Denis d'Oléron** with its pleasure port. From St Denis it is but 3km (2 miles) to the tip of the island and the black-and-white striped **Chassiron** lighthouse. 224 steps in a spiral staircase wider than many lead up to a platform from which there are views of the islands of Ré and Aix, and of la Rochelle itself, not too far away across the Straits of Antioche. On the shore below, the ridges of the fish locks can be seen at low tide.

From Chassiron the road south skirts a wild rocky coast lashed by Atlantic

Port des Salines

Take a walk

At St Trojan, the road ends beside a dyke at the Pointe de Manson. You can leave the car here and take the signed footpath that rounds the headland and continues along the coast to the Plage de Gatseau. The path faces the Seudre estuary and with views of the bridge to Oléron on one side and the wooded Arvert peninsula on the other, seascapes don't come any better than this!

rollers and appropriately named the Côte Sauvage. Sand makes its appearance as you travel on, but there are still the rocks, as can be seen at the Plage des Sables Vigniers, backed by the Forest of Domino. Farther south, **la Cotinière** is the most attractive of fishing ports, filled with brightly coloured boats, many of them carrying the cheerful pennants used to mark out the lobster pots. Once sardines were the main catch of la Cotinière, but in the 1960s shrimps took over and today it is the 'noble fish' (lobster, sea bass, sole). Every afternoon sees the boats arriving at the quayside beside the *criée* (fish auction) to unload their catch. The auction starts at 4pm precisely, and the public are invited to watch from a special viewing gallery.

Beyond la Cotinière the road first follows the coast and then swings inland to **le Grand-Village-Plage**, where a collection of low stone buildings houses a museum of traditional life and costume (La Maison Paysanne de la Coiffe et du Costume). Further on, the southern tip of the island is covered by pines and holm oaks, the Forest of St Trojan. Through its depths wind footpaths and cycle tracks, and at its most southerly part, a little train crosses the forest from **St Trojan** itself, delivering holidaymakers to the beach. The Grande Plage and its northern extension the Plage de Vert Bois are wide sweeps of golden sand pounded by the huge waves rolling in from the west.

The main road does not go through the forest, but rather skirts its edge to reach St Trojan. The pretty resort has other, less exposed, beaches facing the Straits of Marmusson, and it is possible to follow the coast south to the finest of them all, the **Plage de Gatseau**. Thick woodland backs this white sandy bay. A little restaurant tucked under the pines attends to the needs of the many summer visitors, but Gatseau is at its most beautiful when deserted.

Leaving St Trojan there is one last call to be made on the island. Approaching Grande Village Plage, follow signs to **Port des Salines** and you will quickly arrive at a group of coloured huts on the edge of the marshes. This superb ecomuseum is centred on salt and oysters, and three of the huts contain exhibits from both industries. One delivers a push-button commentary (in English if desired) on the work of the oyster farmers. Other features of this most photogenic site are working salt pans, an excellent restaurant, signed nature-trail footpaths, and the little port where boats can be hired to explore the extensive network of marshes.

Marennes and the Seudre

Back on the mainland the white spire of the church at **Marennes** stands high above the flat marshy countryside, a landmark used by boats navigating

Oyster culture

There is nothing new about eating oysters – and nothing essentially exotic about it either. In the Middle Ages, the flat oysters that could be gathered wild from the shores of Britain and France were a staple food of the people, and particularly of the poorer classes. Eventually, at the time when it became possible to transport oysters inland, there just weren't enough to go round, and oyster farming, formerly practised only by the Romans, began again in Europe.

The Marennes-Oléron basin is an ideal place for oyster farming because it is protected by the offshore island, and has shallow, warm waters that are reduced in salt content by the fresh water arriving from the River Seudre. In 1868, fate dealt the area a trump card. A Portuguese ship carrying oysters to Britain was forced by bad weather to take shelter in the Gironde, and after several days decided to dump its cargo of dead and dying oysters. Some survived, and it was these large oysters that were cultivated so successfully in the basin until the late 1960s, when a disease almost wiped them out. Japanese oysters were imported to replace them, and it is this strain you see here today.

Whole families are involved in oyster farming. Their 'farm' is a piece of seabed leased from the government, which they usually mark out with coloured flags, and they may have a brightly coloured hut on the quayside where the oysters are scraped and sorted. The cycle of farming begins in early summer when oysters eject eggs and sperm into the sea for fertilisation. The spats so formed attach themselves to carefully placed 'collectors' (tubes of plastic, oyster shells or slates) which are left in place for a year before being separated and laid out on racks in low water. After another year the collectors are taken in, and the oysters are scraped off and put into cages or sacks. These are again fixed on tables lifting them above the seabed to reduce attacks from predators. In these cages the oysters feed on plankton filtered from the seawater and so grow fat – but they require regular turning to ensure uniformity.

After around 15 months in the cages the oysters are taken in and washed in fresh water to get rid of impurities. In the Marennes-Oléron area there is then another stage – the oysters are transferred to the *claires*, which are the former salt pans. This is where they mature, and acquire their characteristic green colour (and possibly unique taste) from the Blue Navicule algae in the water. Oysters known as *fines de claires* spend a month in a sack in this way – others spend longer and may be more spread out to improve their quality, and the very best *pouses en claires* are thrown individually into the *claires* to refine there for six months.

Oysters are best eaten fresh, garnished with a little lemon juice or vinegar – and the traditional accompaniments are crusty or rye bread and a glass of white wine. They can also be cooked, which may mean poaching in white wine or baking in some delectable sauce. If you buy them from the quayside or market, you must take care opening them, because there are too many casualties from those sharp-pointed knives (thick gloves advised for amateurs). But there are more than enough restaurants with oysters on the menu – just choose yourself a quiet corner with a sea view, sit back, and enjoy!

Oyster platter

Seafood platter

the Seudre estuary. From the viewing platform beneath the spire, the islands, estuary, bridges, oyster beds and all the twists of this complicated shoreline are laid out before you. The story behind the model sailing ship hanging above the nave has long been forgotten, but the straits between Marennes and Oléron (the Pertuis Maumusson) are renowned for their treacherous currents.

The name Marennes is synonymous with oysters, and visitors can view the work of the oyster farmers by taking one of the conducted tours that leave regularly from the port of Marennes,

la Cayenne. La Cayenne is at the end of a long causeway stretching from Marennes into the wide estuary of the Seudre. Beside the road, the water channel is lined with fishing boats tied to rickety jetties, with the colourful huts of the oystermen alongside. The most recent addition to this scene is an ecomuseum by the name of **la Cité de l'Huître**. While one part of this is a workaday farm, the other is a cheerful collection of huts on jetties, each revealing by an ingenious hi-tech 'show' some aspect of oyster-culture. A little train plies between the two parts, a discovery trail winds between the

Château de la Gataudière

La Cayenne

claires and naturally there is a restaurant serving oysters!

More feverish oyster activity can be seen north of Marennes at **le Chapus**, a finger of land that points into the straits beneath the bridge to Oléron. Beyond this tip of land stands another fort (Fort Louvois), so positioned to augment the defence of the arsenal at Rochefort. The causeway that connects it to the mainland serves as a jetty for the oyster boats, which make a fine scene as they race in on the rising tide when work on the beds is no longer possible. The fort itself can be visited in summertime and, not surprisingly, contains a small exhibition on oyster farming.

Returning from le Chapus to

Marais aux Oiseaux

Marennes, signs on the left direct you to the **Château de la Gataudière**. This handsome pale-stoned eighteenth-century château was built by engineer and botanist François Freneau, who made his fortune by discovering the *hevea* rubber tree in Guyana and realising its potential. Today the château is owned by Prince Anatole de Chasse-loup-Laubat, a descendant of Fresneau, who takes many of the visits himself, and can deliver a very rapid salvo in English as he does so. Since the château is lived in, three rooms only are open to the public – the wood-panelled pastel blue dining room with its crystal chandelier, a fine drawing room and the Grand Salon on whose stone-carved walls are representations of the arts, the sciences and the seasons. The stables house an exhibition of carriages and upstairs there is a display of model ships and much more. Running a château is a costly business, and the newest venture here is Châteaubranche Aventure, an arboreal adventure park, with tree-walking routes to suit all ages.

From Gataudière the marshes stretch for miles inland. The most impressive road across them is the D18 (off the D728) from St Just Luzac. Flat grass-land extends on either side, cropped by roaming cattle, with herons and egrets peering from every sunken watercourse. **St Just Luzac** itself is worth a pause. The huge grey church on the corner has a curious sixteenth-century triangular porch in front of the nave, the base of an intended bell tower. Seen from the nave, mirrors have been used to produce curious effects in the modern stained glass windows. In an alley behind the church, an inconspicuous model railway

museum boasts 2,500 steam locomotives and other rolling-stock both French and foreign, dating back to 1875.

Back to Marennes again now, and if you leave the town on the little road to the west, you will join the main road (D728E) at an attention-diverting roundabout on which a child in bathing

Keep your eyes on the road ahead

In this south-west corner of Charente-Marime, imagination seems to know no bounds with regard to roundabouts. As a challenge, see how many of the following you can spot (all are within 30km/20 miles of Marennes)

- 2 folded paper boats
- A monk holding a window
- Deckchairs and umbrellas on a beach
- A crane lifting a block of stone
- Lock gates running water
- Three colourful oyster huts
- Two hands opening an oyster

trunks tows a model boat.

On the opposite side of the roundabout roads lead down to **Marennes-Plage**, an off-the-beaten-track little place that concentrates all its energies into two months of the year, when children romp in its beach club and bathe in its shallow water lagoon.

Towering above Marennes-Plage, a high bridge takes traffic over the mouth of the Seudre. Turning left on the far side, you arrive in **La Tremblade**, the smaller counterpart of Marennes, where once again oysters fill the universe. From the town the drive to the port is shorter, but again there is a boat-filled channel, an assortment of restaurants alongside and an abundance of oyster shells, stacked neatly in crates, scattered on the banks and crunched underfoot. From the parking area at the end of the quay you can watch the flat-bottomed boats plying the channel and the scene is compelling. Back on the quayside in town, La Tremblade has a small oyster museum, a single room filled with old photographs, bits of equipment and pinned French texts, the simplicity of which has more impact than many a high-tech show.

Beyond La Tremblade the banks of the Seudre are lined by little ports and scattered with oyster huts. For a glimpse of an attractive yet working harbour make your way to **Chatressac** (7km/4.5 miles south) where boats and huts are extra-colourful, and jetties on the narrow channel seem to wobble even more vigorously with the incoming tide.

Further up the estuary, **Mornac-sur-Seudre** is also a working oyster port, but pretty Mornac is one of the designated *plus beaux villages de France* (see P81) and has become a honey-pot for tourists. Narrow streets of blue-shuttered whitewashed houses with pink hollyhocks round their doors lead down to a picturesque harbour – where even the boats are blue and white! Mornac has a twelfth-century Romanesque church, a narrow-gauge railway (it is on the line from la Tremblade to Saujon) and a handful of really top-quality craft shops with lots of browsing potential. You won't be alone here in high summer, but it won't be as crowded as the other side of the peninsula, around Royan.

Take a walk

From the harbour at Mornac, two signed trails lead out between the oyster *claires* to the banks of the main channel – you can pick up a leaflet at the Office de Tourisme on the quayside. Viewed in one way, this is just a muddy, messy area, and yet it is also beautiful, with pink *salicornes* (glassworts) down by the water, white egrets haunting the *claires* and always a wide sky above the flat horizon.

The Gironde

In the long sweep of sun-baked golden sand that edges the Bay of Biscay, there is one break, a deep slash into the hinterland – the estuary of the Gironde. And that in itself is an anomaly, because there is no River Gironde. The name is given only to the estuary formed from the confluence of the Garonne and the Dordogne, an estuary that is the largest of its kind in Europe, draining all south-west France from the Massif Central to the Pyrenees. Shallow and wide, the Gironde has many sandy islets, and its brown waters have been likened to thick gravy, with a 'muddy plug' ever-present where the down-flowing river meets the incoming tide. Most of the eastern shore of this estuary is in Charente-Maritime, and it is a fascinating region to explore, getting more and more off the beaten track as you head upstream.

Royan, at the mouth of the estuary, was a small fishing harbour until the mid-1800s, when the new vogue for sea-bathing caused it to transform almost overnight into a fashionable resort. The arrival of the railway in 1875 brought yet more visitors, who stayed in the lavish hotels that were springing up along the seafront, or built stylish villas to their own design. Days were spent on the promenades and beaches and long evenings in the newly-established casino. Royan had its heyday, but it all came to an end with the Second World War.

At the end of 1944, the retreating German forces dug in hard around Royan. On the night of 5 January 1945, the misdirected bombing attack of a weary allied airforce reduced the town to rubble. On the night of 14/15 April the performance was repeated, and this time surrender came two days later – just three weeks before the armistice. The story is told with mannequins, tanks, photographs, manuscripts and a lot besides in the Musée de la Poche de Royan, 10km (6 miles) north at le Gua.

Royan was subsequently handed over to the enthusiastic planners of the 1950s. Long geometric lines of white apartment blocks appeared along the seafront, above arcades where restaurants, shops and ice-cream bars flourished. A wide avenue was created to lead up to a market hall apparently disguised as something from outer space. The most conspicuous new arrival was the Église Notre-Dame on high ground above the port. The architects Gillet and Hébrard followed the zeitgeist in choosing reinforced concrete for their medium, but had it covered in resin to protect against the elements in this exposed spot (in vain as it turns out, because the concrete is now cracking). The design of this church is still unusual

– a solid grey building with a strange saddleback roof, it has a 60m (200ft) belfry rising like the high prow of a ship at the east end. Love it or hate it, it has interest value, and the inside has even more. The huge space created by the high single nave is best appreciated from the top-of-staircase entrance at the west end. The tall narrow side windows admit a pale light, thus making all the more striking the brilliant triangle of colour that pours down over the simple altar. And well in keeping, the organ by Robert Boisseau has a case of hammered pewter.

Below the church, harbours surround the headland. From the outermost jetty, car ferries leave to cross the estuary to the Pointe de Grave, the tip of the Médoc peninsula. Next comes the harbour for the fishing boats, with the fish auction rooms alongside. Nearest to the long beach is a harbour for the pleasure boats, and at the promenade alongside you can book a boat trip around the estuary or to the distant Cordouan lighthouse.

Royan's other attractions include four beaches, a town museum and the newly-opened and liberally-signposted Jardins du Monde. The latter can be visited on foot or by boat (extra charge), butperhaps deliberately lack colour other than in the tropical greenhouses and butterfly habitats at the start of the visit. Of the beaches, the longest by far is the busy Grande Conche, and the streets backing it (where the likes of Emile Zola and Sarah Bernhardt once lived) still retain some of their Belle-Époque glory. A more peaceful corner to survive the bombing raid is the suburb of Pontaillac, whose little cove of white sand is overlooked by yet more elegant villas tucked among the pine trees

The Cordouan lighthouse

The Cordouan lighthouse perches on a rock some 7km (4.5 miles) out to sea – you may or may not get wet feet as you land depending on the tide! This is the oldest lighthouse in France – its lower ornate section was constructed between 1584 and 1611, while the more austere upper part was added in 1789. The older part contains furniture dating from Napoleon III, the marble-floored royal apartments and even a chapel with stained glass windows. Audioguides (in English) describe both the architecture and the work of the resident wardens, while 311 steps lead up to the level of the lantern for a magnificent view!

Phare de Chassiron (it does rain!)

mingos divert passing motorists, while inside the gates the polar bear seems to be the star of the show. Animals here are generally well kept with adequate space, and watching a scene such as the ruffed lemurs flinging themselves freely between the pine trees is pure magic.

Beyond la Palmyre the road goes on into the forest that clothes all the tip of this Arvert peninsula. The red and white **Phare de la Coubre** pushes its head above the treetops to look along the length of the coast – a mere 300 or so steps will allow you to share its view. The coast, now known as the Côte Sauvage, is more suited to the needs of surfers than swimmers and is most readily accessible to the cyclists, who soar gleefully along miles of dedicated track. Eventually the road itself bends east and, with many a tropical scene of umbrella pines shading a silvery shore, reaches the little resort of **Ronce-les-Bains**, at the foot of the bridge across the Seudre.

Take a walk

A well-marked footpath (white on red bars, as this is a *Grande Randonnée*) skirts the shores for some 10km (6 miles) to the north of Royan before striking off into the forest. To enjoy just a short section of this you could join it beside the beach at Pontaillac, from where it rounds the cliffs and crosses a cleft in the rock by the Pont du Diable (Devil's Bridge). Further on it reaches the Plage du Platin before passing the Terre Neuve lighthouse and then the viewpoint of la Grande Côte.

Going north by car, the **Grande Côte** viewpoint with its telescopes is soon followed by the resort of **La Palmyre**, most renowned for its large zoo. Brilliantly-coloured Caribbean fla-

A drive up the estuary

Back at Royan again, you are only at the start of the Gironde estuary. Heading south you first pass through the family resort of **St Georges-de-Didonne** on whose outskirts is the new Parc de l'Estuaire. A high-quality educational ecomuseum, it seems to be aimed mainly at school parties, and a level of French that extends to scientific detail is necessary to get the best from it. Nevertheless it commands a splendid view of the bay and boasts an observation tower for seeing yet further.

The holiday crowd begins to thin just a little as you next approach **Meschers-sur-Gironde**. Meschers has cliffs of yellow limestone, the highest on the estuary, and those cliffs are tunnelled with caves that have been inhabited in their time by Saracens, Vikings, pirates, smugglers, wreckers and even a few with less evil intent. By the end of the nineteenth-century, the caves had become centres of entertainment, with cafés and theatrical and musical performances. All was closed down in 1976. Today many of Mescher's fifty or so caves are privately owned. Vying for your custom, two adjacent (and not unsimilar) complexes can be visited, the Grottes de Régulus (municipal) and the Grottes de Matata (private, including a hotel and crêperie). From the caves, the cliff road eventually drops down to Mescher's substantial port, a jumble of pleasure and fishing boats, and the departure point for a boat taking passengers to view the caves and coastline from the water.

After Meschers the next place south is **Talmont-sur-Gironde,** and it cer-tainly attracts the visitors at the height of summer. Talmont is another of the elite *plus beaux villages* (see P81), with white-washed blue-shuttered cottages showing off pink hollyhocks around their doors. But, pretty as they are, in Talmont it is the eleventh-century church of Ste Radegonde that steals the show. Balanced precariously on a rocky spur jutting into the sea, it is an architectural gem, a geometrically satisfying blend of curves, arches and right-angles, all worked in pale stone under pink-tiled roofs. Pilgrims en route for Santiago de Compostela once came here to worship, and they must have taken the memory of this lovely church with them all the way to Spain.

From Talmont, a road will take you out to Barzan and the Gallo-Roman site at the **Moulin du Fâ**. Guided visits take an hour and a half – a long time under the hot sun or pouring rain – and are in French only. But this extensive site is quite remarkable and is still undergoing enthusiastic excavation.

Back on the D145, **Les Monards** is a pretty port with lots of boats. Even prettier and totally unspoilt is **St Seurin-d'Uzet**, whose church stands alongside the harbour on a long inlet that fills and empties with the tide. From here you can walk out on a path (past the excellent little campsite) to the edge of the estuary where the sun magically sets into the sea.

On south to **Mortagne-sur-Gironde** – and there are lovely views as the road winds over hills before descending into the town. Mortagne itself is rather grey, but once you turn down to the port, all is life and colour. Along the coast road from the port is l'Hermitage, four bare rooms in the cliff face, once sheltering pilgrims who crossed the estuary here on their way to Santiago de Compostela. The fifth room is a rocky chapel dating from the ninth-century, kept locked apart from the occasional tour in high season. A staircase cut through the cliff leads to its summit and views across the estuary.

Below Mortagne the coast road goes on, with low marshes and flat fields of sunflowers and maize now separating you from the estuary. **Port Maubert** is another beautiful harbour, quiet even in high summer, with boats lined along pontoons on the wide channel and a pleasant little crêperie from which to watch the peaceful scene. The estuary itself is out of sight and accessible only on foot (10 minutes) or by bike. From Port Maubert you might like to head inland through the vineyards to **St Fort-sur-Gironde** to see one of the classic Romanesque churches. This church dates from the latter half of the twelfth-century and has a rose window and a plethora of carvings both inside and out – the main doorway is curiously framed by horses, heads.

Just down the road now is **St Dizant-du-Gua**, another sleepy pale-stoned village. In its main street, a glimpse of the gardens of the Château de Beaulon lures visitors to enter – beyond the well-groomed lawns and bright floral borders the woodland conceals brilliant blue pools that are fed by underground springs. The elegant château itself was once a palace belonging to the Bishops of Bordeaux. Today you can possibly enter just one room to sample the cognac and pineau produced in the distillery at nearby Lorignac.

South of St Dizant the D145 runs through farming country with good views over the marshes to the west and a windmill on the heights at Conac. At **St Thomas-de-Conac**, the prominent church is another typical of the Saintonge – although the façade is nineteeth-century, the interior is Romanesque, with some finely carved capitals. St Sorlin, St Bonnet and St Ciers have more views and from each, little roads lead out across the marsh to ports that are mere inlets on the side of the brown estuary. All of them are off the beaten track and all are worth a visit, but **Vitrezay**, right on the border of Charente-Maritime is a gem not to be missed. Vitrezay has recently been developed as a Pôle-Nature (Nature Focus) and there are exhibitions on the life of the estuary fishermen, and paths on which you can walk off into the marshes and observe the birds and other wildlife. It is possible to take sailing or fishing lessons, and even to hire a *pêcherie* (one of those spindly-legged fishing platforms) for the day. The new restaurant here has pledged itself to serve local fare in season, including estuary fish. Excellent, informal and inexpensive, it is rapidly becoming very popular with locals as well as visitors.

Vitrezay in its way typifies Charente-Maritime's current thinking with regard to tourism. A lot of money has been spent here in encouraging visitors to appreciate the real essence of the area, the natural history, gastronomy and traditional way of life of these banks of the Gironde. It seems a fitting place to take leave of one of the most fascinating regions of France.

Places to Visit

Offices de Tourisme

St Pierre d'Oléron

Place Gambetta – BP 46
17310 SAINT PIERRE d'OLÉRON
☎ 05 46 47 11 39

Marennes

Place Chasseloup-Laubat
17320 MARENNES
☎ 05 46 85 04 36

Royan

Palais de Congrès - BP 102
17206 ROYAN Cedex
☎ 05 46 23 00 00

Places of Interest

Île d' Oléron

Musée de l'Île d'Oléron (St Pierre)

☎ 0546 75 05 16
Open Jun to Sept daily 9.30am–1pm, 2–7pm; Apr, May and Oct daily except Mon 10am–12noon, 2–6pm; rest of year daily except Mon 2–5.30pm.

Phare de Chassiron

☎ 05 46 75 18 62
Open daily – Jul and Aug 10am–8pm; Apr to Jun and Sept 10am–12.15pm, 2–7pm; rest of year 10am–12.15pm, 2–5pm.

Maison Paysanne de la Coiffe et du Costume (le Grand-Village-Plage)

☎ 05 46 47 43 44
Open Jul and Aug only, 10am–12.30pm, 2.30–6pm daily except Sun (and closed Mon mornings).

Ecomuseum of the Port des Salines

☎ 05 46 75 82 28
Open Jul to Sept daily 9.30am–1pm, 2.30–7pm (but closed Sun morning); Apr to Jun daily 9.30am–12.30pm, 2.30–6pm (but closed Sun and Mon mornings).

Marennes

La Cité de l'Huître

☎ 05 46 36 78 98
Open Jul and Aug 10am–8pm daily; Apr, May, Jun, Sept and autumn half term 10am–7pm daily; Febr, Mar, Oct, Nov and Dec Fri, Sat and Sun only 12noon–7pm. Last entry 1½ hours before closing.

Boat trips around the Marennes-Oléron basin – destination according to tide

☎ 05 46 85 20 85
Boats depart from the port of La Cayenne daily in Jul and Aug at 10.30am, 2.30, 3.30 and 4.30pm; May, Jun and Sept at 2.30pm daily except Sat. English translation offered. No reservation required.

Fort Louvois

☎ 05 46 85 07 00
Open Jul and Aug daily 10.30am–6.30pm (ferry boat put on when tide too high for causeway); Jun and Sept open at low tide only.

Château de la Gataudière

Château

☎ 05 46 85 01 07

Open Jun to Sept daily 10am–12noon, 2–6.30pm. Mar to May, Oct and Novr daily except Mon 10am–12noon, 2–5pm.

Châteaubranche Aventure

☎ 05 46 85 01 07

Open Jul and Aug daily 10am–8pm (last tickets 3 hours before closing); Apr, May, Jun, Sept and Oct, Sat and Sun only, 2–6pm; Easter and All Saints' holidays daily 2–6pm.

St Just Luzac

Model railway museum

☎ 05 46 85 33 35

Open mid-Jun to mid-Sept daily except Mon 3–6pm.

La Tremblade

Musée Maritime (oyster culture museum)

☎ 05 46 36 30 11

Open Jul and Aug 2.30–6.30pm daily except Sun; Apr, May, Jun and Sept daily except Tue and Sun 3–6pm and public holidays 10am–12noon.

Boat trips on the estuary – to the oyster beds at low tide and the oyster ports at high.

☎ 05 46 02 06 92

Leave from the port, duration 1 hour. Jul and Aug departures at 10.30am, 2.30, 3.30, 4.30 and 5.30pm daily; Apr, May, Jun and Sept daily at 3pm.

Royan

Musée de Royan

☎ 05 46 38 85 96

Open daily except Tue mid-Jun to mid-Sept 10am–12.30pm, 3–7.30pm; rest of year 9am–12noon, 2–6pm.

Musée de la Poche de Royan (le Gua)

☎ 05 46 22 89 90

Open daily, Jul and Aug 10am–7pm, rest of year 10am–12noon, 2–6pm.

Jardins du Monde

☎ 05 46 38 00 99

Open daily Jul and Aug 10am–8pm, rest of year 10am–6pm. Last ticket 1 hour before closing.

Zoo de la Palmyre

☎ 05 46 22 46 06

Open daily Apr to Sept 9am–7pm; rest of year 9am–6pm.

Phare de la Coubre

☎ 05 46 06 26 42

Open mid-Jun to mid-Sept 10am–12.30pm, 1–6pm.

St Georges-de-Didonne

Parc de l'Estuaire

☎ 05 46 23 77 77

Open Jul and Aug daily 10am–1pm, 2–7.30pm; Apr to Jun and first half of Sept 10am–12.30pm; 2.30–6.30pm; Feb, Mar and mid-Sept to mid-Nov 2–6pm. Open some days in Christmas holidays.

(cont'd overleaf)

(cont'd from previous page)

Places to Visit

Meschers-sur-Gironde

Grottes de Regulus

☎ 05 46 02 55 36

Guided visits from mid-Jun to mid-Sept daily; Apr to mid-Jun and mid-Sept to early Novevery afternoon.

Grottes de Matata

Tel 05 46 02 70 02

Guided visits from Apr to beginning of Nov, between 10am and 7pm.

Barzan

Moulin du Fâ (Gallo-Roman site)

☎ 05 46 90 43 66

Open Apr to Sept daily 10am–7pm; rest of year Fri to Sun (school holidays daily) 2–5.30pm.

Mortagne-sur-Gironde

St Martial Hermitage

☎ 05 46 90 62 95

Open every afternoon in summertime.

St Dizant de Gua

Château de Beaulon

☎ 05 46 49 96 13

Open May to Sept daily 9am–12noon, 2–6pm; rest of year weekdays only at the same times.

Vitrezay

Pôle-Nature

☎ 05 46 49 89 89

Open Jun to Sept daily 10.30am–12.30pm, 1.30–7pm; Apr, May and school holidays daily except Mon and Thur 10.30am–12.30pm, 2–5.30pm; Feb, Mar, Oct and Nov Wed, Sat and Sun only 10.30am–12.30pm, 2–5.30pm.

For the family

Beaches

There is a huge choice of bathing beaches, many of them supervised. Those directly facing the Atlantic have the bigger waves, and are therefore less suitable for young children. Do not hesitate to ask any Tourist Office for their advice regarding beaches for your family

Cycling

There is a good network of cycle tracks on Oléron and in the Arvert peninsula. Bike hire is omnipresent, and if you are thinking of more than a couple of days, it is worth looking at weekly rates. Of course it is a big saving if you can bring the bikes from home!

Birds and Animals

For children who love animals and birds, you can get quite close to plenty of both in the Marais aux Oiseaux. Not far away (off the road to la Cotinière) is another bird park (Parc d'Oiseaux) with many exotic species. And, of course, there is a whole day's entertainment in the Zoo of la Palmyre (north of Royan).

A rainy day?

Head for the Cité de l'Huître

It will take you at least an hour and a half to see all the shows, and you can always linger longer in the gift shop and restaurant. When the sun shines again you will be all genned-up for a boat trip to the oyster beds.

Visit a Château

If it's still raining, go on to the nearby Château de la Gataudière and after the visit, spend as much time as you like browsing all the bric-a-brac in the attic of the barn. There are old books for sale here, too.

Take a drive & dine

Take a meandering drive down to Vitrezay and linger over a four-course lunch in the restaurant overlooking the estuary. If it doesn't clear up, you get to see a very wild place in wild conditions – if it does you can walk out across the marshes and unpack your camera for the way home (Talmont is obligatory).

A taste of the region

Oysters, of course

The local green oysters really are special – take every opportunity to indulge (and see P169)

Wines

Grapes grown on Oléron were once used only for cognac. Nowadays the vineyard produces its own wine, which is mostly white. Oléron white wine is dry, perfect with oysters, and ideal for quaffing in the garden at home on a warm day. The Cave du Port at le Château can advise about purchases.

Fish from the estuary

Shrimps and prawns certainly, but the estuary is also prime fishing ground for lamprey and shad in spring and eels that return from the Sargasso Sea in autumn. Whatever is in season should be on the menu at Vitrezay.

How to get there

Options are by land, sea and air

By land

Which in this case means Eurostar for those who are not taking a vehicle, and le Shuttle for everyone else.

Eurostar

There are at least a dozen trains every day from London Waterloo to Paris-Gare du-Nord (2¾ hrs.approx.). From there a TGV will speed you to La Rochelle in less than 3 hours, so it is perfectly possible to leave London at 9am and arrive in La Rochelle by teatime. Information for services throughout France can be obtained by phoning Rail Europe (☎ 08705 848848) or on the website www.raileurope.co.uk. But to take full advantage of the recommendations of this book, you are probably at some time going to need your own transport.

Le Shuttle

Staying with your vehicle all the time, this is probably the 'least hassle' way of getting to France, and almost a must for those who are seasick, in a hurry or have pets with them. With several departures every hour, only in high season do you need to purchase your ticket ahead of time. Nevertheless, you may be able to take advantage of offers by doing this – and should you arrive at the check-in early, you have a pretty good chance of getting an earlier train. Crossing time is about 35 minutes and both loading and unloading are carried out with admirable efficiency. But from Calais, you would face a journey of approximately 450 miles to La Rochelle.

By sea

This is the leisure way to travel, and most people still feel it marks the start to the family holiday. At least it gets everyone out of the car for a while! A wide choice of crossings is on offer

Eastern crossings

Dover-Calais is the shortest and quickest and (usually) cheapest crossing of the Channel. Regular ferry services are offered by Sea France, P & O and Norfolk Line (to Dunkerque) with a crossing time of about 90 minutes. But you will then have a long drive through France (approx. 700km/430 miles to la Rochelle)

Western crossings

The western crossings are all longer and generally a little more expensive – but, depending on your home location, you may save considerably on mileage and even time. All the western crossings have overnight options, and since reveille always tends to be on the early side, you could be in the Vendée for lunchtime! LD Lines cover the crossing from Portsmouth to le Havre (5½ hours), while Condor Ferries operate on the Portsmouth to Cherbourg route (5 hours) with fast craft from Poole and Weymouth shuttling via the Channel Islands to St Malo in summertime (4½ hours). Brittany Ferries have crossings from Portsmouth to Caen (5¾ hours), Poole to Cherbourg (4¼ hours), Portsmouth to Cherbourg (5½ hours), Portsmouth to St Malo (overnight out, 10+ hours return in daytime), and Plymouth to Roscoff (6 hours). All except the last two crossings have high-speed options in summertime that can reduce times by about 50%. La Rochelle is 204 miles (328 km) from St Malo, and approximately 290 miles (465 km) from Cherbourg, Caen or Roscoff.

By air

This could be preferable from a cost point of view if there are not too many of you, but today there are also 'green' considerations.

La Rochelle is served by Ryanair flying from Stansted and in summer only, by Easyjet operating from Bristol and Jet2 operating from Leeds Bradford.

Car hire is available from the airport, but it would be as well to arrange this in advance (possibly in a package with the flight). Expect to spend the first couple of hours reaching for the gear lever and/or handbrake with the wrong hand!

Onward travel in France

Whatever your point of arrival in France, you will probably find that it is quickest and most convenient to continue by *autoroute*. Most of these incur a charge (the one from Caen to Rennes is an exception), but are far less congested and offer better services than motorways in Britain. They have a generous provision of pull-offs known as *aires*, which at their most basic have picnic tables and toilets, and at their most sophisticated have petrol stations, top class restaurants, fitness courses and even regional museums to take your mind off the road for a while. An *autoroute* is normally free of charge while it is bypassing a big city.

Other points to remember in connection with driving are listed below –

Before you leave home, make sure you have your passport, driving licence, insurance certificate and log book (including a letter of authorisation from the owner if the vehicle is not registered in your name), and keep them all with you whenever you are out in the car. The French police are very keen on spot checks, and being on the road without these documents is an offence.

It goes without saying that you drive on the right! This sounds simple enough, but your weakest moments are first thing in the morning, and when turning out of a car park or one-way street into an empty two-way road. Known precautionary measures include putting a red spot on your windscreen and wearing your watch on the other wrist while in France – perhaps you can think of something better!

It is compulsory to carry a red warning triangle. This should be used in conjunction with hazard flashers if you break down on the road. Since July 2008 it has also been compulsory to carry visibility vests, to be put on if you have to step out of the car.

Car headlights must be fitted with appropriate beam deflectors – it is an offence to drive without these even in daylight. And dipped beams must be used when the visibility is poor.

Carrying a spare set of lightbulbs for your vehicle is recommended.

Seat belts must be worn by front and rear seat passengers, and children under 10 years of age may not travel in the front seat. As in the UK, young children must be belted into seats that are appropriate for their weight and age.

Speed limits are 130kph/81mph on motorways in good weather conditions, 110kph/68mph on dual carriageways and on motorways in bad weather, 90kph/56mph on all other roads. In towns and villages, the speed limit is 50kph/31mphmph from the name sign at the entrance to the sign where the name is crossed out at the end, even though no limits may be displayed. And added to all that, there are many sections of road marked with their own peculiar limits, which you need to remember. Police are empowered to impose on-the-spot fines for speeding, and to confiscate the driver's licence if the limit was exceeded by more than 25kph.

France has had to crack down very hard on drunken drivers – limits are now much more strict than in the UK and punishments are severe. Do not touch even a drop before getting behind the wheel!

The old rule of *priorité à droite* (you should give priority to any vehicle arriving from the right) lingers in some town centres – and also in the minds of some older drivers. Since the rule is not yet extinct, look out for signs telling you who has priority at junctions and roundabouts – and if you don't know, err on the safe side. *Cédez le passage* means Give Way!

When you are there
Accommodation

This can be divided into hotels, *chambres d'hôtes* (bed and breakfast), *gîtes* (country cottages) and campsites (with hostel accommodation in *auberges de jeunesse* and *gîtes d'étapes* for the young at heart on a budget). For peace of mind, it is advisable to book ahead all accommodation needed in high season. Any tourist office will be able to supply you with lists of what is available in their area.

Hotels

Nationally, these are graded from 0 to 5 stars, and usually perform as their grade would lead you to expect. The most highly favoured guide is the *Michelin Red Hotel and Restaurant Guide* (in English) – which also rates a few thousand restaurants as well. Hotels listed in the *Logis de France* catalogue (available to order from the website www.logis-de-france. fr) are of guaranteed quality and not necessarily expensive. Ratings here vary from 1 to 3 'hearths' and whatever the grade, you are likely to find a good standard of regional cuisine. For overnight stops, you could consider one of the motel chains (Campanile, Ibis, Novotel are the most upmarket) to be found near most big towns. In contrast to their British counterparts, these motels generally serve high quality imaginative food, again with regional emphasis, and are more than generous with the buffet parts of set menus. If you are staying for several nights in a hotel and thinking of eating in, look for their *demi-pension* (half-board) rates. These usually represent an overall saving (not invariably, so look hard!), but you are generally expected to eat from the humblest of the menus on offer.

Chambres d'hôtes – B&B

Many of them also offer an optional evening meal *en famille* – an opportunity to meet people and try out your French in an informal setting. *Fermes auberges* offer something of the same. *Gîtes-de-France* catalogues also contain information on *Chambres d'hôtes* (see below for details).

Gîtes Ruraux – country cottages

(Not to be confused with *gîtes d'étapes*, which are more like youth hostels).

There are quite a lot of these available in this holiday area. British owners of properties in France generally advertise with Brittany Ferries (The French Collection), Chez Nous or Owners in France (among others); French owners seem to prefer to deal directly with *Gîtes de France*, who have a vast number of properties listed and catalogued by *département*. Go to their website (www.gites-de-france.fr – there is an English version), order a catalogue and browse. All the facts are there, the only thing you can't predict is the owner. A few will give you a brief tour, meet you at the end and add up the electricity bill; most go well beyond that and some will lavish wine, regional gifts and free firewood upon you and spend as much time as you care to give them extolling the virtues of their region, thus providing you with a wonderful opportunity of improving your French whatever its standard. This is definitely the best option for getting the feel of French life, although satisfaction can't be entirely guaranteed.

Camping

The French love camping and you will probably see three-generation families that have evidently moved under canvas for the duration of summer, taking with them what appears to be the entire contents of their house and assorted livestock as well. Campsites in France are plentiful and of varying quality – municipal sites usually represent good value for money and are of a high standard. The catalogue of choice is probably Michelin's *Camping France*, obtainable at bookshops in the UK, with a new edition released each spring. Nevertheless, there is virtually no descriptive text in the Michelin book (and a few sites of perfectly reasonable quality are unaccountably absent) so you might like to equip yourself also with the AA *Camping and Caravanning France*, or even the French *Camping Caravaning Guide Officiel*, which lists everything that could with abundant imagination be deemed an outdoor place to spend the night, and needs reading with care (in French). Tourist Offices in Vendée and Charente-Maritime should also be able to provide you with details of all campsites in their area.

Money matters

The euro in your pocket

Money can usually be exchanged without commission in the UK before you leave, and top-ups can be obtained from any ATM with the appropriate logo for your card. In practice, holders of the major cards will have no problem at all, but note that, in addition to the commission on the exchange, a fee is usually charged even for debit card withdrawals, and taking out small amounts is therefore relatively costly. If you cannot find a bank, larger post offices will always have a cash-point (*distributeur de billets*). The other option is travellers' cheques, and you may be lucky enough to obtain them without commission – but of course they can only be cashed during banking hours. These are something like Monday to Friday, 9am–5pm but – some banks close for two hours in the middle of the day, some close on Mondays, some open on Saturday mornings, all close for designated public holidays, and if the latter fall within one day of a weekend, many will not miss the obvious opportunity have an extended holiday.

Card purchases

Major credit cards are widely accepted in hotels, restaurants, supermarkets and petrol stations. It will normally be possible to use the British chip-and-PIN cards in French machines, but success will depend on whether the individual merchant is using the same system. If not, he should nevertheless be able to swipe the card as it will still have a magnetic strip. It should be said that, particularly in off-the-beaten-track areas, some supermarkets seem to have trouble with this swiping, but it is usually successful eventually, if everyone remains patient (including the lengthening queue).

Shopping

Markets

When in France, do as the French do (at least traditionally) and buy your fresh produce from the market. Almost every small town holds one at least once a week, and it is almost always all over by midday. But markets are by no means just a source of fruit and veg. – almost anything, animal, vegetable or mineral, can be found in some of the larger ones.

Supermarkets

At the other end of the scale are the supermarkets, which are becoming more popular with the busy housewives of today. Worst scenario opening hours are 9am–12noon, 2–6pm Tuesday to Saturday. Many, though not all, now open on Mondays, some open on Sunday mornings, but not one opens on a Sunday afternoon.

High Street

High Street shops have hours similar to supermarkets, give or take a bit. Bread at least is usually obtainable on a Sunday morning, and even on public holidays – to find it, you have only to look where all those carrying their breakfast bundles are coming from.

Electricity

The electric current is 220 volts and two-pin circular plugs are the norm. If you are going to use your own electrical devices, make sure you get an adaptor before you leave home (or at the ferry terminal) because they are not so easy to come by once you are in France.

Enjoying your holiday

Regional Offices de Tourisme

If you contact these before you leave, you can get all the up-to-date information about the area you will be visiting.

Vendée

Comité Départemental du Tourisme de la Vendée

8 Place Napoléon BP 233

85006 LA ROCHE-SUR-YON

☎ 02 51 47 88 20

Charente-Maritime

Comité Départemental de Tourisme

85 Boulevard de la République

17076 LA ROCHELLE Cedex 09

☎ 05 46 31 71 71

Holiday Pursuits

Museums

Published opening hours for museums are given in the information section at the end of each chapter – some establishments prefer to keep things more general by saying that they are open in the 'morning' or the 'afternoon'. And, of course, even where times are stated, they can change (although not usually radically) over the years. You could always telephone to check when timing is critical. Generally speaking, museums are quite likely to be closed on either a Monday or a Tuesday out of season and when open they may well take a longish lunch-break. In many places museum entry is free on the first Sunday of the month. And most museums are open all day every day in July and August.

Festivals

Local festivals can be wonderful entertainment. There are so many in this area that it has only been possible to detail one or two of the most important ones in their appropriate places. But any tourist office should be able to provide you with dates and times of what's on.

Walking

This is another popular French pastime, and almost every Office de Tourisme will be able to offer you maps of short circular walks in their area. These *Petites Randonnées* are usually waymarked with flashes of paint (yellow is the most common) on rocks, trees, walls etc., making them relatively easy to follow. A painted X indicates that you have taken the wrong way. The other type of path that you will commonly meet is the long-distance route, the *Grande Randonnée*. These are marked with bars of white on red and following one can be a great adventure, but first of all equip yourself with the appropriate map and decide how you are going to get back at the end of the day (with the help of OT for e.g. bus routes and taxis). Anyone with really serious intent should get on to the website of the French walking organisation, the *Fédération Française de la Randonnée Pédestre* (www. ffrandonnee.fr) who produce several truly excellent *Topoguides* covering this area. Attractive, colourful and with maps good enough to compensate for the lack of English translation, they describe both short local routes (PR) and long-distance trails (GR) and can be obtained by post from the FFRP headquarters in Paris.

Cycling

This is almost the French national sport – witness the popularity of the Tour de France. Routes for road bikers wanting to explore the local countryside can usually be obtained from any tourist office – although their idea of what constitutes a quiet country road might not entirely agree with your own. But in this region there are miles upon miles of designated cycle track, safe for all the family. By contrast this is probably not the best area for mountain bikers, although there are good circuits marked out in the Mervent-Vouvant Forest and in one or two other places. Mountain bikes are known as VTTs (*vélos tout terrain*) and the circuit logo is two wheels topped by a triangle pointing the direction. Tourist Offices should have all the necessary maps and information on bike hire.

Watersports

There are more than enough beaches, but you don't have to go to the seaside to swim in a pleasant outdoor environment – a *Plan d'eau* will do just as well, and there are several mentioned in the text. A *plan d'eau* is simply a small man-made lake with recreation facilities – perhaps a beach of imported sand, some children's play equipment nearby and possibly pedalos or other boats for hire. In many ways a *plan d'eau* is much safer for young children – it's easier to keep eyes on them for a start and the swimming area is usually supervised in the summer months. Other popular French pursuits are canoeing and kayaking, possible here on rivers, *marais* and sea, and many of the resorts also provide facilities for sailing.

Eating out

Eating out is very popular in France and even small villages that have no shops may have their own restaurant. If you are in a place where there is a choice of restaurants, go for one that is full – the locals are in the know.

Have no doubts about taking the children – they are always very welcome, and restaurants are usually happy to adapt to their needs (dividing a meal, or bringing an extra plate) if there is no children's menu.

Fixed menus are usually the best value and there are particularly good bargain feasts to be had at lunchtime – but of course you may put yourself out of action for the rest of the afternoon!

Take note that the cheese course comes before the dessert in France (i.e. don't leave as soon as you've had it), and a tiny cup of coffee (not usually included in the meal price) rounds everything off very nicely.

If you want to study form before you venture out, the *Michelin Red Guide* is the generally recognised authority, but also useful is the *Guide du Routard - Hotels and Restaurants*, of which there is an English version, and Dorling Kindersley have thrown in a glossy tome (*France – Best Places to Eat and Stay*) which interestingly details the regional specialities to look out for, as well as where to eat them.

And on leaving the restaurant tips are not strictly necessary, although 2 or 3 euros does register appreciation of a particularly good meal or service.

Public Holidays

The French year is scattered with public holidays and even more festivals that require ritual observance. On Rameaux (Palm Sunday) you will see people waving palm fronds (or stand-ins for the same); on Toussaint (All Saints' – 1 November) they are carrying huge pots of chrysanthemums to put on the graves of their loved ones; on 25 November (St Catherine's Day), unmarried 25-year-old girls become Catherinettes and wear outrageous bonnets on 1 May *muguet* (lily of the valley) is given to friends and sold in the streets and on Bastille Day (14 July), every town will be brought to a halt for the triumphant procession. And that's not even a fraction of it! But, for practical purposes, expect everything to be closed on the 12 official public holidays – 1 January, Easter Sunday, Easter Monday, 1 May, 8 May (Armistice 1945), Ascension Day, Whit Monday, 14 July (Bastille Day), 15 August (the Assumption), 1 November (All Saints), 11 November (Armistice 1918) and 25 December. And where these fall on a Sunday, the Monday following will also be taken as a holiday.

Telephoning

Card-operated telephones are far more common than those that will take cash. Telecartes can be obtained from any Post Office or from any shop displaying the sign 'Tabac' and come in two different sizes, 50 and 120 units. Many phones will now also accept the major credit cards.

You may be able to use your mobile phone in France if you have made arrangements in advance, but both calls and texts can be costly (texts are usually double the internal cost).

To call the UK from France, begin with the international code 0044, followed by the required number with the first zero omitted.

Emergency numbers are

15   Ambulance (SAMU – paramedics)

17   Police

18   Fire-brigade *(sapeurs-pompiers)*, who will deal with just about anything

112   A number that can be used throughout the EEC covering all three emergency services. You can expect to be connected to someone who speaks English

Medical Treatment

Before you leave, make sure you have an EHIC (European Health Insurance Card) – you can obtain one online, by phone or by post, and your local Post Office should be able to give you details. You would also be ill-advised to travel without extra medical insurance.

If you consult a doctor or dentist, you will be expected to pay and then be given a *feuille de soins* (medical treatment form) and a prescription, both of which should be taken to the chemist. To reclaim a proportion of costs, the *feuille de soins*, the sticky labels from drugs prescribed and your passport should be taken to a Caisse Primaire Assurance Maladie (CPAM) – the local OT should be able to direct you (the items can be sent later with the passport photocopied if you prefer). It is sometimes possible to get a refund immediately, although more usually it will be sent to your UK address in about 6 weeks.

In France, chemists are very used to dealing with minor ailments – coughs, colds, sprained ankles and more. It might well be worth consulting a chemist first to see if he can help – but you will not get the cost of his treatments reimbursed.

Historical Table

Date	French history	Associations
In the beginning		
215-65 million years BC	The Age of dinosaurs	Footprints on the beach of Veillon
7500-2500BC	Neolithic period	Many menhirs and dolmens, erected, especially around Avrillé in Vendée
56BC	The Romans under Crassus conquer Aquitaine	Saintes became capital of the Santons under occupation
The Middle Ages		
5th and 6th Centuries	Franks gradually take over from Romans	Gaul becomes France!
844	Bones of St James found in Galicia	Start of the pilgrimages to across France to Santiago de Compostela
900-1200	Romanesque architecture	Churches and monasteries built along pilgrim route
1152	Marriage of Henry of Anjou and Eleanor of Aquitaine	Together they own all western France
1154	Henry of Anjou becomes Henry II	Half France, including the Vendée and Charente-Maritime, in English hands
1337-1453	Hundred Years War between England and France with ultimate loss of English territories	Vendée and Charente-Maritime under French rule again
1431	Death of Joan of Arc	
1404-1440	Life of Gilles de Rais (Bluebeard)-a lieutenant in Joan's army	Practises alchemy at Tiffauge
16th century		
1517 onwards	The Reformation (a movement to reform the Catholic church)	1520-1523, Rabelais and other humanists unite at Fontenay-le-Comte
1515-1547	Reign of François I, great patron the arts. Time of the Renaissance	1494, François I born at Cognac
1562-1598	Wars of Religion	1573, Duke of Anjou besieges Protestant La Rochelle
1598	Edict of Nantes gives Protestants freedom of worship	Welcomed in La Rochelle
17th century		
1610-1643	Reign of Louis XIII, reinforces power of the monarchy	Richelieu bishop of Luçon (1606-1623)
1624-1642	Richelieu prime minister	1628, Siege of La Rochelle. Destruction of Protestant strongholds like La Garnache and Apremont ordred
1643-1715	Reign of Louis XIV (the Sun King) War at sea with France and Holland	1666, Building of Rochefort arsenal begun
1685	Edict of Nantes revoked. 400,000	Huguenots leave France
18th century		
1715-1774	Reign of Louis XV	
1774-1793	Reign of Louis XVI	
1789	French Revolution. France becomes a Republic	Massive social upheaval. expectations of a fair deal for all soon disappear
1793	Louis XVI and Queen Marie	Vendéans deem this to be a Antoinette executed step too far. Conscription is the last straw.
1793-1796	Vendéan War	Massacres and other incidents throughout the Vendée
19th century		
1804-1814	First Empire (Napoleon I). Napoleon exiled to Elba	
1814-1815	Louis XVIII restored to throne	
1815	Napoleon lands in south of France and returns to power for a'Hundred Days' before defeat	Napoleon spends his last days in France on Île d'Aix before exile in St Helena
1815-1848	Monarchy restored. Louis XVIII, followed by Charles X, then Louis-Philippe	
1848	Louis-Philippe forced to abdicate. Napoleon III (nephew of emperor) becomes new leader of Second Republic Later becomes 'Emperor'	
1870	France defeated by Prussians. Third Republic ensues	
1894	The Dreyfus affair. Jewish Army Captain Deyfus wrongly convicted of treason	Dreyfus imprisoned on Île de Ré before being sent to Devil's Island Clemenceau Publishes Zola's 'J'accuse'
20th century		
1914-1918	First World War	1919, Clemenceau signs the Treaty of Versailles for France
1939-1945	Second World War.	Under German Occupation. Oléron liberated 1st May 1945. Jean de Lattre De Tassigny accepts German surrender, 8th May
1946-1951	Marshal Pétain (leader of Vichy government) imprisoned on Île d'Yeu	
1947	De Gaulle proposes constitution for Fourth Republic.	
1962	Algerian crisis results in another constitution – the Fifth Republic	

Index

Published in the UK by
Landmark Publishing Ltd,
The Oaks, Moor Farm Road West, Ashbourne, DE6 1HD
Tel: (01335) 347349 Fax: (01335) 347303
e-mail: landmark@clara.net
website: www.landmarkpublishing.co.uk

2nd Edition
ISBN 13: 978-1-84306-430-5

© Judy Smith 2009

British Library Cataloguing in Publication Data: a catalogue record for this book is available from
the British Library.

Print: Gutenberg Press, Malta
Design: Michelle Hunt, **Cartography:** Mark Titterton, **Editing:** Ian Howe

Front cover: Quayside at St Gilles
Back cover, top: Arçais; **Back cover, middle:** Chateau de la Guignardiere
Back cover, bottom: Oyster platter

*If you have enjoyed Judy Smith's book,
she has also written
Undiscovered France.*

*Widely acclaimed and covering 20
different areas. Published as a
Landmark Visitor Guide.*

ISBN 13: 978 1 84306 161 8

336PP

£12.99

LANDMARK VISITORS GUIDE
Arrive Informed
Undiscovered
France
Judy Smith

All photography supplied by the author

DISCLAIMER
While every care has been taken to ensure that the information in this book is as
accurate as possible at the time of publication, the publishers and author accept no re-
sponsibility for any loss, injury or inconvenience sustained by anyone using this book.